The Afrocentricity Trajectories of Looting in South Africa

The Afrocentricity Trajectories of Looting in South Africa

Edited by Mfundo Mandla Masuku,
Dalifa Ngobese, Mbulaheni Obert Maguvhe
and Sifiso Ndlovu

LEXINGTON BOOKS
Lanham • Boulder • New York • London

Published by Lexington Books
An imprint of The Rowman & Littlefield Publishing Group, Inc.
4501 Forbes Boulevard, Suite 200, Lanham, Maryland 20706
www.rowman.com

86-90 Paul Street, London EC2A 4NE

British Library Cataloguing in Publication Information Available

Library of Congress Cataloging-in-Publication Data

ISBN 9781666919905 (cloth)
ISBN 9781666919912 (ebook)

Contents

Chapter One

Alooter Continua!

Tracing Historical Trajectories of Looting from Pre-colonial, Colonial and Postcolonial in South Africa

Dalifa Ngobese

INTRODUCTION

Looting in South Africa has taken place intermittently for decades in the context of an ongoing crisis of poverty, inequality and unemployment. It occurred under apartheid and continued to take place in democratic South Africa in 1994. But it has traditionally been largely confined to marginalized urban and peri-urban areas. One reason to make this argument at the outset is to review the historical legacy of the continent looted: trade by force dated back centuries, slavery that uprooted and dispossessed Africans, land grabs, precious metals and artifacts spirited away, and the nineteenth-century emergence of racial ideology.

Looting remains an important insight for the debates today as Africans struggle for the recovery of African humanity against the ravages of Eurocentrism and coloniality. At the core of Simphiwe Sesanti's discussion on these matters is the argument that tapping into (subjugated) African knowledge is essential to dismantling neo-colonialism in education and other spheres. For Sesanti, in this process, Afrocentrism is the absolute key. Sesanti (2016) speaks of an almost universal, historically unbroken African culture as 'central' to an Afrocentric education. Afrocentricity is a philosophical perspective associated with the discovery, location and actualizing of African agency within the context of history and culture, a quality of thought and practice rooted in the cultural and human interests of African people (Sesanti 2016, 35).

The primary aim of this chapter is to trace the historical trajectories of looting from precolonial, colonial and postcolonial times in South Africa.

This chapter attempts to infuse the history of looting into the implications of looting in modern society and argues for those seeking genuine information about looting in South Africa, the events above were useful in so far as they revealed global elite hypocrisy and power relations that remain impervious to advocacy, solidarity and democracy.. This chapter requires an effort to discover within the political violence and the contest of power the stern laws of the economic process. It argues that engaging with white supremacy and settler colonialism reveals the enduring social, economic and political impacts of white supremacy as a materially grounded set of practices. It illustrates the systemic and structural production of white privilege and supremacy through a range of looting practices.

The chapter reflects on the manner in which colonialism has become a part of the discourse concerning the South African epoch of 1652. Dembele (2012, 179) provides another dimension of colonialism. In doing so, he explains that the colonial administration replaced slavery in the nineteenth century with the occupation of Africa by Western powers. This has led to systematic looting of its natural resources and the exploitation of its cheap labour, which served to industrialize Western countries.

One has to argue that within the historical discourse there is a blind spot to the significance of white supremacy and the white racial identities produced through a taken-for-granted logic of settler colonialism. Bonds and Inwood (2016) have argued that white supremacy is a central organizing logic of Western modernity, legitimating both European colonization and settler projects. It is therefore foundational to the historic development of settler-colonial states, but also to contemporary postcolonial societies

Colonization, from the settler-colonial perspective, is a kind of permanent occupation that is always in a state of becoming. This unfolding project involves the interplay between the removal of First Peoples from the land and the creation of labour systems and infrastructures that make the land productive. Settler colonialism licenses the disappearance of indigenous peoples, the expropriation of indigenous spaces, and makes others infinitely exploitable and/or expendable, for example, through slavery, immigrant labour, and imprisonment.

LOOTING: A VIEW FROM ACROSS

This ongoing project requires the continued displacement of indigenous and other marginalized peoples who are an impediment to capitalist development, as well as particular forms of labour exploitation that extract value from appropriated land. The purpose of this chapter is to broaden and refine our understanding of the nature, historical scope, and frequency of looting and to place looting in a global perspective. Firstly, the overwhelming majority of countries in Africa have experienced looting first-hand on more than one occasion; secondly, looting is in fact a globally pervasive problem.

Bond (2013, 15) renders an African view of what the word *looting* means; he argues that Africa is poor, ultimately, because its economy and society have been ravaged by international capital as well as by local elites that are often propped up by foreign powers. The public and private sectors have worked together to drain the continent of resources that otherwise if harnessed and shared fairly could meet the needs of the peoples of Africa (Bond 2013, 16). Changes in governance revolutions, for example, are desperately needed for social progress, and this entails not only the empowerment of civil society but also the strengthening of those agencies within African states which can deliver welfare and basic infrastructure.

One reason to make this argument forcefully at the outset is to remind ourselves of the historical legacy of a continent looted: trade by force dating back centuries; slavery that uprooted and dispossessed around twelve million Africans; land grabs; vicious taxation schemes; precious metals spirited away (Bond 2013, 16). Development and exploitation of natural resources might be pursued where the industrial potential is limited for institutional or other social and political reasons.

In this chapter, Bond argues that for those seeking genuine information about Africa's situation, the events above were useful mainly insofar as they revealed global-elite hypocrisy and power relations that remained impervious to advocacy, solidarity and democratization (Bond 2013, 24). The events also revealed the limits of strategies aimed at intra-elite persuasion rather than pressure. Tragically, the actual conditions faced by most people on the continent continued to deteriorate.

Dembele (2012, 179) points out that Africa is among the 'poorest' regions of the world. The reality is that Africa is not poor but rather impoverished. This impoverishment dates back to the dawn of capitalism when slavery was one of the key elements of capitalism'. One has to reemphasize that looting is a system driven by the capitalist institution of Western countries. Bond (2013, 38) argues that Africa is poor because its economy and society have been ravaged by the international capital as well as the local elites who have been propped up by the foreign powers.

The question as to who and what is responsible for African underdevelopment can be answered at two levels. The first view is based on the idea that the imperialist system bears major responsibility for African economic retardation by draining African wealth and by making it impossible to develop the resources of the continent. The second view has to deal with those who manipulate the system and those who are either agents or unwitting accomplices of the said system.

In order to understand present economic conditions in Africa, one needs to know why it is that Africa has realised so little of its natural potential, and one also needs to know why so much of its present wealth goes to non-Africans who reside for the most part outside of the continent.

NEW DAWN AFTER WHITE'S MAN ARRIVAL

The relationship between the Southern African societies and the wider world changed dramatically in the sixteenth century with the arrival of Portuguese ships at the Cape of Good Hope. It was in the following centuries that contact with Europeans intensified. As noted by Skinner (2017, 6), Colonial expansion had a particularly negative impact on the Khoisan, whose social cohesion was founded on the basis of patronage connected to the wealth in livestock. The loss of colonial trade resulted in declining power, possession of land and identity. Skinner also points out that colonial society in the Cape was well established as a result of the expansion of colonial agriculture by the end of the eighteenth century (6).

The colonization of African countries by European powers in the nineteenth century sealed the fate of the continent for centuries to come. In addition to the looting of its resources, its citizens were transformed into cheap labour for colonial companies. The Khoisan along with the San hunting communities gradually merged into a colonial power. This certainly facilitated and accelerated the economic and social changes that occurred on the continent during the colonial period.

The breakdown of indigenous political independence was compounded by increased competition over power, land, water, diseases, and scarcity of resources. Skinner (2017, 6) recognises that the histories of the African societies in the late eighteenth and nineteenth centuries had centred on the emergence of the Zulu kingdom under Shaka and its exceptional expansion.

Zulu-led warfare, known as *Mfecane*, resulted in chaos, strife, dispossession, and dominated histories until the late 1880s. As Skinner puts it, this narrative of warfare locates the political and social transformation in political and military developments and reinforces a sense of separation between colonial and African historical trajectories. One may conclude that sparks of looting emanate from the oppressive and inhuman treatment of Africans by the colonizer during that period.

It should be noted that the global colonization of resource-rich lands became the new project for European economic and military powers. Hence the scramble for Africa culminated with the Berlin Conference of 1885 that divided up the continent (Dembele 2012, 181). When formal independence was granted to African countries in the 1960s, hopes were high that with independence, the long period of economic exploitation would come to an end and Africa would then be on the path toward economic growth and development (181).

Dembele's analysis of African developmental impasses brings into focus the hopes of accession to independence from the 1960s; one might have thought that looting Africa would come to an end and its development be stepped up (Dembele 2012, 179). It was the opposite that occurred because, in many countries, foreign domination had been reinforced in connivance with the new African leaders.

But the withdrawal of the European powers was only strategic. They left behind minefields of problems that were set during colonial times. One of these problems was the unbalanced treatment of Africa's ethnic groups. Another one was the birth of new classes that were nurtured on the shallow materialism encouraged by capitalist production. This new dawn reminds Africans of the day when South Africa was looted. As of today, South Africa and Africa are still getting progressively poorer.

LOOTING THE LAND OF THE ANCESTORS

Morris (2012, 23) states that the origin of looting can be traced to the construction of an Afrikaner identity from the second half of the 1800s and steady activities occurred between Britons and Afrikaners in the late 1800s and gradually led to the South African War. From the intrusion of the indigenous African community, it was noted that a large number of the European population settled over the Cape in 1806, numbering from 27,000 to 1.2 million.

Their task was not only to grow wheat and grains and breed cattle and sheep in order to supply the sailing ships with fresh vegetables, meat, water, and other necessities en route to the East Indies but to loot the mineral resources belonging to the indigenous people prior to the colonization of South Africa (Feinstein 2005, 1). The settlement of Europeans on this large scale differentiated South Africa from the rest of Africa.

From the onset, Feinstein (2005, 2) argues that there was a fundamental division between these two groups, Blacks and the new white minority, with massive and enduring implications for land, water, and other resources ownership. Looting is believed to have started after the appearance of the settler community who needed arable land for grazing at the Cape.

Feinstein (2005, 15) asserts that conflicts over land brought the Khoisan into a dispute with the Dutch immediately with the establishment of a European settlement. Despite their sporadic resistance, the herders lost their grazing land, their livestock and their independence. Their discontent was inflamed by the venality, greed, and looting of African land in order to develop large estates and acquire significant wealth, leaving a great majority of indigenous people poor and discontent (25).

The land-as-commodity paradigm indeed presents important moral arguments that should not be taken lightly. Vorster (2019, 3) suggests that the moral claim that land is a financial asset and a source of income for property owners means that the state has the obligation to compensate persons who are deprived of property (through expropriation) for losses incurred. Arbitrary deprivations of the land amount to a form of unacceptable coercion because the property is taken without the consent of the owner. The proprietor is harmed, both emotionally and physically (in terms of livelihood), to a degree that endangers his or her fundamental dignity.

In line with their understanding of land as an exchangeable commodity, this approach emphasizes the right to private ownership as a fundamental feature of a free and open society. Private property rights were presented as an important precondition for human dignity. The land is a space that provides historical meaning and cultural identity to African people.

Vorster (2019, 4) claims that many traditional African groups view land as an inalienable 'inheritance' that should be passed on from one generation to the other. In fact, for most South Africans, access to land is not primarily about finding a livelihood, but about reconnecting to historical roots. Seventy percent of Black respondents in Gibson's survey (2009, 40) indicated that they regard the symbolic value of land and the issue of dignity as more important than monetary considerations.

The successful attainment of the looting strategy of conquest and dispossession was embodied in the notorious Native Land Act of 1913. This made it illegal for Africans to acquire or rent any land outside the existing reserves (Feinstein 2002, 43). This Act also established the principle of land segregation and became the 'homeland' of the apartheid era. By 1910, Deegan (2011, 4) adds, South Africa became a powerful 'settler' state in which around 20 percent of the population of the newly formed territory could be classified as whites or European.

Another way of examining the impact of looted South Africa is Heldrin and Robinson's (2012) study of the wages of gold miners in South Africa between 1911 and 1969. Heldring and Robinson (9) show that the impact of the Native Land Act of 1913 in South Africa and the spread of such institutions as the Colour Bar led to a steep decline in the nominal and real wages of Black gold miners. Vorster (2019, 7) claims that the Africans lost land through the Land Natives Act of 1913, and the dignity of their descendants can only be restored by giving the land back to its rightful owners. Government is the rightful owner of the land, and it should redistribute land through title deeds.

LOOTING OF MINERAL DISCOVERIES

Mpofu (2013, 2) argues that the history of Africa was disputed, and the humanity of Africans was denied. Accompanying the disputation of history and the denial of humanity were the physical violence and forced labour that was inflicted on Africans while their minerals, wildlife and lands were forcibly appropriated by the colonists. In order to understand the present economic conditions in South Africa, one needs to investigate the historic discourse of why mineral resources and natural potential go to non-Africans.

There is no doubt that South Africa possesses rich mineral resources, particularly gold and diamonds. This mineral wealth differentiated South Africa from other regions of European settlement with large indigenous populations. Prior to the discovery of mineral wealth, South Africa was almost dependent on agriculture. As Feinstein (2005, 3) concludes, this unique combination of populations and mineral resources resulted in a process of conquest, dispossession, discrimination and development of rapid economic progress.

The situation in South Africa transformed dramatically after the discovery of diamonds in 1867. The subsequent discovery of gold on the Witwatersrand in 1886 was to have a more profound impact. As more capital was required to dig deeper for diamonds, the multitude of small-scale miners gave away to the dominance of large companies (Feinstein 2005, 28).

The discourse of looting began to shape its course, firstly, by the amalgamation and consolidation of more than three thousand individual claims until they were all owned by a large, joined stock company, called De Beers Consolidation of Mines under the control of Cecil John Rhodes (Feinstein 2005, 99). Secondly, there was the revolutionary development from agricultural sustainability to mining operations with the emergence and recruitment of Black laborers, working deep underground. Over the decades, African mineral resources and treasures slowly became controlled by the minority.

As Bond (2013, 8) correctly point out, the denial of Africans' access to food, medicine, energy and even water is a common reflection of the colonized economic system that perpetuates African subordination. Maphosa (2012, 5) introduces an unequal distribution and access to natural resources in which less powerful groups in the society, relative to other groups, are without equal access to particular resources.

It is advisable to argue that agriculture and mining exports certainly expanded relative to what they were at the time of the scramble for Africa. Heldring and Robinson (2012, 3) have no doubt that Europeans brought technology, such as railways and mining techniques, and integrated their colonies more fully into world trade, taking advantage of existing patterns of comparative advantage.

Africans experienced a severe deterioration in living standards as a consequence of colonialism. Indeed, given the extent of land expropriated from Africans by Europeans, living standards might have fallen by about 50 percent (Heldring and Robinson 2012, 4). Even in the absence of colonialism, technology diffuses across countries, including agricultural and medical technology, emanating from the indigenous/local knowledge that played a significant role in the spread of education before and during the colonial period in Africa.

Today, resources concentrated are in the hands of a few elites, while the rest are subjected to greater scarcity. Such unequal social distribution does not presuppose actual shortage if the resource were to be distributed evenly. In many countries in Africa, the colonial governments segregated local citizens, and this was one of the major causes of violent nationalist movements. In South Africa, for example, the system of apartheid provided whites with 87 percent of the land, while almost 75 percent of the country's Black population lived in squalor and within restricted areas that accounted for only 13 percent of the land (Maphosa 2012, 5). One has to conclude that resources were also inequitably distributed within the restricted areas, as local elites controlled access to productive agriculture and grazing land.

APARTHEID AS A NEW LOOTING PHENOMENON

A major grief amongst South Africans was the establishment of a segregation policy called apartheid. The debates about its origin or formative years of segregation traced back to the nineteenth century and the policies of the British colonial administration. It should be noted that looting has a variety of political meanings that cannot be severed from the violence that looting entails. Importantly, historical incidents are to be considered in redefining the resistance to desegregation in South Africa by looting.

Discrimination by race in South Africa is as old and pervasive as European settlement. It can be traced back to the treatment of slaves and extermination of the San and Khoisan people. The constitution adopted in the 1850s by the Transvaal republics stipulates that no African people desire to permit equality between the coloured people and white inhabitants and also makes a provision for the new looting phenomenon (Feinstein 2005, 74).

The fundamental reason for these restrictions was the white government's desire to protect their jobs and their large income differentials. These differentials were introduced originally in the diamond field in the 1870s and then reproduced in the gold mines in the 1890s. As Feinstein (2005, 75) notes, the economic motives for preserving skilled work for whites were powerfully reinforced by white supremacy and its long-standing idea that whites should not have to perform unskilled work.

The rise of Afrikaner nationalism was noticeable from 1910 onward when South Africa's control was in the hands of a Nationalist government led by Botha and Hertzog (Saul and Bond 2014, 37). They moved briskly to advance the interest of the Afrikaner community, whom they chiefly represented. Racial and class laws created cheap African labour for the mining magnates and white skin privileged labour for the white workers.

Saul and Bond (2014, 39) believe that legislations such as the Mines and Works Act of 1911 and the Industrial Conciliation Act of 1924 were crafted to service the capital along racial lines. It is noted that the Native Land Act of 1913 also deepened the reach of capitalist production in the new South Africa. To make things worse, the introduction of the Native (Urban Areas) Act of 1923 laid down the principles of residential segregation in urban areas and the reinforcement of the doctrine that Africans had no permanent rights in the town (39). Indeed, in adopting these legislations, the white government established two of the key pillars of segregation.

But one law after the next from the 1913 Native Land Act and the Mines and Works Amendment Act of 1924 to the notorious laws of 1936, entrenched looting, including land dispossession, tightening influx control, and removing Black voters from the voter roll. Morris (2012, 44) concludes that the idea of the white government was to limit the Black people's presence in the urban areas and to create a migratory labour system that would rely on Black workers living in the homeland reserves.

As Deegan (2011, 9) notes, racial segregation is imperative not only in the interest of native culture, tradition and institutions not being swamped by the more powerful organization of the whites. The mixing of whites and Blacks led to unhappy results such as racial miscegenation, moral antipathy and clashes, and other forms of social evils. There is no doubt that political, social and economic revolution would eventually lead to looting in the near future.

One has to view white supremacy not as an artifact of history or as an extreme position, but rather as the foundation for the continuous unfolding of practices of race and racism within settler states. Concurring with Bonds and Inwood (2013, 720), if privilege and racism are the symptoms, white supremacy is the disease. The idea of race is mediated on and through local histories that not only have come to define different groups but are also the result of historically grounded structures and struggles.

Mounting pressure on Black communities deepened the spirit of resistance, spurring the growth of opposition and the development of a new kind of looting. Bond (2013, 5) attests that force, fraud, resistance and looting are openly displayed without any attempt of concealment. Africa needs to overcome her brutal infrastructural barriers, including poverty and dearth of capacity, in order to overcome the 'resource curse' and build resource-based linkages.

LOOTING OF AFRICAN KNOWLEDGE

The challenge levelled against African indigenous knowledge (AIK) that it is inferior to Western scientific knowledge (WSK) has its roots in two important antecedents. Ogungbure (2013, 14) explains that the looting of African knowledge can be traced to the colonialist agenda in Africa and the self-acclaimed conceptual superiority of its benefactors over the conquered territories. African indigenous knowledge can be said to be scientific or share the same quality as Western scientific knowledge when it is Western concerns and paradigms that direct the thrust of the African system of thought (Ogungbure, 2013: 13). It is from these two perspectives that the knowledge produced by Africans (AIK) has been criticized as being inferior to the Western alternatives.

Edward Said (1978, cited in Nabudere 2011b, 12) also mentions that Eurocentric knowledge is not produced for its sake. Its purpose throughout the ages has been to enable them to 'know the natives' in order to take control of their territories, including human and material resources for their benefit. Such control of knowledge was used to exploit the non-European peoples, colonize them both mentally and geo-strategically, as well as subordinate the rest of the world to their designs and interests.

Through Afrikology, as Dastile (2013) argues, a universal, restorative transdisciplinary paradigm, an assumption of African originality from a psychological, social, spiritual, cultural and political vantage emerges. Dastile (2013, 100) continues to envisage that the above would lead to knowledge generation that has both epistemic significance and related community contributions and relevance. In turn, what this would require is deep involvement and commitment to the initiation of dialogue with the community and a regard for the community members as repository sites for knowledge generation (100).

Mpofu (2013, 105) discusses how coloniality, as a toxic power is embedded in the African imagination and knowledge production that goes with the knowledge climate of Western modernity, continues to influence views on African knowledge and disrupt even what on the outside might appear to be liberated and liberating African discourses. Mpofu (2013, 107) also points out that Eurocentric and racist naming and descriptions of Africa in its colonial mode are not a monologue on Africa. Just as the scramble for Africa's lands and resources was met with fierce nationalist, Marxist and pan-Africanist resistance, Eurocentric scrambles for African knowledge and its distortions have been challenged and are still being challenged.

Mpofu cited Chinua Achebe (1977, 106), who states that there are no apologies to the West for what Africa is. They have to see Africa as it is, a continent with a people who have their failures and their hopes and who are equal citizens of world society. Western stereotypes of Africa as a continent of wants, deficits, and defects must be dismissed for what they are: the racism that is designed to justify colonialism and imperialism. Ogungbure (2013, 12) states that it is simply an undisguised form of ethnocentrism, an offshoot of the colonial mentality, that believes that Africans lack the general knowledge to transcend certain basic environmental limitations.

African intellectuals and thinkers who, like Chinua Achebe and others, are sold on producing intelligent excuses for colonialism and who confabulate lofty denials of the continuing colonial 'wound', only witness half the tragedy that coloniality presents in Africa and its academy. Mpofu (2013, 109) strongly states that the dehumanization and trinification of the African appear to be part of the imperial project of justifying colonialism and coloniality by presenting the African as a condemned object that deserves exploitation by the imperial white colonizers throughout the ages. Noticeably, Africans have responded to and resisted colonial knowledge of Africa with combative thought and knowledge in the shape of negritude, Pan-Africanism, nationalism, Marxism, Afrikology and Afrocentrism, including Black consciousness.

A DECOLONIAL PARADIGM

The struggle against Euro-centricity in all its many manifestations is real. As real is the necessity of resistance against the suppression of African histories, traditions and epistemologies. In fact, 'epistemocide', like genocide, is not at all hyperbole, and the seriousness of this historical situation should not be trivialized under the weight of academic purity (Boesak 2020, 3).

Eurocentricity does indeed capture this accurately, and it should remain the focus of these new struggles provided that we take the critical and self-critical elements in Black consciousness and spirituality seriously. One should think of Afro-centricity and Afro-plurality together as agents of indigeneity, the recovery and rediscovering, the gathering and harnessing of all our resources in all of their diversities and pluralities would be a formidable force in the struggle not only for the decolonized African mind but also for a decolonial humanism (Boesak 2020, 4). The scars of slavery and the wounds of colonialism are still being felt within the African political, economic, social and indeed spiritual conditions.

The African economic renaissance paradigm, as advanced in this paper, has a historical foundation and contemporary implications. Gumede (2016, 94) argues that the African economic renaissance implies that Africans should decide on the African economy and the socioeconomic system that works for them. The point of departure is that Africans have had, prior to colonialism and imperialism, an economy and an economic system that worked well for them.

The aforementioned epochs of an African-centred decolonial paradigm, as described by Dastile (2013) serve to identify the alterity of existing African discourses. Afrocentrism, Africanity and Afrikology seek to unmask Eurocentric hegemony, which floats on African scholarship to explain African experiences. This is because African scholars continue to rely on imported paradigms of universalism and essentialism of African experiences that continue to dominate locally produced bits of knowledge. The contours described above argue for the scholarship that aims at liberating, emancipating, and decolonizing existing knowledge about African subjects and subjectivities through the lived and embodied experience. (Dastile 2013, 103).

This explication, in part, portrays the rejection of African indigenous knowledge as inferior to its Western equivalent. The implication is that all indigenous forms of knowledge must be similar to other Western categories of thought in order to qualify as meaningful. There is no doubt that Indigenous Knowledge is unique to a particular culture and society. It is the basis for local decision-making in agriculture, health, natural resource management and other activities. It is embedded in community practices, institutions, relationships, and rituals

Researchers in low- and middle-income countries (LMICs) often feel they are 'not adequately appreciated' when they partner with researchers from wealthier countries. O'Grandy (2022) cites local experts who are too often not listed as authors, cannot access data they gathered, and don't have the power to steer research to local priorities. Such 'scientific colonialism' uses the same tactics as colonialism has historically. It extracts data instead of raw materials—and undermines and underfunds local infrastructure and skills. Her presses for equity when scientists from wealthy nations do research in poorer ones (O'Grandy 2022, 1). This leaves researchers in LMICs without the publications, patents, and skills of their wealthier counterparts.

Sebola (2019, 5) alerts Africans that coloniality never left with the colonizer when he left his office, unfortunately, he left his identity in the character of a new democrat, culture, norms, and values that are something permanent in his colonial office occupied by a new African democrat. By looting, it is clearly articulated in the African public administration which continues to highlight the character of a colonial setting at the expense of precolonial Africa. In attempting to create an African state that is supposed to be based on African values, Sebola (2019, 6) proposes that Africans should create an African state of an 'alien character' devoid of ethics with complete reliance on the Western conception of institutions and power.

CONCLUSION

The elite ruling class, which is mostly white and wealthy, ensures the maintenance of private property by violence. In the context of South African white supremacy, Black lives are collectively found less valuable than property. This chapter has attempted to contribute to the discourse of looting by reintroducing the unanswered questions: Who is doing the looting? Where does looting begin? What South African minerals have been looted? And What communities are being hurt?

Africa's dismal economic situation and perennial social and political instability are inextricably linked to its impoverishment since the dawn of capitalism. Africa has paid a heavy price to Western industrialization. Since independence, African countries have experienced a host of models and strategies, most of which were inspired from abroad, the latest being the neoliberal model. All these models, within the capitalist system, have only contributed to the further impoverishment of African countries (Dembele 2012).

For Africans, land has become a symbol of dispossession and social alienation in South Africa. They classify land as a locus of social resistance and therefore call for stringent redress and land redistribution. There is a call for the nationalization of land, the abolishment of private ownership, and a fair reorganization of the ownership structures in South Africa through a system where citizens lease property from the state. It is believed that all the ancestral inheritance of traditional communities must be returned to the communities.

While the need for land reform and deracialising commercial farming is acknowledged by the land as a commodity paradigm, proponents of this paradigm generally do not regard land reform as a quick fix for rural poverty. South Africans who attach social meanings to land generally tend to consider land as a space of rootedness, a locus of life and a place of history-making where identities are formed. Some traditional Southern African societies, for instance, bury the umbilical cord of a new-born baby near the location of the birth to root that person in a place of origin, which is shared with the ancestors.

Expropriation without compensation mechanisms should be used to transfer land to dispossessed communities, while their African traditional authorities/councils should be allowed to decide on how the land would be utilized. At the same time, land currently owned by traditional leaders should be left alone. Countries should invest more in manufacturing and service industries to improve wider governance conditions within the exploitation of natural resources.

Dembele (2012) suggests that there is a need for the political dimension of the paradigm shift which would create real democratization of African societies, with the building of truly democratic institutions and the rise of an enlightened and democratic leadership capacity to implement policies that reflect the fundamental aspirations of the African people. Sovereignty over development policies means the restitution to the African people of the right to participate in the formulation of economic development policies that affect their lives.

REFERENCES

Achebe, Chinua. 1977. *An image of Africa*. Johannesburg: Penguin Books.

Boesak, Allen. 2020. In search of our human face: Black consciousness, Black spirituality, inclusive humanity and the politics of vulgarity. *HTS Teologiese Studies/ Theological Studies* 76(3): 1–10.

Bond, Patrick. 2013. *Looting Africa: The economics of exploitation*. Zeth Book Publishers.

Bonds, Anne, and Inwood, Joshua. 2013. Beyond white privilege: Geographies of white supremacy and settler colonialism. *Progress in Human Geography* 40(6): 715–33.

Dastile, Nontyatyambo. 2013. Beyond Euro-Western dominance: An African-centred decolonial paradigm. *Africanus* 43(2): 93–104.

Deegan, Heather. 2011. *Politics South Africa*. 2d ed. Harlow, UK: Pearson Longman.

Dembele, Demba Moussa. 2012. Africa's developmental impasse: Some perspectives and recommendations. *Africa Development* 37(4): 179–96.

Feinstein, Charles Hilliard. 2005. *An economic history of South Africa: Conquest, discrimination and development*. Cambridge: Cambridge University Press.

Gibson, James. 2009. *Overcoming historical injustices: Land reconciliation in South Africa*. New York: Cambridge University Press.

Gumede, Vusi. 2016. Towards a better socio-economic development approach for Africa's renewal. *Africa Insight* 16(1): 89–104.

Heldring, Leander, and Robinson, James. 2012. *Colonialism and economic development in Africa*. Cambridge: National Bureau of Economic Research, Unpublished work, pp 1–40.

Maphosa, Bongani. 2012. Natural resources and conflict: Unlocking the economic dimension of peace-building in Africa. AISA POLICY Brief Number 74, 1–8.

Morris, Michael. 2012. *Apartheid: An illustrated history*. Cape Town: Jonathan Ball Publishers.

Mpofu, William Jethro. 2013. Coloniality in the scramble for African knowledge: A decolonial political perspective. *Africanus* 43(2): 105–17.

Nabudere, Wadada Dani. 2011b. *Afrikology and Transdisciplinarity: A Restorative Epistemology*. Pretoria: Africa Institute of South Africa.

Ogungbure, Adebayo Anthony. 2013. African indigenous knowledge: Scientific or unscientific? *Inkanyiso, Journal of Human and Social Science* 2013 5(1): 12–20.

O'Grandy, Cynthia. 2022. 'Helicopter research' comes under fire at the Cape Town conference. Proceeding on World Conference on Research Integrity, held in Cape Town, South Africa, 6 June 2022.

Said, Edward. 1978. *Orientalism: Western Conceptions of the Orient*. London: Routledge & Kegan Paul.
Saul, John, and Bond, Patrick. 2014. *South Africa, the present as history: From Mrs. Ples to Mandela and Marikana*. New York: James Currey.
Sebola, Mokoko. 2019. African States' post-colonial dream: Tough battles won in the bush, simple war lost in the public office. *African Journal of Public Affairs* 11(1): 1–13.
Sesanti, Simphiwe. 2016. Afrocentric education for an African renaissance, philosophical underpinnings. *New Agenda: South African Journal of Social and Economic Policy* 2016(62), 34–40.
Skinner, Rob. 2017. *Modern South Africa in world history: Beyond imperialism*. London: Bloomsbury.
Vorster, Nico. 2019. Land and identity in South Africa: An immanent moral critique of dominant discourses in the debate on expropriation without compensation. *HTS Teologiese Studies/Theological Studies* 75(4).

Chapter Two

Looting of Indigenous Knowledge Systems through Patents and Intellectual Property Policies

Dina Mokgadi Mashiyane

INTRODUCTION

African indigenous knowledge is the informal knowledge, values and beliefs transmitted orally from one generation to the next in various contexts to support local communities and their people. Indigenous knowledge systems (IKS) has been harnessed, preserved, and disseminated through African cultural expressions embedded in the traditional customs, rituals, ceremonies, artifacts and oral traditions and indigenous healing practices concerning nature that are embedded within the collective memory of the indigenous elders and practitioners. Due to colonialism and globalization, indigenous people's valuable knowledge and cultural practices have come under threat and are at risk of eroding or being exploited by foreign sponsors, institutions and the government. Intellectual property policies and regulations have been implemented to mitigate the exploitation and looting of IKS; however, they also exacerbate intellectual theft and cultural appropriation through patency and trademarking. Furthermore, Eurocentric Intellectual Property Rights (IPR) policies perpetuate the notion of individualism, wherein indigenous knowledge and cultural resources are privatized and monopolized, thus minimizing accessibility for all to represent African communality as enshrined in the philosophical principle of Ubuntu. Biopiracy has also created a dichotomy in Africa, resulting in IK holders resorting to developing hoarding mechanisms to protect and safeguard their indigenous knowledge.

The Southern African diaspora is endowed with a plethora of knowledge that may be applied to improve the quality of life in various areas, including medical care, social services, education and economic development. This is supported by Oyewale, Adelowo and Ekperiware (2018, 2), with the notion that the development of any nation is not dependent solely on its natural resource endowments but also on the stock of human capital, the available knowledge and how that knowledge is used to be used to solve practical developmental problems. Firstly, it is imperative to comprehend the concept of indigenous knowledge (IK) to dissect further issues related to this phenomenon. According to the literature, this type of knowledge relates to understandings, skills and philosophies acquired by indigenous people who have had a long history of interfacing with their natural surroundings (Thompson, Lantz and Ban 2020; Zidny, Sjöström and Eilks 2020, 147). It is "stored in people's memories, used in their activities, and expressed in stories, songs, folklore, proverbs, dances, myths, cultural values, beliefs, rituals, community laws, agricultural practices, equipment, materials, plant species, and animal breeds" (Sharma 2012, 141–66).

Furthermore, various concepts have been used to refer to this type of knowledge as traditional ecological, aboriginal, traditional and folk knowledge (Thornton and Scheer 2012, 4; Grey 2014; Eckert et al. 2018, 158). African indigenous people have been transmitting and harnessing knowledge from one generation to the next before the dawn of civilization on the continent. It has been argued that IK is shared or "*communal*" and has historically not been in the control of any individual (Ismail and Fakir 2004, 190). Furthermore, Grey (2014) states that rather than individuals, it resides in social activities and reciprocal interactions—it should be viewed as a dynamic engagement rather than a static understanding. Such knowledge can enhance socioeconomic developments, except that IK keepers are acknowledged and given ownership rights. According to Amusan (2017, 103), IK is threatened by commercialization, where patenting and trademarking take ownership rights from original owners. Janke and Sentina (2017) further add to this, as they argue that the law has limited requirements to share benefits with communities who provide access to their IK; also, not sharing its benefits with that community can be offensive and propagates dispossession.

DOMINANT SOCIAL PARADIGM (DSP) VS. UBUNTU PHILOSOPHY

This chapter embeds the philosophical principle of Ubuntu as a restorative justice mechanism in arguing against IK patenting and intellectual property policies, where the Dominant Social Paradigm (DSP) is questioned as an enabler of IK looting. DSP is associated with the notion that humans are superior and in charge of all the resources (Gollnhofer and Schouten 2017, 143). This concept has contributed to Africa's looting of resources for decades, including IK. The patenting of African indigenous practices and natural resources has left the natives destitute, while their resources continue to generate profits and add to commercial outputs in both Eurocentric and Westernized countries (Orozco and Poonamallee 2014, 277; Munyonga 2020, 99). African indigenous communities are seldomly consulted before patenting their physical and intellectual capital. This paradigm can be complemented by the principle of Ubuntu to ensure that all the resources are free from being exploited and commercialization without benefiting indigenous communities. Ujomu and Bature (2018, 176), argue that the notion of DSP has caused value clashes in Africa, where the continent's leaders have normalized corruption and looting of resources. This assertion shows that African leaders have sold out their countries and heritage as far as IK is concerned by agreeing to patency and IPR policies placed on communal knowledge. An example is a traditional healer signing an agreement with large corporations transferring ownership and the rights of community knowledge. According to a study conducted in Mali on "improved medicinal practices," the traditional healers whose preparations processes were used requested to be accredited as the owner of that IK instead of the community at large (Willcox et al. 2015, 284). This perpetuates a behaviour of individualism instead of community in line with the Ubuntu principle. In addition to this, Chennells (2013, 178) argues that it is considered unethical for community healers to claim ownership of the knowledge they have received rather than ascribe it to the communities they serve. Their wisdom is from healers and diviners before them, who acquired it from their predecessors. The tribal leaders, as gatekeepers of specialized knowledge and policymakers, ought to rethink and decolonize how IK is protected, as it is evident that patents are not doing justice to indigenous communities; instead, they take away the heritage, practices, and systems of traditional people. Feris (2004, 243) argues that though there is a remedial mechanism that enshrines the elements of Ubuntu, such as justice, equality, fairness, freedom and dignity, the African Charter provides for a variety of rights that safeguard traditional knowledge bearers. However, the human rights-based approach to traditional knowledge has been generally ignored.

PROVERBIAL PRESERVATION OF INDIGENOUS KNOWLEDGE

IK's characteristics are the wealth of knowledge and wisdom hidden behind proverbs, idioms and metaphors. This has always been how indigenous people have communicated and provided guidance and cultural practices by using these elements. This is supported by Omoera and Inegbeboh (2013, 17), asserting that proverbs are symbolic statements that preserve and propagate a society's rich history and culture. Thus, proverbs can be used to protect IK from looting because they are a type of collective knowledge that is difficult to copyright and patent. According to Chilisa (2020, 187), a community's cultural traditions and folklore are passed down through the usage of proverbs, which are used to explain and express social events and activities and to communicate expected norms of behaviour from one generation to the next. In addition, the findings of the study conducted by Chiparausha and Mavhunduse (2018, 707) show that Shona folktales can preserve IK through song and dance as well as idioms and proverbs. By performing and reciting folktales, one can keep the information the storyteller is supposed to pass on to the audience from being forgotten. Goduka (2000, 76) concurs that proverbs are brimming with cultural, spiritual and intellectual treasures that necessitate a keen eye, in-depth analysis and a fundamental transcendence of the rational Newtonian-Cartesian epistemologies that have previously marginalized our indigenous sociocultural and linguistic treasures.

There is no doubt that proverbs have guided and provided insight to indigenous communities for years and are still a source of knowledge within the twenty-first century. Proverbs were found to be an effective means of conveying information about leprosy in a study examining attitudes toward the disease. (Ebenso et al. 2012, 208). Furthermore, another study was conducted in South Africa, where proverbs were utilized to ascertain if they could enhance the receptiveness of HIV and AIDS messaging to young adults (Lubinga 2014, 16). This demonstrates the versatility of proverbs in being relevant throughout time in solving social, economic, educational, political and cultural problems.

Some African proverbs have been linked to the Sustainable Development Goals (SDGs) by Majange (2015) as follows:

Goal 1: No Poverty (Poverty is slavery.—Somalian Proverb)
Goal 2: Zero Hunger (Hunger is felt by a slave, and hunger is felt by a king.—African proverb)
Goal 3: Good Health (Health is wealth.—African proverb)
Goal 4: Quality Education (Learning expands great souls.—Namibian Proverb)
Goal 5: Gender Equality (Women are part of the origin of life's big mystery on earth; they know the secret of a good life.—Kuba Proverb)
Goal 6: Clean Water and Sanitation (Filthy water cannot be washed.—African Proverb)
Goal 8: Decent Work and Economic Growth (By labour comes wealth.—Yoruba Proverb)
Goal 13: Climate Action (Do not call the forest that shelters you a jungle.—African Proverb)

Goal 14: Life Below Water (Where water is the boss, there the land must obey.—African proverb)
Goal 16: Peace and Justice (Peace is costly, but it is worth the expense.—Kenyan proverb)
Goal 17: Partnerships for the Goals (If you want to go quickly, go alone. If you want to go far, go together.—African proverb)

With the wisdom embedded and transferred through proverbs echoing justice, fairness, equality, peace, commitment, collaboration, unity and respect, indigenous communities have been attaining the goals of the SDGs for decades. Thakhathi and Netshitangani (2020, 408) emphasize that indigenous African proverbs which adopt the Ubuntu-as-Unity philosophy contain principles and values the continent can benefit from in its pursuit of integrated sustainable development where African identity through indigenous proverbs can be used as re-education tools for fostering continental well-being.

INTELLECTUAL PROPERTY RIGHTS AND IKS

Intellectual property rights and patents are intended to deter piracy and exploitation of intellectual property and resources. However, they have become vehicles for plundering common traditional knowledge from the third world's poor and appropriating it for the exclusive "property" of Western scientists and businesses. Masango (2020, 329) asserts that due to the absence of codification of Africa's IK practices in traditional medicine, Western pharmaceutical corporations, which generate enormous profits from IK in medicinal plants, have a strong desire to acquire this information and take exclusive ownership through patency. In addition, De Jonge (2011, 140) argued that IP rights generally do not apply to indigenous groups or agrarian communities. Communities' traditional practices and production methods are not eligible for IP protection, even though they are human inventions. This is supported by the World Intellectual Property Organization (WIPO, 2022) with the assertion that the informality and orality of IK make it impractical for protection through conventional IP laws.

Article 31 (2007) of the United Nations Declaration on the Rights of Indigenous peoples stipulates the protection of IK and its individuals as follows:

> Indigenous peoples have the right to maintain, control, protect and develop their cultural heritage, traditional knowledge, and traditional cultural expressions, as well as the manifestations of their sciences, technologies, and cultures, including human and genetic resources, seeds, medicines, knowledge of the properties of fauna and flora, oral traditions, literature, designs, sports, and traditional games visual and performing arts. They also have the right to maintain, control, protect

and develop their intellectual property over such cultural heritage, traditional knowledge, and traditional cultural expressions.

As there are several IKS laws within the South African context, it is therefore imperative that these be consulted before the patenting and copyrighting of IK. The Protection, Promotion, Development, and Management of Indigenous Knowledge Act 6 of 2019, is one of the new developments which seeks to guard against the exploitation of IK.

LOOTING OF IKS

The colonial power used looting to assert domination over the colonized people by eliminating culture and identity and creating a sense of inadequacy among the subjugated. Van Beurden (2022) believes that as colonial authorities grew, so did the looting of IK tangible resources. Commercial networks grew as demand for objects grew. Colonialism boosted the African art market. Sculptors, weavers and others began producing for local use and sale to outsiders. Some commercial dealings were pressured, while others were African led. There is overwhelming evidence in the literature of looting and appropriation of IKS through patents and IPR. Biopiracy has its grips in African IK history, where patents and IPR policies have had the upper hand and have stolen from marginalized communities legally. This is supported by Wyatt and Brisman (2017, 326) with the assertion that globalized legal patent systems help companies deny any wrongdoing when uncompensated and unrecognized IK has resulted in patented valuable items. Furthermore, Chen (2006, 2) asserts that narratives of biopiracy are notoriously bad at pinpointing the episodes of the purported "stealing."

Researchers frequently use traditional knowledge about plants, animals or chemical compounds to find novel bioresources. Biopiracy is the exploitation by researchers of traditional knowledge without permission (Robinson 2012, 77–94; Rose 2016; Foster 2017).

Therefore, it is imperative to highlight some of the cases of IKS looting within the African region, particularly those that benefited Eurocentric and Westernized counties.

In 2004, the Netherlands and Germany patented Ethiopia's teff flour as an 'innovation.' Health benefits and the absence of gluten have made teff a popular food choice. The patent was revoked in the Netherlands in 2018 and waived in Germany in 2019 after a series of legal cases over license fees (Tesgera 2019, 63–89; Seleshie, 2021). Moreover, the University of California and Lucky Biotech, a Japanese company, used a patent system to take ownership and loot African people's rights of the sweetening proteins from two plants, namely the katempfe and serendipity berry (Roht-Arriaza 1995, 923; Doyle 2018). There were no benefits shared with the rightful owners either. Not forgetting the South African case of the Khoisan Hoodia plant, which was claimed and commercialized without benefitting the San community. The court case between the San community and the patent holders dragged on for years until a benefit-sharing agreement was signed (Wynberg, 2019).

For years, the theft and illegal trafficking of African art pieces resembling stories behind the continents' traditional knowledge has been a concern. Theo-Ben Gurirab, as quoted by Kiwara-Wilson (2013, 375), refers to the looted African artifacts as follows:

> These works are essential in defining our identity and personality as a family, as an African family. We communicate with them. They communicate with us. We come into contact with them at various points in our lives, from birth to death. They are the conduits through which the living spirits of our people, our history, and our culture interact and interact with us. They are not present, thus the void in our minds and hearts. We continue to beg them to return home, to fill that cultural and spiritual void.

Colonial nations have used their powers to take ownership of tangible and intangible IK resources for commercial purposes. Apoh and Mehler (2019) concur with the notion that during the precolonial era, a significant proportion of the artifacts that originate from what we now refer to as "transborder communities" were obtained through coercion. Western museums house African artistic works that should be returned to their rightful owners. A famous Benin ivory mask remains secure in the British Museum's labyrinths. It was looted in the legendary sacking of the Benin Kingdom by a British expeditionary force in the late nineteenth century in retaliation for a humiliating confrontation between Captain Phillips and King Overawhen, whose heritage was Yoruba according to folklore (Kunkun and Olokun 2007).

A version of the traditional Basotho blanket used and commercialized by Louis Vuitton designs caused controversies, highlighting challenges still faced by African countries due to cultural and design appropriation (Bagley 2017, 985). Nonetheless, Lunde (2018) asks whether this constituted cultural appropriation, as the Basotho blankets have been made available for transcultural consumption, not just Sotho culture. Their distribution is shared by numerous cultures and customers; therefore, they are not entirely Basotho. Design appropriation is an unethical practice that profits from traditional communities' cultural identities.

One of the recent novel developments has been the *Open Restitution Africa Project*, which seeks to empower all involved stakeholders to make informed decisions about the restitution of African material culture and human ancestors, as there are uncertainties concerning the process and procedures to be followed (African Digital Heritage, 2020).

INDIGENOUS KNOWLEDGE HOARDING

A goal of the United Nations Convention on Biological Diversity and the FAO International Treaty on Plant Genetic Resources for Food and Agriculture is for countries to share in the benefits that users obtain from their plant genetic resources and traditional knowledge (De Jonge 2011, 127).

Fear of IK misappropriation and looting has resulted in hoarding practices, with indigenous communities hesitant to share their ways of life. The orality of IK has created opportunities for developed communities to exploit and commercialize indigenous practices. This practice results in loss and lack of preservation as when the knowledge holders die. This aligns with the proverb, "*When an old person dies; a library burns to the ground.*" IK holders and communities are also reluctant to record their traditions and practices based on their lack of acknowledgment and credibility as the original rightful owners. This is evident in a statement made by Khomani San leader Andries Steenkamp, as cited by Chennells (2013, 172): "Our knowledge is oral. We reject the idea that for it to be true it must be written down and recorded by white academics." Based on the theft of IK, this has created feelings of fear in IK communities, and holders have resorted to knowledge hoarding. This is supported by Chennells (2013, 166), who asserts that indigenous people rarely accept experts or academic researchers as the final arbiters of their knowledge. San leaders have declared their distrust of the Western system of written knowledge in response to calls from governments and corporations for traditional knowledge proof in the form of publication. However, the unwillingness of indigenous tribes to have their knowledge recorded is detrimental, as this enhances susceptibility to theft and extinction. An African proverb says, "*Until the lion learns to write, every story will glorify the hunter.*" In the context of this chapter, this means that Africans should take responsibility for having their heritage and traditions recorded so that they are appropriately credited. This is supported by Ubungu (2019, 64), stating that there are so many stories to be told, especially those of the lion, that have never been heard before.

The notion of "fair and equitable benefit-sharing" can be used as a hoarding mitigation strategy, where IK keepers are made aware and encouraged to share their practices widely for the benefit of all. This element aligns with the principle of Ubuntu as it represents communality and justice for all. Chabalala Matsabisa and Gqaleni (2021, 41) mention the uBu-Ntu bio-innovation model, which supports indigenous technology transfer and demonstration by empowering African natural medicine practitioners as owners of the means of production through holistic enterprise development activities and suitable entrepreneurship skills development, which also encourages conscious commercialization based on sustainability models, green economies, and organic products, resulting in fair access and benefit sharing for socioeconomic development.

However, "fair and equitable benefit-sharing" has also been criticized as being ambiguous, focusing more on the financial benefits rather than respecting the rights of indigenous communities (De Jonge 2011, 135; Morgera 2019, 1114).

DECOLONIZATION OF INDIGENOUS KNOWLEDGE

Conversations and initiatives around the decoloniality of IKS are pertinent to transforming and correcting the wrongs of the past. Oliver (2020) cautions guarding against using the term *decolonization* haphazardly, without a frame of reference, and further goes on to say that the true definition of decolonization within the context of IKS is to pay attention to the voices of indigenous communities and to alter the balance of power.

For years, IKS and practices have been looked down on, considered of low quality, and regarded as public scientific property. Colonizers found no fault in taking and using knowledge belonging to traditional communities. Bruchac (2014: 3814–24) states that

> Western practitioners posed a serious threat to the integrity of indigenous cultural traditions and territory, by regarding them as public scientific property. Archaeologists conducted investigations in destructive and ethically questionable ways. The damage included: desecration of burial places; theft of cultural property; imposition of nationalist ideologies; interference with traditional activities; damage to local ecosystems; misrepresentations in museums; and general disrespect for indigenous culture and property.

IK communities have been made to feel and perceive themselves as inferior and their practice as barbaric, while most were being looted instead. Therefore, it is also essential to note that our heritage should be reclaimed and protected. Shizha (2010) noted the anticolonial project, which focused on reclaiming, rethinking, reconstituting, rewriting and validating IK and indigenous languages and repositioning them as integral parts of the academy in universities where teaching and learning reinforce hegemonic and oppressive paradigms that allocate Western and IK differential social locations. Though IKS has not been acknowledged as having been scholarly and scientific based on its oral nature, it has contributed to enhancing the socioeconomic factors of its people. There have been developments in academia in incorporating Afrocentric lenses and practices suited to the continent's needs. African scholars are making strides in transforming and decolonizing teaching and learning, science and research. Some of the developments have seen the Ubuntu principle as a core, identifying and solving challenges using Africanised methodologies. According to Sharma (2021, 25), coloniality has reconfigured itself by using scientific-rational methods, and the colonial question must be reframed beyond epistemology and ontology to unravel traditional knowledge as a source of valid knowledge. Ndlovu-Gatsheni (2018:2), citing what his book *Epistemic Freedom in Africa* is about, states the following in support of this:

> Epistemic Freedom in Africa is about the struggle for African people to think, theorize, interpret the world and write from where they are located, unencumbered by Eurocentrism. The imperial denial of common humanity to some human beings meant that in turn their knowledges and experiences lost their value, their epistemic virtue. Now, in the twenty-first century, descendants of enslaved, displaced, colonized and racialized peoples have entered academies across the world, proclaiming loudly that they are human beings, their lives matter and they were born into valid and legitimate knowledge systems that are capable of helping humanity to transcend the current epistemic and systemic crises. Together, they are engaging in diverse struggles for cognitive justice, fighting against the epistemic line that haunts the twenty-first century.

Therefore, it is pertinent for Africans to look beyond the past injustices and tackle and question Western practices, which have gained superiority and universal recognition over IKS. Repatriation of looted physical African indigenous resources thus forms part of decoloniality efforts.

OPEN ACCESS TO INDIGENOUS KNOWLEDGE AND UBUNTU PHILOSOPHY

As IK is regarded as communal knowledge, it enshrines the element of sharing and openness. The movement of Open Access has proven to enhance widespread accessibility of knowledge, closing the gap between the information-rich and the information poor.

IK's preservation and digitization have been identified as a solution to curbing looting and misappropriation of indigenous African heritage and practices (Maasz et al. 2017, 29; Mdhluli et al. 2021, 4). This is supported by Tapfuma and Hoskins (2020), asserting that there is a need for IK to be documented, codified, accessed, shared and disseminated through the utilization of institutional repositories for sustainable living. In addition to this, Balogun and Kalusopa (2021, 2) developed a framework for guiding digital preservation strategies and procedures for the long-term preservation of IKS content online.

By using open access repositories for preserving IK, the next generation will be able to access their ancestral knowledge and practices for sustainable living. This will also ensure that African knowledge is applied, enhancing global practices, where the rightful owners are also acknowledged.

Ubuntu philosophy will thus be embedded and applied beyond continental borders, where the world will be perceived as a universal community with the common goal of sharing and benefiting African IKS. This is supported by Van Norren (2014, 256), with the assertion that there is no valid reason why Ubuntu should be restricted to the continent of Africa just because it was born there, nor does it need to be an ideology that is unique to Africa. Therefore, this communal principle is regarded as a vehicle for managing and preserving IK. The study conducted by Nansubuga and Munene (2020), where the Ubuntu knowledge management model has been proposed, assumes the legitimacy of experience as a source of knowledge. Irrespective of IK being orally in nature, measures can be put in place to record and preserve this knowledge to enhance its accessibility.

Open access thus has the benefit of limiting the patenting of such knowledge to make it openly accessible to everyone, where the rightful IK holders will be acknowledged accordingly. Mhlongo and Ngulube (2020, 284) stress the importance of libraries as information provision institutions to play their role in recording and capturing IK to ensure accessibility. There is no doubt that some of the libraries in Africa are still under-resourced; however, collaboration in sharing resources for digitization purposes can ensure that marginalized indigenous communities and their knowledge are sustained and protected from issues of intellectual theft and patent systems.

CONCLUSION

The wealth of a community is judged based on its heritage and culture. Indigenous groups have been adopting diverse methods and procedures to improve their lives and have mechanisms to transfer this knowledge from generation to generation. The codification channels offered by song, dance, folklore, proverbs, idioms, and artifacts allowed these groups to store and communicate information. Besides depriving Africa of its dignity and freedom, colonization has aided the plundering of IKS for commercial gain. Traditional African groups still have a long way to go to reclaim what they lost in the colonial hands.

The patenting and copyrighting of knowledge emanating from indigenous practices without adequate acknowledgment and benefit sharing is an act against humanity. The African continent is rich in resources, yet it is one of the poorest in the world, and there is no doubt who the beneficiaries are. The narrative that Africa is a poverty-stricken continent should change, as developed nations have kept on taking and enriching themselves from what should be beneficial to indigenous communities.

Therefore, this chapter recommends embedding the principle of Ubuntu in developing policies and guidelines for curbing patenting mechanisms and IPR policies that solely benefit individuals, companies and organizations at the expense of IK communities. In addition to this, there should be advocacy and awareness programs targeting marginalized indigenous groups in managing their knowledge better through participating in codification and digitization projects for preservation and ownership purposes. Information provision organizations such as libraries, museums and archives should collaborate with IKS initiatives in cultivating digitization processes. Restitution policies and guidelines for African looted IKS resources should be developed according to Ubuntu principle elements as they represent peace and justice. Lastly, African citizens should collaborate with IKS practitioners to ensure that restitution of looted IK occurs and re-educate the new generation on the importance of preserving and protecting our heritage.

REFERENCES

African Digital Heritage (ADH). 2020. Open restitution Africa project. https://africandigitalheritage.org/open-restitution-africa-project/.

Amusan Lere. 2017. Politics of biopiracy: An adventure into Hoodia/Xhoba patenting in Southern Africa. *African Journal of Traditional, Complementary and Alternative Medicines*, 14(1): 103–9.

Apoh, Wazi, and Mehler Andreas. 2019. Restitution of art objects: Bringing in African perspectives. *Trafo* (blog). https://trafo.hypotheses.org/17811.

Bagley, Margo. 2017. Ask me no questions: The struggle for disclosure of cultural and genetic resource utilization in design. *Vanderbilt Journal of Entertainment & Technology Law* 20: 975.

Balogun, Tolulope, and Kalusopa, Trywell. 2021. Web archiving of indigenous knowledge systems in South Africa. *Information Development*, 1–14. https://doi.org/10.1177/02666669211005522.

Bruchac, Margaret. 2014. Indigenous knowledge and traditional knowledge. In *Encyclopedia of Global Archaeology*, edited by Claire Smith, 3814–24. New York: Springer.

Chabalala, Hlupheka, Matsabisa, Motlalepula, and Gqaleni, Nceba. 2021. African natural medicine: Toward a health preservation theory and systematization model for clinical application: African natural medicine and health preservation theory. *Journal of Traditional Chinese Medical Sciences* 8: S32–S43.

Chen, Jim. 2006. There's no such thing as biopiracy . . . and it's a good thing too. *McGeorge Law Review* 37: 1–33

Chennells Roger. 2013. Traditional knowledge and benefit sharing after the Nagoya protocol: Three cases from South Africa. *Law, Environment and Development Journal* 9:163.

Chilisa, Bagele. 2020. *Indigenous research methodologies*. Thousand Oaks, CA: Sage.

Chiparausha, Blessing, and Mavhunduse, Frederick. 2018. The role of folktales in the preservation of indigenous knowledge among the Shona: A review based on Aaron C. Hodza's Ngano Dzamatambidzanwa. *Southern African Journal for Folklore Studies* 24(2): 707–19.

De Jonge, Bram. 2011. What is fair and equitable benefit-sharing? *Journal of Agricultural and Environmental Ethics* 24(2): 127–46.

Doyle, Anastasia Roxane. 2018. Access and control of biodiversity in the context of biopiracy: The case of pelargonium sidoides in the Raymond Mhlaba Local Municipality. http://vital.seals.ac.za:8080/vital/access/manager/PdfViewer/vital:30547/SOURCE1?viewPdfInternal=1.

Ebenso, Bassey, Adeyemi, Gbenga, Adegoke, Adegboyega, and Emmel, Nick. 2012. Using indigenous proverbs to understand social knowledge and attitudes to leprosy among the Yoruba of southwest Nigeria. *Journal of African Cultural Studies* 24(2): 208–22.

Eckert, Lauren, Ban Natalie, Frid Alejandro, and McGreer, Madeleine. 2018. Diving back in time: Extending historical baselines for yelloweye rockfish with indigenous knowledge. *Aquatic Conservation: Marine and Freshwater Ecosystems* 28(1): 158–66.

Feris, Loretta. 2004. Protecting traditional knowledge in Africa: Considering African approaches. *African Human Rights Law Journal* 4(2): 242–55.

Foster, Laura. 2017. Reinventing hoodia: Peoples, plants, and patents in South Africa. Johannesburg: Wits University Press.

Goduka, Ivy. 2000. African/indigenous philosophies: Legitimizing spiritually centered wisdoms within the academy. In *African voices in education*, edited by P. Higgs, N. Vakalisa, T. Mda, and N. T. Assié-Lumumba, 179–93. Kenwyn, South Africa: Juta

Gollnhofer, Johanna F., and Schouten John. 2017. Complementing the dominant social paradigm with sustainability. *Journal of Micromarketing* 37(2): 143–52.

Grey Sam. 2014. Indigenous knowledge. In *The Encyclopedia of Quality of Life and Well-Being Research*, edited by Alex C. Michalos, 3229–33. Dordrecht: Springer. https://doi.org/10.1007/978-94-007-0753-5.

Ismail, Zenobia, and Fakir, Tashil. 2004. Trademarks or trade barriers? Indigenous knowledge and the flaws in the global IPR system. *International Journal of Social Economics*, 31 nos. 1–2: 173–94.

Janke Terri, and Sentina, Maiko. 2017. Indigenous knowledge: Issues for protection and management. https://www.ipaustralia.gov.au/sites/default/files/ipaust_ikdiscussionpaper_28march2018.pdf.

Kiwara-Wilson, Salome. 2012. Restituting colonial plunder: The case for the Benin bronzes and ivories. *DePaul Journal of Art, Technology and Intellectual Property,* 23: 375426.
Kunkun, Olori, and Olokun, Oli. 2007. A preamble on menu, service, and table manners at the devil's dinner table. In *You must set forth at dawn: A memoir*, edited by Wole Soyinka, 221–332. Ibadan, Nigeria: Randon House Trade Paperbacks.
Lubinga, Elizabeth. 2014. Exploring the possibility of including African proverbs in HIV and AIDS messages to influence reception by the South African youth. *South African Journal of African Languages* 34(sup1): 15–22.
Lunde, Kristin Scheel. 2018. Ancient, indigenous and iconic textile motifs in contemporary fashion case study: Defining concepts through textile designs—appropriation, collaboration, provenance and identity. In *The Social Fabric: Deep Local to Pan Global; Proceedings of the Textile Society of America 16th Biennial Symposium.* Presented at Vancouver, BC, Canada; September 19–23.
Maasz, Donovan, Winschiers-Theophilus, Heike, Stanley, Colin, Rodil, Kasper, and Mbinge, Uriaike. 2018. A digital indigenous knowledge preservation framework: The 7C model—Repositioning IK holders in the digitization of IK. In *Digitisation of culture: Namibian and international perspectives*, edited by Dharm Singh Jat, Jürgen Sieck, Hippolyte N'Sung-Nza Muyingi, Heike Winschiers-Theophilus, Anicia Peters, Shawulu Nggada, 29–47. Singapore: Springer.
Majange, Gwadamirai. 2015. Amazing African proverbs that can be linked to the new Global Goals. https://www.one.org/international/blog/amazing-african-proverbs-that-can-be-linked-to-the-new-global-goals/.
Masango, Charles Akwe. 2020. Indigenous knowledge codification of African traditional medicine: Inhibited by status quo based on secrecy? *Information Development* 36(3): 327–38.
Mdhluli, Tsetselelane D., Mokgoatšana, Sekgothe, Kugara, Stewart, and Vuma, Lucky. 2021. Knowledge management: Preserving, managing and sharing indigenous knowledge through digital library. *HTS Teologiese Studies/Theological Studies* 77(2): 1–7.
Mhlongo, Maned, and Ngulube, Patrick. 2020. Resource provision and access to indigenous knowledge in public libraries in South Africa. *Information Development* 36(2): 271–87.
Morgera, Elisa. 2019. Under the radar: The role of fair and equitable benefit-sharing in protecting and realising human rights connected to natural resources. *The International Journal of Human Rights* 23(7): 1098–139.
Munyonga Alex. 2020. Global coloniality through science and technology: the theft of African traditional medicinal knowledge. In *Decolonising Science, Technology, Engineering and Mathematics (STEM) in an age of technocolonialism: Recentring African indigenous Knowledge and Belief Systems*, edited by Artwell Nhemachena, Nokuthula Hlabangane and Joseph Matowanyika, 99–124. Bamenda: Langa Research & Publishing Common Initiative Group (RPCIG).
Nansubuga, Florence, and Munene, John. 2020. Awakening the Ubuntu episteme to embrace knowledge management in Africa. *Journal of Knowledge Management* 24(1):105–19. https://doi.org/10.1108/JKM-09-2018-0603.

Ndlovu-Gatsheni, Sabelo. 2018. *Epistemic freedom in Africa: Deprovincialization and decolonization*. New York: Routledge.

Oliver, Owen. 2020. Decolonization can't happen without the input of indigenous communities. The Aspen Institute. https://www.aspeninstitute.org/blog-posts/decolonization-cant-happen-without-the-input-of-indigenous-communities/.

Omoera, Osakue Stevenson, and Inegbeboh, Bridget Obiaozor. 2013. Context of usage and aesthetics of selected proverbs from Southern Nigeria. *Journal of Language, Technology & Entrepreneurship in Africa* 4(1): 16–30.

Orozco, David, and Poonamallee, Latha. 2014. The role of ethics in the commercialization of indigenous knowledge. *Journal of Business Ethics* 119(2): 275–86.

Oyewale, Adesina, Caleb Adelowo, and Moses Ekperiware. 2018. Patenting and technology entrepreneurship in Nigeria: issues, challenges and strategic options. *Journal of Economics, Management and Trade* 21(2): 1–14.

Robinson, Daniel. 2012. Biopiracy and the Innovations of indigenous Peoples and Local Communities. In *Indigenous Peoples' Innovation: Intellectual Property Pathways to Development,* edited by Peter Drahos and Susy Frankel, 77–94. Canberra: Australian National University ePress.

Rose, Janna. 2016. Biopiracy: When indigenous knowledge is patented for profit. The Conversation. https://theconversation.com/biopiracy-when-indigenous-knowledge-is-patented-for-profit-55589

Roht-Arriaza, Naomi. 1995. Of seeds and shamans: The appropriation of the scientific and technical knowledge of indigenous and local communities. *Michigan Journal of International Law*, 17: 919–66.

Seleshie, Loza. 2021. Biopiracy: How can African countries protect their plants and traditions? The Africa Report. https://www.theafricareport.com/135045/biopiracy-how-can-african-countries-protect-their-plants-and-traditions/.

Sharma, Ananya. 2021. Decolonizing international relations: Confronting erasures through indigenous knowledge systems. *International Studies* 58(1): 25–40.

Sharma Piyush. 2012. Indigenous knowledge of plants in India and biopiracy. In *Plant Taxonomy: Past, present, and future*, edited by Rajni Gupta, 141–66. New Delhi: The Energy and Resources Institute (TERI).

Shizha, E. 2010. Rethinking and reconstituting indigenous knowledge and voices in the academy in Zimbabwe: a decolonization process. In *Indigenous Knowledge and Learning in Asia/Pacific and Africa,* edited by Dip Kapoor and Edward Shizha, 115–29. New York: Palgrave Macmillan. https://doi.org/10.1057/9780230111813_8.

Tapfuma, Mass, and Hoskins, Ruth. 2020. Visibility and accessibility of indigenous knowledge on open access institutional repositories at universities in Africa. In *Digital Libraries and Institutional Repositories: Breakthroughs in Research and Practice*, 454–72. Hershey, PA: IGI Global. https://doi.org/10.4018/978-1-7998-2463-3.ch028.

Tesgera, Beka Melkamu. 2019. Patenting developing countries' traditional knowledge as new invention: An examination of the teff processing patent claim by a Dutch company and the way forward. In: *Ethiopian Yearbook of International Law 2018*, edited by Yihdego Zeray, Melaku Desta and Martha Belete Hailu, 63–89. Cham, Switzerland: Springer. https://doi.org/10.1007/978-3-030-24078-3_4.

Thakhathi, Andani, and Netshitangani, Tshilidzi. 2020. Ubuntu-as-Unity: Indigenous African proverbs as a 're-educating' tool for embodied social cohesion and sustainable development. *African Identities* 18(4): 407–20.

Thompson, Kim-Ly, Lantz, Trevor, and Ban, Natalie. 2020. A review of indigenous knowledge and participation in environmental monitoring. *Ecology and Society* 25(2): 1–10. http://dx.doi.org/10.5751/ES-04714-170308

Thornton, Thomas, and Maciejewski Scheer, Adela. 2012. Collaborative engagement of local and traditional knowledge and science in marine environments: A review. *Ecology and Society* 17(3): 1–26

Ujomu, Philip Ogo, and Bature, Anthony. 2018. Conflicting values, Ubuntu philosophy and peace building: An African experience. *Culture and Dialogue* 6(2): 174–90.

Ubungu, George Okello. 2019. Museums: Geopolitics, decolonisation, globalisation and migration. *Museum International* 71(1–2): 62–71.

United Nations (UN). 2007. United Nations declaration on the rights of indigenous peoples. https://www.un.org/esa/socdev/unpfii/documents/DRIPS_en.pdf.

Van Beurden, Sarah. 2022. Loot: Colonial collections and African restitution debates. Ohio State University. https://origins.osu.edu/read/loot-colonial-collections-and-african-restitution-debates?language_content_entity=en.

Van Norren, Dorine Eva. 2014. The nexus between Ubuntu and Global Public Goods: Its relevance for the post 2015 development Agenda. *Development Studies Research. An Open Access Journal* 1(1): 255–66.

Willcox, Merlin, Diallo, Drissa, Sanogo, Rokia, Giani, Sergio, Graz, Bertrand, Falquet, Jacques, and Bodeker, Gerard. 2015. Intellectual property rights, benefit-sharing and development of "improved traditional medicines": A new approach. *Journal of ethnopharmacology* 176: 281–85.

World Intellectual Property Organization (WIPO). 2022. Traditional Knowledge and Intellectual Property—Background Brief. https://www.wipo.int/pressroom/en/briefs/tk_ip.html.

Wyatt, Tanya, and Brisman, Avi. 2017. The role of denial in the 'Theft of Nature': Comparing biopiracy and climate change. *Critical Criminology* 25(3): 325–41.

Wynberg, Rachel. 2019. San and Khoi claim benefits from rooibos. https://mg.co.za/article/2019-11-01-00-san-and-khoi-claim-benefits-from-rooibos/.

Zidny, Robby, Sjöström, Jesper, and Eilks, Ingo. 2020. A multi-perspective reflection on how indigenous knowledge and related ideas can improve science education for sustainability. *Science & Education* 29(1): 14585.

Chapter Three

Land Dispossession and Food Insecurity in Contemporary South Africa

Consequences of Land Looting Institutionalized through the Natives Land Act 27

Mfundo Mandla Masuku, Mbongeni Shadrack Sithole and Bhekani Ngwenya

INTRODUCTION

The Natives Land Act of 1913 was introduced by the Apartheid regime to regulate the acquisition of land owned by Blacks and thus served to provide a foundation for segregation and apartheid, with state institutions used to evict and dispossess Blacks, Africans in particular, from better-endowed land. The current incidents of land and other properties' expropriation may be attributed to the historic legacy of colonial land looting of Africa, resulting from the Berlin Conference. This conference, popularly known as "Scramble for Africa," served as a foundation that orchestrated the major Western powers' competition over control of Africa (Bond 2008; Oliver and Oliver 2017). South Africa, with its unique history, was not spared from these unjust practices. The colonial and apartheid systems used institutionalized strategies, to advance the nature and extent of colonial land expropriation that was faced by the indigenous people. The authors purposely use the phrase *land looting* to advance the nature and extent of indigenous people's socioeconomic injustice manifested through food insecurity and dispossession of their land. Blacks, Africans in particular, had been steadily and systematically deprived of access and ownership of land for more than 261 years since the arrival of white Dutch settler communities on South African shores (Dye and La Croix 2020).

For most people, Africans in particular, land plays various roles, namely a commodity, a social space, a cultural artefact and a divine inheritance (Vorster 2019). Land is therefore an entity, which communities' aspirations are dependent upon. Landless people will never be able to survive, particularly at the economical level, but will always serve the interest of those with the land. Historical trends on the land question show that the colonizers were not ready to give up land without a fight. In fact, to (forcefully) deprive people of their land may be regarded as the highest form of dehumanizing (Vorster 2019). An example is Algeria, where the French had to exit after what was termed 'revolutionary terrorism' organized by the Front de Liberation Nationale (FLN) (Steele 2017). Another example is Mozambique, where the Portuguese had to leave (Funada-Classen 2012), and Zimbabwe, where Ian Smith suffered defeat in the hands of Robert Mugabe in 1980 (Eppel 2004). The land question is not only an African problem, considering, as Faulkner (2017) reports, that the revolutions in Russia, organized by the Bolsheviks under the leadership of Lenin and Trotsky, and China, under Mao Ze Dong, confiscated the land through land reform. In this regard, the land was redistributed to the peasants, forming collectives in order to increase the production of food; in the process, the socialists' approach was viewed to have managed to narrow the gap between the rich and the poor.

In South Africa, the adoption of a capitalist economy has had negative impacts on the livelihoods of ordinary South Africans and has widened the gap between the rich and poor; hence, South Africa has been and is still regarded as one of the most unequal societies in the world. Moreover, the negotiations on the road to democracy resulted in white landowners keeping the land that they had acquired through 'looting'. Therefore, white people will not give up the land without a bloody fight. Attempts by the government of South Africa to acquire land voluntarily, through the 'willing seller' and 'willing buyer' approach has not yielded much success (Lahiff 2007). It is on this basis that the land reform activists are calling for the expropriation of land without compensation after more than two decades with the democratic government in power. Radical measures and compromises from those who own land need to happen to prevent land revolution in South Africa. The looting that happened in July 2021 indicates the violence ordinary people can be subjected to when cornered by poverty, food insecurity and unemployment. Therefore, it is important that the legacies of the Natives Land Act of 1913 and previous land looting be addressed by the African National Congress government and other stakeholders.

HISTORICAL BACKGROUND ON LAND LOOTING

As indicated in the introductory section, the looting of land in South Africa is traceable from the arrival of settlers in 1652 under the auspices of Dutch East India Company. The Dutch East India Company is a private company that in 1602 received a charter from the States General of the Dutch Republic to act on its behalf in its overseas territories (Fourie, Jansen & Siebrits 2013 51). As the agent of Dutch activities at the Cape and in the East, this private company is reported to have applied three principles that guided its commercial and economic policies, namely monopoly, maximum profit and strongly oriented to short-term profiteering (Fourie et al 2013). This assertion reflects that this company was not different from other colonial masters like Britain and Portugal, since they were all driven by wealth, greed and profits. When the first settlers landed in the Southern tip of Africa, they neither had land nor livestock, as their primary goal was that of trading with India, Malaysia and Indonesia through the sea via the Southern part of Africa (Oliver and Oliver 2017).

Apparently, they raided the local indigenous African population not only for livestock but to dispossess them of land as well. The first European settlements had no formal governmental structures; land was grabbed with impunity and, in the process, the African people's lifestyles, livelihoods and economic survival patterns were destroyed. In this regard, the sharecropping farmers were turned into labourers in white-owned farms. This could be viewed as having provided the labour base for the supply for the Industrial Revolution that was kick-started with the discovery of diamonds in Kimberly in 1886 and later the discovery of gold in Witwatersrand. This economic sector transformation in Southern Africa necessitated the beginning of transporting and supplying of labour from one area to another to work in the minerals sector; thus began the migrant labour system, which in a way destroyed not only the livelihoods but the social fabric and cohesion of family units and affected the whole social units. The survival of the Khoi San and other indigenous people depended on whites, to whom they had to sell their labour. The white settlers became rich landowners, with their food security becoming guaranteed at the expense of the dispossessed (Beinart and Delius 2014). The formation of the Union of South Africa in 1910 laid the foundation for institutionalized land grabbing through legislation by the Union government after the decolonization by the British government (Houston et al. 2013).

The first legacy of the Union government was to regulate land ownership through the enactment of the 1913 Natives Land Act. "The Act laid the foundation for segregation and apartheid through most of the rest of the century" (Hall 2014, 1). It is through this very same Act that at a later stage the apartheid regime institutionalized the regulation of land looting. The parliament that promulgated this Act was not legitimate in the eyes of the Khoi, San, the Xhosa and other indigenous groups in Southern Africa, as they were not party to it in the land of their birth and of their forefathers. People's livelihoods and their food security were destroyed as they had to destock their livestock and live in areas that were infertile in perpetuity up until today. Interestingly, the first opposition to the Union Bill in 1910 and the 1913 Natives Land Act by the South African Native National Congress, which later became the ANC in 1924 had no connection with the local peasantry; they were missionary-educated elites who only wanted to become British subjects and pay their allegiance to the queen of England.

CONFLICT FROM CAPE TO THE INTERIOR OVER LAND

Conflict in the Cape can be traced as far back as the 1650s by the arrival of the Dutch, then the French Huguenot settlers, who also had nothing, and finally the British in 1795 and 1806 in the Cape; which was an entry point for the dispossessors. The arrival of the British brought them into conflict with the Boers because of their Anglicization policy. This conflict saw African people being disposed of land from the East through frontier wars with the Xhosa and other land looting by the Afrikaners when they trekked from the Cape into the interior. This great movement of the Afrikaners from 1834 to 1838 led to massive looting of the interior starting in Natal, the Transvaal and the Orange Free State and would lead to the destabilization of the interior involving the Afrikaners in skirmishes with the Dingane, Moshoeshwe and other tribal groups. This chapter will argue that the Natives Land Act of 1913 laid the foundation for organized and institutionalized state looting of the land in Southern Africa. Rich provides a perception by Sol Plaatje that the African was reduced to the condition of "pariah in the land of his birth," and it was further argued that "the authorities were waging a war of extermination against the blacks; and that they were bent upon reducing the independent black peasantry to a state of thralldom" (Rich 1976, 1).

LOOTING IN THE CONTEMPORARY ERA

In July 2021, South Africa was hit by a wave of devastating violence that left over 350 people dead and caused massive economic damage (Maluleke, Mphatheni and Nkosi 2022). It is unfortunate that different people attributed different causal factors to this incident, namely civil unrest, looting, food riots, uprising, rebellion and counterrevolution. Maluleke et al. (2022) are among few authors who have described this riot to have started as a result of sentencing and detention of South Africa's former president, Jacob Gedleyihlekisa Zuma. They further describe this incident to have "swiftly degenerated into looting and destruction, driven by widespread anger over the hardship and inequality that nearly three decades of democracy since the end of apartheid have failed to address" (Maluleke et al. 2022, 591). For eight days, South Africa experienced violent protests linked with widespread looting, shop burning and destruction of public and private property, primarily in the provinces of Kwa-Zulu-Natal and Gauteng. Protests resulted in the loss of properties, business stock, employment and livelihoods, as well as the destruction of farming, financial services facilities, infrastructure and food distribution centres (Vhumbunu 2021). The South African economy is particularly vulnerable to such disruption; during the unrest period, nearly 100 malls, 200 shopping centres, 300 banks and 90 pharmacies were closed (Elumalai et al. 2022). The unrest contributed to increased food insecurity and price inflation, which severely impacted a number of households due to their low socioeconomic status.

This looting was described by the media as barbaric and senseless, as it wreaked havoc throughout the economy of the province. While it is true that acts of violence and looting should have been and were condemned in the strongest terms; it is worth pointing out that naturally Black people are not looters. History has shown that Black people have lived and coexisted for centuries, some living nomadic lifestyles working in harmony with nature. However, one would not dispute the fact that there were wars fought between the tribal groups where of course livestock would be taken as spoils of war. Therefore, in a sense, this was not looting but a wartime event which did not involve taking the land. People lived off the land by grazing their livestock, fetching firewood for survival and plant crops in order to survive and maintain their livelihoods as any social grouping. Ownership of the land was not paramount, as there was also a belief that anyone could use the land and move on to another piece of land since the land was owned by the king. All people had to do was to pay allegiance to a particular king and claim citizenry.

A new theory of land ownership was introduced which was alien to indigenous Black African communities, and they were caught flat footed on the issue of land. Apartheid and colonialism were constituents of capitalist development, and their economic systems were described as an attack on the livelihoods of the poor and economic sabotage (Cottle 2021; Ngwane 2021). Depriving the indigenous African population of their land was a definite way of destroying their livelihoods. Access to land by Black Africans prior to dispossession yielded positive results in their lives (Hall 2014). The arrival of settlers and their land grabbing and the imposing of forms of governance foreign to and not representative of the indigenous was absolutely a form of looting. This looting was not only confined to the land but extended to other properties, including livestock and resources, which belong to the rightful indigenous population of Southern Africa. The July 2021 looting of shops and businesses thus was an expression of frustration by the dispossessed South African communities, who found themselves at the receiving end of poverty, unemployment and marginalization in what the world described as a rainbow nation.

THE EFFECT OF THE NATIVES LAND ACT OF 1913

Modise and Mtshiselwa (2013) argue that before this Act, Black Africans did not experience many socioeconomic challenges, namely poverty and food insecurity, as their economic wellbeing was grounded by full access and ownership of arable land. This chapter describes the Natives Land Act of 1913 as a state-driven looting mechanism used by European settlers to gain control over the lives and properties of African people. Furthermore, the Act was biased toward the needs of white commercial farmers and their counterpart Black farmers steadily became farm labourers and landless to destabilise the economy of Black farmers. A great deal of food insecurity and the continuation of looting in a legitimised manner came into being as a result of the enactment of the Natives Land Act of 1913, reminding us that the apartheid regime was rooted in it.

The Land Act of 1913 restricted the African majority to only 7 percent of the land, which was estimated to be about nine million hectares. The Act prohibited Black Africans from buying and owning land anywhere other than in their designated reserves, which were degraded and non-productive. This prohibition exacerbated poverty and food insecurity amongst the Black majority. The forceful removal from arable land to degraded land made it difficult for Blacks to farm and reduced avenues of the source of income. Despite the existence of International Human Rights Conventions including the International Convention on the Elimination of All Forms of Racial Discrimination of 1965, the International Covenant on Civil and Political Rights of 1966 and the International Covenant on Economic, Social and Cultural Rights of 1966, the apartheid regime was still receiving backing from some Western international communities. Akinola (2016) raises great concern that this Act was a violation of the human rights of the South African majority to access and own their forefathers' land, which caused hunger among Black Africans. Furthermore, Akinola argues that land is a natural capital that enhances economic sustenance and social sustainability, and the Act therefore increased inequality and made white commercial farmers generate income while Black farmers were mainly producing for consumption. The white population owned 72 percent followed by Coloured at 15 percent, Indians at 5 percent, and Black Africans at 4 percent; other unidentified by race were at 3 percent and co-owners at 1 percent (Department of Rural Development and Land Reform 2017). Furthermore, this inequitable distribution of land was informed by the 1913 Natives Land Act of racial land dispossession. This created economic dependence and turned the Black populace into consumers, thus providing the market for white farmers. Tshishonga (2020) has raised great concern that the South African government is still unable to address the inequitable distribution of land through land reform programmes to give back to rightful owners.

LAND AS BASIC HUMAN RIGHTS

This chapter argues that the Natives Land Act of 1913 was used as a mechanism to violate the right to property, which led to lack of socioeconomic independence and promoted dependence on the white people (Davenport 2005, 25). The promulgation of the Natives Land Act of 1913 made Black African farmers not worthy, and their effort not recognized to enhance food security but retrogression. Coetzee (2018); Jili and Masuku (2021) attest that more than fourteen million people, the majority Black Africans, in South Africa are food insecure because they are net consumers of purchased food, not producers, due to limited access to and ownership of arable land. Land and food security cannot be separated from socio-political issues, and the government has an obligation to redress the inequitable distribution of land to save the lives of previously disadvantaged groups during the Apartheid regime. The government of South Africa committed itself to bring about equitable access to land for all South Africans and to ensure food security and sharing of natural resources as stipulated in section 25 of the Constitution.

The Natives Land Act of 1913 according to Daniels (1987) had far reaching effects on Black people, it limited rights to land ownership to reserve areas; it legalized and regularized territorial segregation and the 'natural policy'; and it increased the supply of cheap labour to South Africa predominantly white-owned industry. The latter was assured by Black disenfranchisement and by the Black population growth on a fixed amount of land which would eventually result in erosion of the agricultural potential of the land. With virtually no agricultural potential in the reserves or the means to provide that potential, Blacks were required to seek employment in areas where jobs could be found (Daniels 1987, 11). This act was divided into 'Schedule of Native Areas'. Alan-Dodson argues that they were essentially areas which included existing reserves, locations and farms which were set aside for occupation by Africans, consisting of 8 percent of the surface area. Section1 of the Act forbade a 'Native' from entering into any agreement . . . for the purchase, hire or acquisition from a person other than a native' of land outside the Scheduled areas, save with the permission of the Governor General, which for all intents and purposes meant the Minister of Native Affairs (Alan-Dodson 2013, 31). This further outlawed the purchase of land by Europeans from Africans.

Feinberg and Horn estimate that twenty-two million acres of land were brought within the four provinces of the Union to white controlled areas (Feinberg and Horn, 2009). Some different scholars and academics have had different approaches and interpretations of the Natives Land Act. as Davenport (2005) perceives regards these acts as inadequate by the Union government; hence they passed Native Trust and Land Act 1936 which would give them more powers in removing the Black spots in white designated areas. With the 1936 Land Act the government was able to remove blacks in areas where blacks had done well for themselves as in Doornfountein, and at Mgwali in the white corridor between Ciskei and Transkei and among the Mfengu who were removed from Humansdorp to Elukhanyisweni (Davenport 2005, 25). In the Orange River Colony, farming had spread after the South Africa war, producing at the upper reaches comfortably situated peasants and small farmers. According to Bundy, these farmers used state-of-the art and up-to-date machinery, selling a lot of grain directly to merchants, on equal terms with the whites, and ran large herds of sheep, cattle and goats (Bundy, 1972: 384).

The prohibition of sharing crops had negative effects on Black South Africans. Both Black and white people could share the profit from their agricultural activities. According to Feinberg and Horn (2009), Section 7 of the Act of 1936 declared sharecropping or sowing on the shares illegal. As a result, the existing contracts on sharecropping between white landlords and the Black African people were terminated. Such termination had a negative impact on the livelihoods of many Black South Africans, in that they lost their means of making a living. Having lost their source of income, Black South Africans were forced to consider other means of accumulating money. As such, labouring for the white farmers became an option (Feinberg and Horn 2009, 69). Furthermore, Rich (1976) regards the Act as striking a death blow at non-white farming, which had been an earnest wish of every progressive landowner. It would therefore be safe to say that the Act considerably affected labour conditions in many parts of the Union. It meant clearing off a large number of natives from European farms, the natives simply being allowed to work in return for a wage. These would result in landowners becoming rich and acquiring capital which they would invest in another sector of the economy where Blacks were excluded and had to rely on meagre wages for their survival and livelihoods in the land of their ancestors. This argument is also upheld by Modise and Mtshiselwa (2013), who say that the Natives Land Act deprived the majority of Africans of the right to productively own land for their economic wellbeing and sustainability; thus poverty, as experienced in post-apartheid South Africa, can be attributed to the legacy of the colonial and apartheid past, especially with reference to the 1913 Natives Land Act and the resulting dispossession.

Furthermore, this Act compromised further access to land and as it limited the opportunities for the economic development, stability and welfare of the Africans. Therefore, the looting of the land laid the foundation for the Natives 1913 Land Act to institutionalise through the 1910 Union parliament the looting that had been happening since the arrival of white people on South African shores. This destruction of African people's farming activities and independent peasantry who had once been able to support their families led to poverty which is still felt today by landless ordinary South Africans.

LAND REFORM AND LOOTING

Before the arrival of White settlers, Black Africans used to share land and agrarian products. The democratic government led by African National Congress (ANC) had to address the imbalances of the past through land reform. Land reform has been described by Martin as the redistribution of property or rights for the benefit of the landless, tenants and farm labourers (Martin 1999). The South African Constitution, adopted on 8 May 1996 and amended on 11 October 1996 by the Constitutional Assembly has made the land question clear. Section 25 (1). No one may be deprived of property except in terms of law of general application, and no law may permit arbitrary deprivation of property, (2) property may be expropriated only in terms of law of general application, (a) for the public purpose or in the public interests, and (b) Subject to compensation, the amount of which and the time and the manner of payment of which has been agreed to by those or decided or approved by the court.

Therefore, the Constitution of the Republic of South Africa would not directly deal with the damage done prior to and post the 1913 Native Land Act. While section 7 of the Constitution of 1996 states that a "person or community dispossessed of property after 19 June 1913 as a result of past racially discriminating laws or practice is entitled, to the extent provided by an Act of parliament, either to restitution of that property or to equitable redress." This in a nutshell means that all land looted by the white settlers before 1913 can actually be kept and the redress will only be considered after 1913, when Black people had already been deprived of their land. The government had to buy it back from whites, which is not working to benefit the landless Black people of South Africa because the prices are determined by white farmers and have been inflated (Sikwela, Tshuma and Tshabalala 2018). The Department of Rural Development and Land Reform has attempted to address the land issue but has been characterised by several difficulties, as pointed out by Moolman (2017). First, there is a lack of government capacity to manage Land Reform, in that post-1994, the government could not buy land that was voluntarily offered for land reform. Second, under spending of annual financial budgets and successive budget cuts continue as part of National Treasury's policy to apply fiscal control. Third, there is a lack of expert and efficient support for beneficiaries of land reform after land is possessed (Akinola 2020). Moreover, the Department of Land Affairs has attempted to manage land on behalf of rural communities in tribal settlements. Mamabolo, Sebola and Tsheola (2021) argue that this management has denied people access to one of the key virtues of governance. Land reform in tribal settlements continues to be afflicted by disputes between communal property and interest groups within tribal settlements, thereby undermining the original goal of the policy (Mamabolo and Tsheola 2017, 161). All is not doom and gloom, however; when the Land Reform was set up, Maré (2017) points out, the initial target for land Reform that was set by the government was to transfer 30 percent (25 million hectares) of white-owned farmland to 800,000 non-white farmers. Although the target by 2017 had not been achieved, the figures were quite remarkable with roughly nine million hectares distributed through restitution and redistribution. Some South Africans have not realized the dream of looted land being redistributed to the rightful owners; only a few benefitted, although some cannot farm as they lack support and farming experience. Therefore, land reform cannot redress the impact of loss of land taken since 1913 through forced removal by the apartheid state. Changing the constitution is the only answer, but that is a pie-in-the-sky proposal for ordinary South Africans because the governing party (ANC) has lost credibility with the masses in South Africa, with the support dwindling election after election because of corruption.

CONCLUSION

This chapter offered to provide insight into the inequalities and imbalances prevailing in South Africa's economy and trace the current food insecurity and land looting as the consequences of colonization and apartheid. The chapter confirms that the South African democratic government has been unable to address land question and systematic land looting which occurred before 1994. It further argues that looting is un-African and lacks 'Ubuntu' which Black people have had since postcolonial times. Evidence suggests that the democratic South African government through land reform programmes has manifestly failed to address the effects of the Natives Land Act of 1913. Compared to their white counterparts, the majority of Blacks are still characterized by socioeconomic injustice, manifested through food insecurity and lack of access to land for subsistence or commercial farming. This chapter highlights the three aspects worth noting in relation to land looting. First is that lack of access to land deprived indigenous communities' ability to meet their socioeconomic needs, including advancement of their economic development. Second is that the Act contributed to engineering food insecurity due to depriving Black Africans of farming land. Third, the Act was instrumental in depriving them of the development of a sense of identity and linkage with the land. The colonial and imperialist Britain in its looting escapades took advantage of African people's kindness and exploited the hospitality of indigenous people. African people had lived for million years in Africa in harmony with nature, living stable and sometimes nomadic lifestyles without personally possessing land individualistically. This looting was not confined to the Cape but extended to the interior from the competing interests of the Afrikaners and the British, which culminated in the South African War in 1899–1902. The Natives Land Act laid the foundation for Bantustan because the 'schedule areas' became designated as reserves through the Bantu Authorities Act and Group Areas Act. Moreover, to ensure that Africans stay in perpetual poverty, other acts had to be passed; those acts were later regarded as apartheid legislation. An example is the Bantu Education Act and others which prevented an African from fighting for his rights in the country of his birth. The chapter concludes with the view that the redress of imbalances experienced by the dispossessed communities is the inevitable recommendation to empower them in contributing to the country's economy.

REFERENCES

Akinola, Adeoye O. 2016. Human rights, civil society and the contradictions of land reform in South Africa. *Politeia* 35(2): 52–70.

———. 2020. Land reform in South Africa: Interrogating the securitisation of land expropriation without compensation. *Politikon* 47(2): 215–32.

Alan-Dodson, S. C. 2013. The Natives Land Act of 1913 and its legacy. *Advocate*: 29–32.

Beinart, William, and Delius, Peter. 2014. The historical context and legacy of the Natives Land Act of 1913. *Journal of Southern African Studies* 40(4): 667–88.

Bundy, Colin.1972. The emergence and decline of a South African peasantry. *African Affairs* 71(285): 369–388.

Bond, Patrick. 2008. Global uneven development, primitive accumulation and political-economic conflict in Africa: the return of the theory of imperialism. *Journal of Peacebuilding & Development* 4(1): 1–14.

Coetzee, Carli. 2018. "Unsettling the Air-Conditioned Room: Journal Work as Ethical Labour." *Journal of the African Literature Association* 12 (2): 101–15.

Cottle, Eddie. 2021. Potent brew that led to South Africa's urban uprising: pandemic, recession and a crisis of social reproduction. *Daily Maverick*, August 2. https://www.dailymaverick.co.za/opinionista/2021-08-02-potent-brew-that-led-to-south-africas-urban-uprising-pandemic-Recession and-a-crisis-of-social-reproduction.

Daniels, Rudolph. 1987. The nature of the agrarian land question in the Republic of South Africa. *American Journal of Economics and Sociology* 46(1): 1–16.

Davenport, T. R. H. 2005. The Native's Land Act, 1913. *Black Sash Aug* 1983: 24–25.

Department of Rural Development and Land Reform. 2017. *Land audit report. Phase II: Private land ownership by race, gender and nationality*. Pretoria: Department of Rural Development and Land Reform.

Dye, Alan, and La Croix, Sumner. 2020. Institutions for the taking: Property rights and the settlement of the Cape Colony, 1652–1750. *The Economic History Review* 73(1): 33–58.

Elumalai, Vetrimurugan, Godwyn-Paulson, P., Logesh, N., Muthusankar, G., Lakshumanan, C., and Jonathan, M. P. 2022. Burning urban cities of South Africa due to civil turmoil 2021: Socio-economic and environmental consequences. *Cities* 124: 103612.

Eppel, Shari. 2004. Gukurahundi: The need for truth and reconciliation. In *Zimbabwe Injustice and Political Reconciliation*, edited by Brian Raftopolous and Tyrone Savage, 43–62. Harare, Zimbabwe: Weaver Press.

Faulkner, Neil. 2017. *A people's history of the Russian Revolution*. London: Pluto Press.

Feinberg, Harvey M. 1993. The 1913 Natives Land Act in South Africa: Politics, race, and segregation in the early 20th century. *The International Journal of African Historical Studies* 26(1): 65–109.

Feinberg, Harvey M., and André Horn. 2009. South African territorial segregation: New data on African farm purchases, 1913–1936. *The Journal of African History* 50(1): 41–60.

Fourie, Johan, Jansen, Ada, and Siebrits, Krige. 2013. Public finances under private company rule: The Dutch Cape Colony (1652–1795). *New Contree* 68: 51–71.

Funada-Classen, Sayaka. 2013. *The origins of war in Mozambique: A history of unity and division*. Oxford, UK: African Books Collective.

Hall, Ruth. "The legacies of the Natives Land Act of 1913." *Scriptura: Journal for Contextual Hermeneutics in Southern Africa* 113.1 (2014): 1–13.

Houston, Gregory, et al. 2013. *The liberation struggle and liberation heritage sites in South Africa.* Pretoria: Democracy, Governance, and Service Delivery (DGSD) & Human Sciences Research Council (HSRC).

Jili, Nokukhanya N., and Masuku, Mfundo M. 2021. Land expropriation, food security and local economic development (LED) in South Africa. In *The New Political Economy of Land Reform in South Africa*, 101–19. Cham, Switzerland: Palgrave Macmillan.

Lahiff, Edward. 2007. "Willing buyer, willing seller": South Africa's failed experiment in market-led agrarian reform. *Third World Quarterly* 28(8): 1577–97.

Maluleke, Witness, Mphatheni, Mandlenkosi Richard, and Lindani Nkosi, Sphamandla. 2022. A systematic study on stock theft contributory factors during the South African lockdown. *International Journal of Research in Business and Social Science* 11(2): 462–76.

Mamabolo, M. A., and Tsheola, J. P. 2017. Political-economy of land governance in a democratic South Africa: Private interests vis-à-vis rural communities in tribal settlements. *African Journal of Public Affairs* 9(5): 154–67.

Mamabolo, M. A., Sebola, M. P., and Tsheola, J. P. 2021. The economics of communal smallholder farming within South Africa's historical agricultural structure. *Journal of Global Business & Technology* 17(2.

Maré, Frikkie. "Land reform policies-the path to success." *FarmBiz* 3.5 (2017): 16–17.

Martin, Aurora, and Almeda, L. Philippine land reform cycles: Perpetuating US colonial policy. *Philippine Studies* 47(2 (1999): 181–205.

Modise, Leepo, and Mtshiselwa, Ndikho. 2013. The Natives Land Act of 1913 engineered the poverty of Black South Africans: A historico-ecclesiastical perspective. *Studia Historiae Ecclesiasticae* 39(2): 359–78.

Moolman, H. J. 2017. Law minute: Regulations under the PV Act. *FarmBiz* 3(8): 33.

Ngwane, Trevor. 2021. Mall attacks and the everyday crisis of the working class in South Africa. *Global Labour Journal* 12(3.

Oliver, Erna, and Oliver, Willem H. 2017. The colonisation of South Africa: A unique case. *HTS: Theological Studies* 73(3): 1–8.

Rich, Paul. 1976. African farming and the 1913 Natives' Land Act: Towards a reassessment. https://opensaldru.uct.ac.za/bitstream/handle/11090/503/1976_rich_sflcp21.pdf? equence=1.

Sikwela, Misery M., Tshuma, Mengezi C., and Tshabalala, Thulani. 2018. A critical review of South Africa's land reform programme as a tool to address the nation's triple challenges. *Journal of Public Administration* 53(1–2: 474–88.

Steele, Ryan D. 2017. Violence in Algeria: From colony to independent nation. *Students Theses, Papers and Projects (History)* 62: 1–38. https://digitalcommons.wou. edu/his/62. Accessed 12 February 2022.

Tshishonga, Ndwakhulu Stephen. 2020. Rural development and the struggle for land reform in post-apartheid South Africa. In *African Perspectives on Reshaping Rural Development*, 95–117. Hershey, PA: IGI Global.

Vhumbunu, Clayton Hazvinei. 2021. The July 2021 protests and socio-political unrest in South Africa: Reflecting on the causes, consequences and future lessons. *Conflict Trends*, no. 3: 3–13.

Vorster, Nico. 2019. Land and identity in South Africa: An immanent moral critique of dominant discourses in the debate on expropriation without compensation. *HTS Teologiese Studies/Theological Studies* 75(4): 3–13.

Chapter Four

Criminalising Looting and the Quest for Social Justice in Postcolonial South Africa

Perspectives from Twitter Data

Kemist Shumba, Kutenda Trinos and Nirmala D. Gopal

INTRODUCTION

From July 11 to 23, 2021, political and social tensions erupted in KwaZulu-Natal and spilled into Gauteng province. 'South Africa was hit by hostile demonstrations of a magnitude that it had not experienced since the end of apartheid in 1994 (Winning and Wendell 2021). The civil protests were initially considered an expression of displeasure over the judicial detention of former president Jacob Zuma, indicted on charges of state capture and corruption. The former statesman defied a court order to appear before the Zondo Commission of Inquiry into State Capture. The former statesman was sentenced to fifteen months imprisonment for contempt of court. This legal development angered President Zuma's supporters; thus, the incident rekindled a growing split. Pro-Zuma protests were spontaneously triggered, and protesters gathered at the former statesman's Nkandla residence. The demonstrations spilled into the streets, culminating in an orgy of mass looting (Hunter, Kaveel and Wicks 2021).

What started as protests escalated to mass looting, extensive damage to property and loss of life in the crossfire (Mlaba 2021). An expert panel reported that the looting of shopping malls and warehouses was also linked to some elements of the insurgency, as there is evidence of damage to some strategic government offices, such as those belonging to the Department of Home Affairs. The mass looting has socioeconomic implications, given that an estimated loss of more than 20 billion Rand was recorded, with increased urban insecurity, food insecurity and compromised social protection for all.

This chapter explores the divergent views of netizens, particularly Twitter users, to try to understand the stimuli that triggered this historic uprising. Our goal is to illuminate the complex phenomenon that places the economically disadvantaged communities, Frantz Fanon's *Wretched of the Earth*, at the centre of a simmering socioeconomic and political stalemate in postcolonial South Africa. On the one hand, mass looting is considered sheer criminality and inexcusable (Business Tech 2021). On the other hand, this unprecedented social upheaval is conceptualised as a tool for social change and an inevitable result of poverty and deep-rooted inequalities whose roots can be traced to the infamous apartheid-era (Seekings and Nattrass 2005). Writing on the backdrop of protracted demonstrations for Black Lives Matter in the United States, Vicky Osterweil, the author of *In Defense of Looting*, staked out a provocative position, claiming that looting is a powerful tool to bring about real, lasting change in society (Osterweil 2020).

This chapter begins with an overview of the general understanding of crime and violence. The chapter then focuses on how the data were collected from Twitter, a social media platform that is incontrovertibly fast gaining traction as a source of data for social research (Shumba et al. 2020). After an overview of the methodology, the research findings are presented and discussed. Finally, a conclusion is drawn.

UNDERSTANDING CRIMINALITY, VIOLENCE, AND LOOTING

The looting in KwaZulu-Natal and Gauteng provinces started as spates of uncoordinated violence. The big question revolves around what exactly triggered this violent uprising. Garbero (2017) argued that there is a link between violence, poverty, crime and extreme social injustice in every community. Further, he argued that it is necessary to promote social justice for all communities if violence is to be suppressed. Similarly, Young (1985) argued that social justice is the best approach to preventing crime. This leads us to the general explanations for the causes of crime. There are several theories about the occurrence of crime, which are biological, sociological, political, economic and strain theories (Burke 2018).

We briefly reflect on each of the above theories. The biological theory was propounded by Cesare Lombroso, who claimed that criminals are born with such pressures. As espoused by Shaw and McKay (1942), the sociological perspective conceptualises crime as a force triggered by the environment, particularly socioeconomic disadvantages. This view is supported by Merton (1957) through the strain theory, in which crime is attributed to the presence of a gap in material wealth or socioeconomic status. Similarly, Young (1999) cites increasing inequalities between the haves and have-nots as a trigger for crime, which Cohen (1955) equates with status frustration. This perspective dovetails into Frantz Fanon's conceptualisation of violence as a relevant tool rather than a form of crime (Wallerstein 1978). Indeed, the conceptualisation of violence as instrumental and constructive (Imge 2021) aims to address social imbalances that have their roots in the socioeconomic realm (Roberts 2004). Imge (2021) views socioeconomic imbalances as dehumanising to the oppressed. Thus, the unequal distribution of resources fuels anger, expressed in violence to create new humanity (Roberts 2004). Indeed, Frantz Fanon (cited in Roberts 2004) perceives violence as purifying, and not a criminal act.

Looting is perceived differently by different people with different ideological beliefs. Looting is a crucial tool to bring about the much-needed permanent change in the established and 'acceptable' inequalities that characterise most once-suppressed communities (Osterweil 2005). It is the mass appropriation of property and mass shoplifting in the face of a crisis that constitutes an expression of resentment over the unequal distribution of wealth and property (Osterweil 2005). According to those that frame it as functional, looting is conducted by the urban poor who target businesses and all available commercial spaces. Looting is a means to an end, which is to improve the survival of economically disadvantaged groups (Osterweil 2005).

On the contrary, Quarantelli and Dynes (1970) viewed looting as deviant behaviour by community members that naturally express some form of resentment. This definition, of course, emphasises that looting is a form of deviation from the normative code of conduct and recognises that it is a way for those involved to express their displeasure. Thus, looting is a means of compensating for socioeconomic inequalities. For Loghdey and Newalani (2021), nonviolent protests are legitimate. Therefore, looting constitutes a criminal act because it violates people's rights and the property rights of others. In this study, the focus is on exploring looting from a functional perspective, considering it a justifiable expression by the poverty-stricken, unemployed, and urban poor to address socioeconomic imbalances that have roots in apartheid policies and remain normalised decades after South Africa's independence.

METHODOLOGY

This study was conducted using a qualitative research approach based on its social nature. Pathak, Bijayini and Kalra. (2013) refer to qualitative research as an approach to understanding people's beliefs, experiences, attitudes, behaviours and interactions. The primary focus of this study was to explore the causes of looting by the socially, economically, and politically discriminated and marginalised Black communities.

This study adopted a qualitative approach to explore netizens' responses to the historic mass looting in KwaZulu-Natal and Gauteng provinces on

Twitter, a social media platform and real-time communication service. We purposively selected tweets and replies analysis. These tweets reflected the unprecedented mass looting from July 11 to 23, 2021.

Owing to market developments in information communication technology (ICT), recent years have witnessed a burgeoning social media landscape, characterised by such platforms as Facebook, Instagram, LinkedIn and Twitter. By 2020, Twitter had approximately 1.3 billion accounts and 336 million active users, posting 500 million tweets daily (Ahlgren 2020; Shumba et al. 2020). Of late, Twitter has become trendy, given that it provides an easy way of accessing and downloading published posts. Many social researchers analyse Twitter data for many reasons, including detecting users' emotions (Mohammad 2012). In this study, Twitter was chosen because it constitutes the most extensive dataset of user-generated content, which provides a good source of public opinion (Giachanou and Crestani 2016). Twitter users actively engage in topics of interest through tweets, which constitute an essential source of inadvertently available data.

Further, research has shown that Twitter data are a diverse and salient source for researchers and policymakers (Sarker, DeRoos and Perrone 2020; Aladwani 2015). Thus, among other social media platforms, Twitter serves as the most dominant discursive space (Munoriyarwa and Chambwera 2020). Tweets and their replies from July 11 to 23, 2021 were selected to generate relevant data. This period is significant because mass looting was a topical issue in South Africa, as the phenomenon was practically unfolding and trending on various social media platforms. The tweets were thematically analysed according to thematic analysis inspired by Braun and Clarke (2006). Two authors (KS and KT) coded the data and generated relevant themes. Further, it was essential to ensure inter-coder reliability (Nyambuya et al. 2020). One author (NDG) reviewed all the themes, and consensus was established following an extensive discussion and considerable revisions.

THE ANALYTICAL LENS

Theoretically, this study was situated within the ambit of Critical Discourse Analysis (CDA), which is based on the analysis of texts, interactions and social activities of members of a shared society (Mogashoa 2014). The main principle of CDA is to understand the motivation behind any social action. CDA focuses on describing, interpreting, analysing and critiquing social activities reflected in human texts (Armayanti 2019). In this sense, Van Dijik (2006) positions CDA as an analytical framework that aims to understand the motivation behind all pressing social issues.

From the socio-political and socioeconomic perspectives, Rogers et al. (2005) argued that CDA concerns aspects of power and justice and how economics, race, class, gender, religion and social orientation construct, reproduce and change social systems. In this case, the proponents of CDA believe that texts are the most potent weapons that people use to achieve a different meaning and understanding of the world around them (Lucke 1996; Given 2008). For McGregor (2010), CDA helps social researchers to remove the abstractness of texts and see meaning in the social, political, and economic milieu. In this regard, Locke (2004) highlighted that discourse criticism allows researchers to see how standard texts have been formulated based on existing power relations and people struggling to maintain power balances.

Some scholars emphasised that discourse criticism is about identifying the causes of a social problem and its associated effects and finding possible solutions to address the current situation and avoid it in the future (Armayanti 2019; Mogashoa 2014). In this case, Olson (1995) argued that critical discourse seeks to decipher the hidden motivation behind any action and solve social problems by asking ontological and epistemological questions that inquire into the causes and consequences of a problem.

Critical discourse is viewed from a three-part dimension in its practical application: (i) discourse as text—that is, the linguistic features and organisation of the concrete instances of discourse. (ii) Discourse is discursive practice—that is, discourse as something produced, circulated, disseminated and consumed in society. (iii) Discourse as social practice—that is, the ideological effects and hegemonic processes in which discourse plays a role (Blommaert and Bulcaen 2000). Following this, Mogashoa (2014) argued that CDA is inherently corrective; it aims to redress inequalities visible in social, economic and political settings.

CDA can be conducted through thematic, printed and oral text analysis to activate the meaning of texts in any context. In this study, a thematic analysis was conducted in which the researchers attempted to find themes and patterns in the data (Fulcher 2010). The researchers identified a limited data set from Twitter texts (Howitt and Crammer 2010). To assign patterns, the researchers applied the principles of qualitative data analysis outlined by Braun and Clarke (2006) by identifying, analysing, and reporting emergent patterns in the data. This activated the meaning of the texts.

CAUSES OF LOOTING: EXPLORING DIFFERENT NARRATIVES

The demonstrations, dubbed *Ayikhale*, were caused by a constellation of factors and problems. We studied the reactions of different people to relevant tweets. We analysed the tweets using critical discourse analysis and concluded that the causes were perceived differently: (i) looting as economic sabotage, (ii) criminal networks, (iii) an attack on South African democracy—an imminent coup d'*état,* (iv) lack of state security, and (v). socioeconomic imbalances (Vhumbunu 2021). The following section addresses each of the above reasons.

Looting as Economic Sabotage

The search for the real cause is still underway, and the absolute truth is far from clear. A political faction of the South African population, particularly the ruling ANC, believes that there was a planned racketeering scheme to diminish the economic gains of the South African people. This was even voiced by the incumbent president, Cyril Ramaphosa, who attributed the demonstrations to a group of unnamed individuals who not only sided with former president Jacob Zuma but also did their best to cripple the economy (Sparks 2021). Although there is no evidence of this, it brings into play the political connotations in which accusations of state capture and corruption emerged as the undercurrents contributing to this uprising. Indeed, some of the pro-Ramaphosa supporters believed that there was a hidden hand that supported the demonstrations. They thought that those behind the capture were not happy that wealth was flowing into the hands of Black South Africans. However, other factions also believed that nothing had been done about the unequal distribution of wealth and power from the day of South Africa's independence to the present day. The following excerpt supports this:

> It's okay to Disagree with the looting, BUT you don't have to stupefy yourself by saying its criminality: you use this narrative to avoid the fear you feel, the trauma it causes in you because you know the truth: this is about the POVERTY which your absolute privilege is built on. @MbuyiseniNdlozi.[1]

The general political climate is the leading cause of all civil unrest worldwide. The situation in South Africa was triggered by the imprisonment of former president Jacob Zuma for corruption. A pro-Zuma group (the Zumaites [Zuma supporters]) felt that the justice system was unfair to the former president. Therefore, they mobilised for a solidarity demonstration, which initially began as such when the former president appeared in court.

This expression is visible in the following excerpt:

> Can they leave the former President? Now he is no longer a threat to the society please this man is not well she can serve through parole he didn't kill anyone please it enough now. @nkandla.[2]

However, the verdict did not go down well with many, and they mobilised for massive demonstrations to condemn the judgment. This led to political tensions, even to the point of involving the ruling ANC party. This is what one user shared:

> Zuma is being persecuted by Ramaphosa and his captured Zondo Commission and the entire Judiciary using a rule by law method which was used by ED on you, Mr Chinono. Ramaphosa is learning from Zanu Pf how to be corrupt and cling on power using all means available. #zondocommission.[3]

Zuma-ites wanted the verdict overturned and even demanded that President Cyril Ramaphosa pardon his predecessor. These deafening calls were inciting the president of the Republic to move outside his jurisdiction, given that the law is impartial and must be applied without impunity (Sannerholm 2022).

Zuma-ites wanted the former president to be left alone, arguing that he was old and could no longer be humiliated as a former president. The calls culminated in violence and looting at shopping malls and warehouses. The socio-political dimension was not ignored either; *Ayikhale*'s call encouraged tribal warfare. The tribal expression was visible in one of the tweets:

> They were busy bragging that KZN ke country on its own, blah blah they don't protest here on Twitter only, ke bo papa and mama action. @RiotAndattaSA/Twitter.[4]

Social conflicts ensued. The members of the Zulu tribe had to fight alongside their old man and were ready for anything. This was evident in how they spread the word to defend their old man through all available social media—*Ziyakhala*. The loyalty of the Zuma-ites is visible in the following post:

> Can they leave the former President now he is no longer a threats to the society please this man is not well she can serve through parole he didn't kill anyone please it enough now. #FreeZuma@mnqobigatje.[5]

Criminogenic Perspectives

The attempt to free former president Jacob Zuma turned ugly, and people began to engage in criminal activities such as looting, burning down stores and killing each other. This left a trail of devastation where no one could distinguish between a cause for concern and criminal tendencies. People now moved around in groups, looting stores and warehouses. People's belongings were taken, businesses were paralysed, and buildings were set on fire, which was considered riotous.

Some Twitter users believed that this incident was an act of organised crime, with some people taking shelter under the guise of saving President Zuma to commit looting and arson (Lamb 2021). However, this did not go unchallenged as some people began to question the country's police service status. Those who questioned the state of the police even claimed that even those who were supposed to protect citizens were part of dirty tricks in communities where they were bribed or belonged to crime syndicates such as drug lords.

However, some Twitter users noted that looting is not new in South Africa. For example, one claimed that looting was exacerbated by poverty, inequality and high unemployment rates in South Africa, which the country grappled with for decades during and after apartheid. Some users shared this:

> The burning & looting in South Africa has everything to do with how they're being treated in their land. Most black South Africans own nothing. No jobs & no lands. Apartheid never ended in South Africa. The invaders are still controlling everything there @funshographix.[6]

> This is what happens when society and governments fail to empower the poorest to better themselves. @MobilePunch.[7]

Observers also averred that looting occurred during xenophobic attacks and demonstrations challenged poor township services. An important observation was that looting was committed by those involved in xenophobic attacks on foreign-owned businesses.

Critical commentators pointed out that looting foreign-owned stores during xenophobic attacks appeared to be glossed over by a particular group within the South African community. On some social media platforms, the looting of foreign-owned property was socially acceptable and encouraged. Some netizens even claimed that looting, in some cases, was instigated by influential members of communities who believed that it was permissible and justified when it comes to the property of a particular group of people, especially foreign nationals. In this way, intermediary transactions become visible, where manifestations of criminality were socially permissible due to networks. Indeed, some Twitter users observed that looting is contagious because it originates from a few violent citizens and is camouflaged by the collective engagement that turns into group disobedience. For example, it can be argued that the Zulu people initiated the demonstrations to protect one of their own from arrest. However, the looting also involved non-Zulu South Africans, and foreign nationals living in KwaZulu-Natal and Gauteng provinces. Apart from social networks, criminal acts were observed in collectively violent groups. For example, protests, extortion, political murders, taxi conflicts and hostel violence (Mlamla and Shumba 2021).

The general observation here is the economic strength of the population. Taxi conflicts, for example, have their roots in the economic sphere. Every taxi company depends on a thriving business. If competition reduces its revenue, eliminating competitors is an option. This creates a social problem rooted in the socioeconomic and political establishment.

Threat to Democracy: Coup d'état in the Making

The massive looting and demonstrations cannot be explained without the political angle under which the power relations were played out in the power and state security services corridors. In this context, Vhumbunu (2021) highlighted that the massive demonstrations were a socio-political problem. Some saw these actions as discrediting the incumbent president and dissuading him from being the first citizen of South Africa. This was also voiced by President Cyril Ramaphosa, who called the demonstrations an attempted coup d'état, and an insurrection. The Government of South Africa shared this:

> We call for the immediate stop of violent protests and looting in Gauteng and Kwazulu-Natal. The unrest is tantamount to economic sabotage, and criminality will not be allowed to ensue in South Africa @GovernmentZA.[8]

While there was no solid evidence to support these claims, the fact that former high-ranking security officials, such as Zuma's former spy commissioner, appeared to suggest otherwise.

From a socio-political perspective, some Twitter users accused the Zulu State of attempting to undermine South Africa's democracy and its constitutional provisions. For example, some accused the Zulu tribe of portraying itself as South Africa's first tribe, even though the country is made up of many tribes that fought together to liberate the country. Portraying the Zulu as the first tribe is an assault on the notion of a 'Rainbow Nation', and the country's supreme law. Those who were against the demonstrations argued that former president Jacob Zuma, as a former statesman, should be a role model and abide by the provisions of justice. This led to a 'tribal divide' that needs to be patched up socially and politically if South Africa must move forward as a united country.

Poor State Policing and Security in South Africa

In the aftermath of the demonstrations, it has become apparent that some citizens in South Africa do not have confidence in the police and the security sector. For example, some Twitter users believed that security and police personnel collaborate with criminals and use dirty tricks. A section of the South

African population believes that the upper echelon of power in the security and police sector have dirty hands and enjoy dirty money from the hidden hands that promote criminal activities. This expression is shown in the following excerpt:

> How will our ministers and "leaders" bring calm to the situation regarding the #PhoenixMassacre, if they are involved with criminals and drug lords from Phoenix? @Thabile68438954.[9]

In fact, some people believe that all those who instigate social unrest are well endowed and they all keep their hands off the authorities to get away with it. Against this backdrop, some Twitter users lack confidence and believe that the July 2021 looting could have been avoided if South Africa had a police force that served diligently. This is visible in the following tweets:

> All along you have failed to make such a deployment to stop drug trafficking, rapes and gun violence in the townships? @savndaniel.[10]

> Strange how the South African Defence Force can be used to enforce the COVID-19 lockdown in the townships, but are not allowed to defend South Africa and its infrastructure from incalculable damage, looting and arson across the country. @SouthAfricaRiot.[11]

Generally, some sections of South Africans lack trust in the social security provision sections of the government.

Socioeconomic Inequalities

There is a general perception among the South African masses that the national cake is in the hands of a few colonial masters. Most Black South Africans are economically marginalised, excluded, subjugated and disenfranchised (Vhumbunu 2021). Indeed, the World Bank Report concurs with this observation by stating that 90 percent of South Africans live in poverty, while national wealth belongs to only 10 percent of the population (Oxfam South Africa 2020). Moreover, according to the United Nations Human Development Report (2020), 55.5 percent of Black South Africans live below the poverty line. High unemployment rates and economic inequality exacerbate this.

Given the glaring inequalities in South Africa, it is argued that poverty-stricken communities resort to survivalist and motivated violence to extricate themselves from the maw of their suffering. Indeed, Oxfam South Africa (2020) argued that the poor are subject to manipulation by the rich and are vulnerable to being exploited by the rich. This leads to economic, political and social anger. As a result, the poor turn to socio-political violence to show their frustration. Based on the reactions entailed in tweets about the July 2021 looting and vandalism, the poor were not satisfied with the country's socioeconomic situation in which wealth is only in the hands of a few, who exploit the poor to make a profit. This is evidenced by data showing that most of the businesses under attack were owned by large multinational corporations and individuals who accumulated their wealth during apartheid.

Given the socioeconomic imbalances exacerbated by the COVID-19 pandemic, the looting led to the closure of many businesses, from the once-thriving retail and food industries to large companies in the mining and agricultural sectors. The unjust result was the loss of jobs, and breadwinners lost their only source of income. Unemployment soared to 40.3 percent (Statistics South Africa 2021). This triggered economic frustrations as communities were threatened by increasing poverty, unemployment and food insecurity. The call for demonstrations against the imprisonment of former president Jacob Zuma sparked an already soured discussion in which the Black majority viewed itself as being embedded in politically induced poverty (Vhumbunu 2020). Arguably, the incarceration of former president Jacob Zuma, much like the assassination of Archduke Franz Ferdinand of Austria in Sarajevo in 1914, set South Africa on fire. A wave of civic disorder ensued, the first of its kind and magnitude since 1994. South Africa is the most unequal country in the world in terms of wealth distribution (Mlaba 2021; World Population Review 2022).

The politics of the demonstrations cannot be understood without including the views of some South Africans who have a burning feeling that the government has failed the masses in terms of addressing unemployment, poverty and socioeconomic inequality. Some people felt that the current government had done nothing to empower Black South Africans, and they hid by offering social grants. Some users shared:

> It's okay to Disagree with the looting BUT you don't have to stupefy yourself by saying its criminality: you use this narrative to avoid the fear you feel, the trauma it causes in you because you know the truth: this is about the POVERTY which your whole privilege is built on. @MbuyiseniNdlozi.[12]

The general opinion is that the country is still colonised, both politically and economically. Most citizens felt suffocated and provoked by the deep-rooted inequalities that disadvantage the Black majority.

UNPACKING THE IMPACT OF THE LOOTING PHASE

Globally, demonstrations of any kind are known to leave a trail of impact. In this study, we have traced possible effects that the protests may have caused in the social, political and economic spheres. Each of these impacts is described in detail in the subsections below.

Social Impacts

South Africa is a country of diverse races and tribes. The outbreak of the July 2021 demonstrations signalled a new era in which different tribes held different views. Zuma-ites felt that the ruling elite was undermining the Zulu tribe, which considers itself the most important tribe in the country. This did not sit well with the other tribes, who felt that they were equally important as citizens of South Africa and that no tribe should claim supremacy over another. This led not only to tribal wars but also to racial wars, which were sparked by certain community members taking policing into their hands to protect themselves and their businesses, especially the Indian South Africans or 'Indo-Africans' (Mamdoo 2022). Feizel Mamdoo (2022) argued that the term 'Indian' is an alienating name for Africans of Indian origin, proposing that 'Indo-African' is a politically correct identity.

> The #freezuma anarchy disguised as political protest has produced Vigilantism at phoenix, Arson & torching of businesses, Ethic mobilization, Attack on state institutions and Barbarism of the worst kind. This are backward tendencies they call it a "People's revolt" I beg to differ. #ZumaUnrest.[13]

Black South Africans perceived the butchering of their fellow Blacks by the Indo-Africans as racially motivated. In this case, a race war broke out that sacked the police and created another divide among Black South Africans who felt that the law was being selectively applied for racial reasons. One Twitter user shared:

> Ramaphosa gave Indians license to go on a killing spree when he made his reckless statement on ethnic mobilization. It's his fault that black people are being killed and going missing. He should account. #PhoenixMassacre MaLanga@ZandiileL.[14]

The demonstrations also showed that some community members took policing into their own hands to protect the businesses and lives of their community. Business owners and community members turned to self-defence, self-protection and community policing, such as the Phoenix Arrangement. This is shown in the following tweets:

> This time around we will defend our malls, shopping centres and businesses. KZN people, wake up, you are only destroying your province, kuzofiwa indlala. The Zuma family will be fed nicely. Your family members will lose jobs. Toyota said they are leaving should #looting repeat itself. @Buyani_ZN_2.[15]

In reality, this was a good thing, but community policing by untrained individuals was taken to extremes, resulting in mob justice that endangered the lives of many. Considering that the Phoenix community was mainly there for Indo-Africans, this led to racial tensions, as the Black South Africans felt they had been mistreated so far, which led to poor treatment of the Blacks by the economic beneficiaries.

Political Impacts

In any conflict, observers and analysts review a country's political establishment. In this case, South Africa is a democratic country with many political parties. Most of these political parties have different ideologies that they try to adopt in case of conflict. However, the political views of the other political parties have mainly focused on blaming the ruling party for how it handled the Zuma issue. The following excerpt supports this:

> KZN ANC took their #FreeZuma campaign too far. Now their tails are between their legs, they have lost any political capital they had, zero credibility remaining, totally lost any grounds they had to make any demands to National ANC, all in a space of 5 days. @LuzukoMngqibisa.[16]

It is important to note that the looting and demonstrations exposed the ruling party, as members of the ANC held different views. According to constitutional procedures, some sympathized with the former president, and others believed that the case of President Zuma should be handled like any other legal cases. This has exposed the cracks in the ruling party, and analysts believe that the Zuma demonstrations will impact the political stability of the ANC as a ruling party. These fissures in the ruling ANC are evident in the excerpt below:

> When the KZN ANC lost in Nasrec when Ramaphosa emerged victorious, their capital dwindled. As if this wasn't enough, they've lost again when they supported the #FreeZuma campaign. They now have zero credibility & capital. Their inability to think has caused them major losses. @KhulaniQoma.[17]

Economic Impacts

The looting and protests resulted in the loss of businesses, essential social services and infrastructural and financial losses. During the demonstrations, many major roads were blocked, disrupting the commercial transport of goods in and out of KwaZulu-Natal and Gauteng provinces. Some trucks were set on fire, causing a shortage of goods, and resulting in food shortages and essential services such as medicines. Users shared:

> People of Alex vandalizing their own township, looting and destroying all the shops that gives them food, tomorrow they'll complain about lack of service delivery. #GautengShutdow #ShutDownGauteng #Sandton pic.twitter.com/pvCq2IKW7I? @Nemza.[18]

> KZN people had and are still suffering from the results of #looting. They are no longer interested to repeat that nonsense when a loaf of bread was R50, airtime for R5 sold 4 R20 or more. Service stations with no petrol. Jobs lost. Lives lost. We are not taking that route anymore. @mbuli607.[19]

To make the situation worse, the disruption of transportation affected the implementation of the immunization program, as the looting occurred at the beginning of the immunisation period. Road transport was disrupted, but rail transport was also negatively affected.

Looting and demonstrations also caused vital service providers such as Eskom and the telecommunications sector to cease operations. The cessation of Eskom's operations affected the supply of electricity to households and essential industries such as mining and agriculture, which meant that production was scaled back or brought to a standstill. The disruption of the telecommunications industry meant that access to information was also interrupted. This endangered many people's lives, especially during the height of COVID-19.

The looting may have indirectly weakened investor confidence in South Africa, a country suffering from the effects of COVID-19 and in need of more business opportunities than before. The looting and pillaging may have caused waves of shock and distrust among anyone who wanted to invest in the country.

TAKEAWAYS FROM MASS LOOTING AND PROTESTS

From the socio-political and socioeconomic uprising, each community can learn some lessons that it can use to cope with or avoid future similar incidents. First, South Africa must strive to reduce inequality. This can only be achieved if socioeconomic inequalities are eliminated. Blacks must be economically empowered to have a fair share of the economy. Second, the police system must be strengthened to ensure efficient and effective crime-fighting and prevention. To avoid unprofessional policing, the police service must respond quickly to thwart acts of criminality. The situation can then be contained before it gets out of control, saving national resources. The police also need to improve training for neighbourhood watch workers, so that policing is done by trained personnel. This will ensure that all measures are taken to protect the population and comply with the country's constitutional provisions, thus avoiding vigilantism.

CONCLUSION

Ziyakhala/Ayikhale/Azikhale, a movement that expressed displeasure over the imprisonment of former President Jacob Zuma on charges of state capture and corruption, opened up spaces for social, political and economic discussions in postcolonial South Africa. The Twitter data reflects a South Africa marked by glaring socioeconomic inequalities.

In examining the causes of the worst social unrest that led to economic loss and loss of life, we first reviewed the plethora of theories put forward by Twitter users. Various views were presented, mainly from socio-political, and socioeconomic perspectives. However, underlying these views was the desire of South Africans to free themselves from the current economic hardship in which people feel that the national cake is in the hands of a privileged few. The economically disadvantaged population generally feels that post-apartheid has not focused on addressing economic inequalities, which is a trigger for the masses' struggle for survival. Black South Africans feel that their existence is no different from what it was under apartheid. Instead, they wallow in poverty, unemployment, and socioeconomic inequality. These Black South Africans resort to organised violence and crime to free themselves from the economic slavery that has shaped their society decades after gaining independence.

Although the global economy was negatively impacted by COVID-19 and a wave of global recession that led to economic collapse, South Africans still feel that their economy is out of their hands. They prefer a South Africa where they come first, and others come second. This is reflected in how they oppose foreign-owned businesses, whether in the form of xenophobic movements, vigilantism, or such resentment as the Free Zuma protests targeting large corporations.

The results of our study show that the Black majority is angry about socioeconomic inequalities. The pent-up frustration over the pursuit of social and economic justice is both socially and economically devastating. Although we do not advocate criminality, we believe that criminalising the pursuit of social justice has economic, social and political implications. The Black masses have spoken, as they did during apartheid. The suppression of the call for social justice is equivalent to an inhumane situation where the poor are forever trapped in poverty, and any expression of displeasure is equated with criminal acts. *Ayikhale*, Black South Africans must be liberated from economic bondage.

NOTES

1. https://mobile.twitter.com/mavistothechiro
2. https://twitter.com/search?q=%23nkandla
3. https://twitter.com/search?q=%23zondocommission
4. https://twitter.com/riotandattacksa
5. https://twitter.com/search?q=%23nkandla
6. https://twitter.com/funshographix
7. https://twitter.com/mobilepunch/status/1416471758815866880
8. https://twitter.com/governmentza/status/1414525722975252484
9. https://mobile.twitter.com/thabile68438954
10. https://twitter.com/savndaniel/status/1169860302608842752
11. https://twitter.com/search?q=%23SouthAfricaRiot
12. https://twitter.com/nelson_dono/status/1415534468593504256
13. https://twitter.com/search?lang=en&q=%23ZumaUnrest
14. https://mobile.twitter.com/ZandiileL/status/1415410554001403909
15. https://mobile.twitter.com/buyani_zn_2
16. https://twitter.com/LuzukoMngqibisa/status/1415721102832193551
17. https://twitter.com/KhulaniQoma/status/1415919112384098305
18. https://twitter.com/riotandattacksa
19. https://twitter.com/search?q=%23SouthAfricaRiot

REFERENCES

Ahlgren, M. (2020, August 25). 50+Twitter statistics and facts for 2020. Retrieved from https://www.websitehostingrating.com/twitter-statistics/.

Ahmed, Loghdey, and Raman Newalani. 2021. The looting was not a legitimate protest; it was about destruction. News24 (July 28, 2021).

Aladwani, Adel M. 2015. Facilitators, characteristics, and impacts of Twitter use: Theoretical analysis and empirical illustration. *International Journal of Information Management* 35(1): 15–25.

Armayanti, Rika. 2019. Critical Discourse Analysis (CDA) on Qualitative Research. *Journal of Research and Innovation in Language* 1(1): 29–34.

Blommaert, Jan, and Bulcaen, Chris. 2000. Critical Discourse Analysis. *Annual Reviews Publishers* 1(29): 447–66.

Braun, Virginia, and Clarke, Victoria. 2006. Qualitative Research in Psychology. *Journal of Psychology* (3): 77–101.

Burke, Roger Hopkins. 2018. *An introduction to criminological theory*. London: Routledge.

Business Tech Staff Writer. 2021. Looters, gangsters and the 'third force'—the disturbing root of South Africa's violent riots. https://businesstech.co.za/news/government/505840/looters-gangsters-and-the-third-force-the-disturbing-root-of-south-africas-violent-riots/.

Cohen, Albert K. 1955. *Delinquent boys: The culture of the gang*. New York: Free Press.

Fulcher, R. 2010. *Critical discourse analysis*. New York: Longman.

Garbero, R. 2017. Social justice and criminal justice go hand in hand. *Blog Network* (20 February, 2017), blogs.biomedcentral.com/on-health/2017/02/20/social-justice-and-criminal-justice-go-hand-in-hand.

Giachanou, Anastasia, and Crestani, Fabio. 2016. Like it or not: A survey of Twitter sentiment analysis methods. *ACM Computing Surveys (CSUR)* 49(2): 1–41.

Given, Lisa M. 2008. *The SAGE encyclopaedia of qualitative research methods*. Thousand Oaks, CA: Sage Publications.

Howitt, Dennis, and Cramer, Duncan. 2010. *Introduction to Research Methods in Psychology* Second edition. London: Pearson Education Limited. https://www.websitehostingrating.com/twitter-statistics/.

Hunter, Qaanitah, Singh, Kaveel, and Wicks, Jeff. 2021. Eight days in July: Inside the Zuma unrest that set South Africa alight. News24 .https://www.news24.com/news24/books/excerpt-eight-days-in-july-inside-the-zuma-unrest-that-set-south-africa-alight-20211108.

Imge, Oranli. 2021. Fanon's frame of violence. *Interventions: Internationl Journal of Postcolonial Studies* 23(8): 1106–23.

Lamb, Guy. 2021. Why have South Africans been on a looting rampage? Researchers offer insights. The Conversation (July 15, 2021).

Locke, Terry. 2004. *Critical Discourse Analysis*. N.p.: Cromwell Press.

Lucke, A. 1996. *Text and Discourse Analysis*. New York: American Educational Research Association.

Mamdoo, Feizel. 2022. 'Indian' is an alienating name for Africans of Indian origin—call me Indo-African. *Daily Maverick*, January 17. https://www.dailymaverick.co.za/opinionista/2022-01-17-indian-is-an-alienating-name-for-africans-of-indian-origin-call-me-indo-african/.

McGregor, Sue L. T. 2010. *Critical discourse analysis: A primer*. Halifax, NS: Mount Saint Vincent University.

Merton, Robert K. 1957. *Social theory and social structure*. New York: Free Press.

Mlamla, Ntsika Edward, and Shumba, Kemist. 2021. A critical discourse analysis of the voice of Maskandi on hostel killings in KwaMashu, Durban: Implications for community safety, health and well-being. *African Journal of Development Studies* 11(3): 271–92.

Mlaba, Khanyi. 2021. Poverty, inequality, and looting: Everything you need to know about South Africa's protests. Global Citizen (July 13, 2021).

Mogashoa, Tebogo. 2014. Understanding critical discourse analysis in qualitative research. *International Journal of Humanities Social Sciences and Education* 1(7):104–13.

Mohammad, Saif. 2012 # Emotional tweets. In *SEM 2012: The First Joint Conference on Lexical and Computational Semantics–Volume 1: Proceedings of the main conference and the shared task*, and *Volume 2: Proceedings of the Sixth International Workshop on Semantic Evaluatio*n (SemEval 2012), 246–255.

Munoriyarwa, Allen, and Chambwera, Collen. 2020. Tweeting the July 2018 Elections in Zimbabwe. In *Social Media and Elections in Africa, Volume 1*, 75–96. Cham, Switzerland: Palgrave Macmillan.

Nyambuya, V. P., Nyamaruze, P., Dube, M. and Shumba, K. 2021. Rethinking education in the age of 'social distancing': A qualitative inquiry on University of KwaZulu-Natal students' responses to online learning in the context of COVID-19. *Journal of African Education* 2(1): 107–26.

Olson, Hope. 2007. Quantitative "versus" qualitative research: The wrong question. In *Lexical and Computational Semantics–Proceedings of the main conference and the shared task: Proceedings of the Sixth International Workshop on Semantic Evaluation* (246–55). Montreal, QC. The Association for Computational Linguistics.

Osterweil, Vicky. 2020. *In defense of looting: A riotous history of uncivil action*. New York: Bold Type Books.

Oxfam South Africa. 2020. 'Reclaiming power: Women's work and income inequality in South Africa. https://www.oxfam.org.za/wp-content/uploads/2020/11/oxfam-sa-inequality-in-south-africa-report-2020.pdf.

Pathak, Vibha, Bijayini, Jena, and Kalra, Sanjay. 2013. Qualitative research. *Perspectives in Clinical Research* 4(3): 192.

Quarantelli, Enrico L., and Dynes, Rusell R. 1970. Property Norms and Looting: Their Patterns in Community Crises. *Phylon (1960-)* 31(2): 168–82.

Roberts, Neil. 2004. Fanon, Sartre, violence, and freedom. *Sartre Studies International* 10(2): 139–60.

Rogers, Rebecca, Malancharuvil-Berkes, Elizabeth, Mosley, Melissa, Hui, Diane, and O'Garro Joseph, Glynis. 2005. Critical discourse analysis in education: A review of the literature. *Review of Educational Research* 75(3): 365–416.

Sannerholm, Richard. (2022, March 17). Responsibility and accountability: AI, governance, and the rule of law. *The Guardian*.

Sarker, Abeed, DeRoos, Annika, and Perrone, Jeanmarie. 2020. Mining social media for prescription medication abuse monitoring: A review and proposal for a data-centric framework. *Journal of the American Medical Informatics Association* 27(2), 315–29.

Seekings, Jeremy, and Nattrass, Nicoli. 2005. *Class, Race, and Inequality in South Africa*. New Haven, CT: Yale University Press.

Shaw, Clifford Robe, and McKay, Henry Donald. 1942. *Juvenile delinquency and urban areas: A study of rates of delinquents in relation to differential characteristics of local communities in American cities.* Chicago: University of Chicago Press.

Shumba, Kemist, Nyamaruze, Patrick, Nyambuya, Venencia P., and Meyer-Weitz, Anna. 2020. Politicising the Covid-19 pandemic in Zimbabwe: Implications for public health and governance. *African Journal of Governance & Development* 9(1.1), 270–86.

Sparks, John. 2021. South Africa unrest: President Cyril Ramaphosa says violence designed to 'destroy democracy' as he visits site of looting. Sky News.

Statistics South Africa. 2021. Youth still find it difficult to secure jobs in South Africa. http://www.statssa.gov.za/?p=14415.

United Nations Human Development Report. 2020. South Africa, human development ndicators. http://hdr.undp.org/en/countries/profiles/ZAF.

Van Dijk, Teun A. 2006. Principles of critical discourse analysis. Amserdam: University of Amsterdam.

Vhumbunu, Clayton H. 2021. The July 2021 protests and socio-political unrest: Reflecting on the causes, consequences, and future lessons. *Accord* (10 December, 2021).

Wallerstein, Immanuel. 1970. Frantz Fanon: Reason and violence. *Berkeley Journal of Sociology* 15: 222–31.

Winning, Alexander, and Wendell, Roelf. 2021. Worst violence in years spreads in South Africa as grievances boil over. Reuters. https://www.reuters.com/world/africa/looting-violence-grips-south-africa-after-zuma-court-hearing-2021-07-13/.

World Population Review. 2022. Wealth inequalities by country 2022. https://worldpopulationreview.com/country-rankings/wealth-inequality-by-country.

Young, T. R. 1985. Social justice vs criminal justice: An agenda for critical criminology. *The Journal of Sociology & Social Welfare* 12(3): 7. https://scholarworks.wmich.edu/jssw/vol12/iss3/7.

Chapter Five

Unemployment as an Instigator of Looting

Tawanda Majoko and Annah Dudu

INTRODUCTION

As South Africa was in the third wave of the COVID-19 pandemic in July 2021, the National State Capture Commission was mandated to identify entrenched corruption cases that were pernicious to its citizens (Calland 2021). The imperative to safeguard human rights and social justice of South African citizens underpinned the appointment of the commission (Buthelezi 2021). This aligns with Ubuntu, which is the 'morality' of care, because of its embedment in human interest and dignity, humanness and welfare, prioritization of human needs and moral values (Majoko 2021). The former president, Jacob Zuma, disputed the legitimacy of the chairperson of the National State Capture Commission, namely, Chief Justice Zondo, and consequently refused testifying at it (Calland 2021). Resultantly, Zuma was charged with contempt of court and sentenced to fifteen months in prison (Calland 2021). This resonates with Ubuntu, which underpins all the values of Africans and involves a collective personhood and a collective morality (Khoza 2004). Waves of riots in the home village of the former president that progressively developed to widespread looting across KwaZulu-Natal and Gauteng provinces ensued with his imprisonment (Reuters 2021; Sidimba 2021). This contradicts Ubuntu, which is enshrined in the proverb of the Nguni, "Umuntu ngumuntu ngabantu." This means that "a human being finds genuine human expression in human relationships with other humans—I am because we are" (Phasha 2016 29). At least three hundred people were killed and property amounting to billions of Rands was destroyed because of the violence (Seekings 2021; Sidimba 2021). This is inconsistent with Ubuntu. Tutu (1999, 34) reveals that "Ubuntu speaks to the very essence of being human." When you intend to give high praise to an individual, you say, "Yu u nobuntu: He or she has Ubuntu." It is style of life of handling others and a code of conduct (Kunene 2009). Although trauma remains fresh in the minds of South Africans, several are seeking for answers that explain this era of chaos and unrest that culminated in looting, hence the current chapter. Also, in discussing Ubuntu, Brown and Shumba (2011, 535) utilizes Nelson Mandela as an illustration. They indicate that "Madiba's humanism . . . is reflected in the qualities of Ubuntu. We can infer this when others are tortured or treated as if they are less than who they are, Madiba feels equally diminished, humiliated and undervalued."

UNEMPLOYMENT AND LOOTING NEXUS: AN UBUNTU PERSPECTIVE

South Africa is among countries with the highest inequality of income, levels of structural unemployment and poverty among emerging economies (Netshitenzhe 2013). This is inconsistent with Ubuntu (Phasha 2016). Despite the nearly three decades of government legislations and policies earmarked to mitigate poverty, not much has changed on average for South Africans who are out of employment, with the state failing to offer basic goods and services to the majority of society (Maringira 2020). This too contradicts Ubuntu (Swanson 2007).

The COVID-19 pandemic has socioeconomically aggravated prevailing developmental calamities and generated significantly immense challenges for the government to resolve including the rampant unemployment (Maringira 2022). The mandate of the government of South Africa to safeguard human welfare resonates with Ubuntu philosophy, which is ensconced in communalism, interdependence and high esteem for human worth and values (Khoza 2004). According to Netshitenzhe (2013), poverty as a result of unemployment is prevalent across the provinces of South Africa. The Gini coefficient was revealed as 0.65 in 2019 nationally, which is relatively consistent since 2006 (Statistics South Africa 2019). This contradicts the values of respect for life, appreciation of nature, concern for others, social cohesion and collectivism that underpins Ubuntu (Mawere and Mubaya 2016). Because of unemployment, approximately 14 percent of households reside in informal settlements, with houses built utilising substandard resources and materials and having limited access to sanitation or piped water in addition to high inequality levels (SERI 2018). Regrettably, nearly three decades into democracy, people surviving in these circumstances are principally from the Black population, which triggers anger that results in their looting (Calland 2021). This is inconsistent with Ubuntu..

The consequences of the apartheid-era Group Areas Act of 1950 of South Africa endure, with persons of colour compulsorily dislocated from prime real estate and relocated to large distances away from the economic centres of towns and cities (Seekings 2021). This is coupled with the segregation of the population of South Africa along racial lines in various domains of life including employment (SERI 2018). However, enunciating on compassion and sharing as traits of Ubuntu, Broodryk (2006) posits that if a person is progressing materially and receiving more than others, the extras are shared with the underprivileged sisters and brothers as "Africa does not allow that some eat whilst others go hungry, or some sleep warm whilst others are left in the cold." The racial distribution of unemployment coupled with poverty in South Africa further intensifies tensions between racial groups, leading to looting and waning social cohesion (Habib 2021). This is inconsistent with Ubuntu, which advances that "Africans must act collectively to free themselves from the bondage of perpetual servitude, and rise to attain the envisaged self" (Biko 2004, 52). Ubuntu is also "a wellspring that flows within African existence and epistemology" (Majoko 2021). Visagie and Turok (2021a) posit that, in South Africa, unemployment triggers societal tensions that culminate in unrest coupled with looting the country over. This misaligns with Ubuntu, which is embedded in collectivism (Phasha 2016) and constitutes humanness, interdependence and communalism (Mawere and Mubaya 2016).

Several people in South Africa question whether the splurge of looting in the country is a protest against the experiences of poverty of the majority as a result of unemployment or due to political dissenters pursuing a systematized campaign to destabilize the republic (Booysen 2021). This is inconsistent with Ubuntu, which fosters pride among African people, their outlook on life, their culture, their value system, and their religion (Kunene 2004). Since the timing of the looting ensues instantly after events that draw national attention, such as the imprisonment of the former president, Jacob Zuma, it cannot also be ignored (Gaxamba 2021). The looting also transpired during a phase branded as an Adjustment Level 4 Lockdown because of the climaxing of the COVID-19 third wave (Maringira 2021). Barnard-Naude (2021) reveals that a confluence of variables including the experiences of extreme hunger, poverty and homelessness due to unemployment instigates looting in South Africa. This contradicts interconnectedness, respect and dignity, collectivism and solidarity, communal enterprise, and leadership legitimacy that informs Ubuntu (Majoko 2021). '[Ubuntu] speaks to the very essence of being human. We belong in a bundle of life. . . . Harmony, friendliness, community are great goods. Social harmony is for us . . . the greatest good. Anything that subverts or undermines this sought-after good is to be avoided like the plague" (Tutu 1999, 34). A state of hopelessness is ubiquitous in communities of people who are poor in South Africa because of unemployment (Habib 2021). This is exacerbated by the ineffective delivery of goods and services that is widespread across the republic, with numerous institutions incapacitated by deep-seated corruption and inept management. Political factions within the ruling political party, particularly, the African National Congress (ANC), also took advantage of these frustrations to incite people who are unemployed into a state of tempestuousness (Habib 2021). According to Letseka (2013), South Africa, which was left fractured with no shared moral discourse, by apartheid, requires Ubuntu.

The factionalism within the ANC also reveals how susceptible the national custodian of democracy has become because of rampant unemployment in South Africa (Booysen 2021). While a disgruntled faction of the ANC triggers the initial social unrest, the underlying pain of the majority of South Africans who are unemployed remain (Gaxamba 2021). This misaligns with Ubuntu, which includes self-protection, in-group collectivism, consensus building, and a 'being your brother's keeper-type' of humane orientations (Sotuku and Duku 2016, 31). The looting will continue in South Africa until the government in collaboration and discourse with other individuals, organizations and institutions addresses the socioeconomic challenges of the country including the rampant unemployment (Gaxamba 2021). This resonates with Ubuntu, in which during hard times for the organization or community, all the members share the burden (Tutu 1999). Although half of the people of South Africa were born after the democratic election of 1994, they particularly experience the legacy of the apartheid system, inclusive of gross inequality in employment (Nyoka 2020). This has intensified after at least a year of repeated lockdowns resulting in acute socio-political, socioeconomic and sociocultural crises (Vally and Motala 2021). This contradicts Ubuntu, which constitutes a spirit of interconnectedness and social cohesion (Majoko 2021). An incomplete political revolution in which the leadership of South Africa adopted pro-capital legislations and policies to the detriment of the working class is the epicentre of the crises of unemployment in the country (Alexander 2003). After nearly three decades of such legislation and policies, the inequalities of the country with respect to employment have extended and social challenges have intensified (Cloete 2014). This contradicts Ubuntu management, which unites both competitiveness and cooperativeness within an iterative and openly communicative model (Sotuku and Duku 2016).

The looting witnessed in South Africa is the logical conclusion for a society struggling with numerous parallel and interconnected challenges including political instability, corruption and well-being as well as unemployment (Levy et al. 2021). This is inconsistent with Ubuntu, which brings to the fore supportiveness, solidarity and cooperation (Swanson 2007). Ubuntu is also the basis of a social contract that manifests from, but transcends, the narrow confines of the nuclear family to be extended into a kinship network, the community (Letseka 2012). The challenges of the crisis of looting in South Africa include the socioeconomic, sociocultural and political tensions emanating from unemployment (Black et al. 2020). Neglecting such a crisis for a protracted retro triggers social unrest (Visagie and Turok 2021a). Visagie and Turok (2021b) reveal that South Africa is a developing an emerging economy grappling with an unemployment crisis and requires a fast-tracked attempt to solve this complicated and multidimensional phenomenon that triggers looting. This misaligns with Ubuntu, which is a lifestyle that is a natural response flowing from a happy approach to life (Sotuku and Duku 2014). Societal conditional variables for social quality, specifically, socioeconomic security, social inclusion, social cohesion and social empowerment buttresses unemployment as an instigator of looting in South Africa (Spaull 2015; Webster and Francis 2019). Normative variables of social quality, particularly, social justice, solidarity, equal value and human dignity inform the moral influence of the crisis in South Africa (Spaull 2015). This is consistent with Ubuntu's spiritual ideal that humans aspire to continuously (Oppenheim 2012). This is because through collaboration and hospitality that are celebrated in Ubuntu, communities strive towards a shared vision (Kunene 2009).

The COVID-19 pandemic intensified the socioeconomic crisis, particularly, unemployment, further highlighting the inequalities and divisions in South African society, instigating looting (Rogerson & Rogerson 2020). This is consistent with Ubuntu which advances that a spirit of harmony can be achieved through sharing human capital (Letseka 2012). Nussbaum and Weichel (2010) also posit that a spirit of harmony can be achieved through sharing human capital. These authors refer to African saying that "when there is peace in an individual, there is peace in a family. When there is peace in a family, there is peace in the community. When there is peace in the community, there is peace in the nation and ultimately in the world." Nelson Mandela, cited in Oppenheim (2012), reveals that in Ubuntu sharing is not only limited to material things but is also linked to human capital, including knowledge and skills. The capitalist system of South Africa has perpetuated inequality in employment offering a basis for a violent response and ultimately looting (Black et al. 2020). The COVID-19 pandemic has exacerbated this social tension, particularly, known as 'societal comorbidity' (Black et al. 2020). Booysen (2020) posits that in periods of social crisis, such as unemployment, people with greater resilience capacities such as social capital, knowledge and income adopt positive responses. Such people exhibit a faster recovery or enhance their level of well-being (Alexander 2013). Contrarily, embedded in the inherent spirit of sharing and caring in Ubuntu, Tutu (1999) reveals that, "We Africans share everything and share nothing." This means that Africans share whatever they possess, even when they possess nothing.

People living in more affluent suburbs in South Africa are more resistant and resilient to the economic shocks, including unemployment imposed by national disasters such as the lockdowns of the government because of the COVID-19 (Buthelezi 2021). Contrarily, low-income households living in vulnerable contexts including squatter settlements and townships of South Africa experience food insecurity and general misery because of lack of financial savings due to unemployment (Visagie and Turok 2021a). This contradicts Ubuntu which enshrines human rights and human dignity (Oppenheim 2012). Analysis of spatial inequalities reveals uneven effect of the COVID-19 pandemic in South Africa (Visagie and Turok 2021b). People who are unemployed who live in shacks in urban settings were most at risk and most severely affected (Visagie and Turok 2021a). The pre-existing inequalities reveal the economic vulnerabilities including unemployment of communities residing in these localities inciting looting (Webster and Francis 2019). This is inconsistent with Ubuntu, which translates as personhood, humanness, justice and morality (Mawere and Mubaya 2016). The challenges in cities including unemployment were more acute, as it is these settings that carry the burden of population of the country since 2 percent of the land supports 40 percent of the population, triggering looting (Visagie and Turok 2021b). Space is an extremely limited commodity in informal urban communities in South Africa (Alexander 2013). This is inconsistent with Ubuntu, which is translated through human rights and social justice (Kunene 2009).

South Africa is among the most unequal countries in the world (Department of Planning, Monitoring and Evaluation 2018). Gender, racial and spatial dimensions with respect to employment generally delineate this inequality that instigates looting (Thomas 2020). Because of unemployment, the majority of people have little access to productive land; basic goods and services such as sanitation, water supply and electricity; and quality education (Alexander 2012). Inequality in employment has been persistent in South Africa for multiple generations, resulting in looting (Booysen 2020). This is inconsistent with a spirit of interconnectedness and social cohesion that informs Ubuntu (Phasha 2016). Because of unemployment, poverty in South Africa positively correlates with racial demographics that are attributable to apartheid legislations and policies (Alexander 2012). The system of apartheid in South Africa instituted low-quality transport networks, basic infrastructure, health care and education in majority communities, which contributes to massive unemployment, prompting looting (Klasen 1997). This contradicts Ubuntu in which Africans care during both times of joy and times of sorrow hence, 'Your joy is my joy, and your sorrow is my sorrow (Sotuku and Duku 2014).

After nearly three decades of democratic rule, the government of South Africa has failed to change racial inequalities in employment, triggering looting

(Alexander 2012). This is inconsistent with Ubuntu, which values humanity and consultation as a value orientation and interdependence as a value to dependence (Khoza 2004). Some of the redistributive legislations and policies of South Africa inclusive of Black economic empowerment, have exacerbated inequality in employment while profiting only a minority of the population (Béné 2020). This misaligns with Ubuntu, in which different talents, qualities and resources of people are shared in a spirit of cooperativeness for positive existence (Majoko 2021). Analysis of inequality entrenched in racial distribution reveals that South African Black economic empowerment legislation and policies on employment lack meaningful effects on Black the majority (Webster and Francis 2019). Rather, legislation and policies support the white capitalist class as regards employment without resolving structural challenges (Beresford 2015). The racial disparities in South Africa in relation to employment trigger outrage, causing tension and ultimately looting (Bhorat et al. 2020). This misaligns with Ubuntu, which is a lived world, a form of reasoning that informs and sustains people who resides in a specific geographic area (Biko 2004). South African wealth inequality is significantly more acute, with only 10 percent of the population possessing 95 percent of all the assets and wealth, while the bottom 80 percent of the population effectively possess none of the wealth of the country because of unemployment (Orthofer 2016). Such a vast gap in wealth underscores the variations in classes that trigger unrest and revolution and ultimate looting (Patel 2021). This is inconsistent with Ubuntu, which constitutes the totality of the attitudes, competencies, knowledge and skills possessed by a specific group of people that facilitate their survival in a specific geographic community (Brown and Shumba 2011).

A repetition of the creation of intergenerational poverty because of rampant unemployment persists to widen the gap between people who are rich and the majority who are poor. (Bhorat et al. 2020). This is inconsistent with Ubuntu, which links people and their nature (Pellerin 2012). In South Africa, children from households that are poor because of unemployment attend poor-quality schools that churn out graduates with low academic performance, who struggle to enrol at university and barely secure employment (Van der Berg et al. 2017). This contradicts Ubuntu values, including supportiveness and open-handedness in response to the individual needs (Pellerin 2012). Only a minority of young people in South Africa can escape from the cycle of poverty emanating from employment (Reyers 2019). Simultaneously, people from affluent homes access higher-quality schools, attain better results and establish pathways through institutions of higher education and training into more productive jobs (Spaull 2015). Because of the high prevalence of unemployed low-skilled workers in the economy of South Africa, workers struggle significantly to secure new jobs in either the informal or formal economy, which triggers looting (Segalo

2015). This trend is persistent despite the informal economy of the country accounting for 80 percent of non-agricultural employment (Mkhize, Dube and Quazi 2014). People in the informal sector also find it difficult to access the social and economic relief funds, such as Temporary Employee-Employer Relief Schemes (TERS), which stirs tension in them, resulting in their looting (Khambule 2020). This contradicts Ubuntu, which emanated from the political tumult before the 1990s as a defining component of a democratic vision (Phasha 2016).

While the informal sector is a buffer for the economy in other countries, with people who lose employment in the formal sector resorting to informal employment, such a trend is uncommon in South Africa (Martin 2021).. South Africa has low rates of absorption of labour, both in the informal and formal economy, causing historically high rates of unemployment (McKinley 2021). These statistics worsen when the cumulative impact of the COVID-19 pandemic is measured (Naidu 2021). The informal sector experienced high losses of jobs because of the lockdown, restricting opportunities of informal business, as workers were actually locked out of employment (Rogerson and Rogerson 2020). In the formal sector, the effect of business closure is that firms become more capital intensive and less dependent on labour in the process of production, culminating in looting by people who are out of employment (Francis Valodia and Ramburuth-Hurt 2020). This is inconsistent with Ubuntu, which postulates that the thumb requires the cooperation of the other fingers so as to work effectively (Majoko 2021). Ubuntu also embraces the African proverb 'It takes a village to raise a child' (Sotuku and Duku 2010).

The increase in the prevalence of hunger across South Africa because of unemployment affects the well-being of the population of the republic (Kalina 2021). For instance, the Mineral Council of South Africa reveals that 45,000 mine workers and their families endured food insecurity when mines were closed (Grobler 2020). This contradicts the spirit of caring, sharing and collective personhood that underpins Ubuntu (Broodryk 2006). In 2020, 40 percent of the population in South Africa consumed less food and 33 percent went to bed hungry because of unemployment (Grobler 2020). Food insecurity is an urgent concern that persists, with complications experienced in food supply, in purchasing power of people and in the quality of production of food (News24 2021). Low-income households are persistently most vulnerable (Naik 2021). Because of the closure of schools in South Africa during the COVID-19 pandemic, supplementary feeding schemes of these institutions were also closed, which transferred the burden of sourcing food back to households that are poor and triggered their anger, resulting in looting (Teresi 2021). Also, the low resilience of unemployed South Africans is because of their lowest levels of emergency savings universally (Casale and Sheperd 2021). According to a multivariate logistic regression analysis, unemployed households have the least financial capabilities, restrained financial knowledge and the lowest amount of emergency savings (Reyers 2019). As a result of the lack of capacity to draw upon savings, unemployed families could not buy groceries in bulk and safely isolate themselves in their homes during the peak periods of the COVID-19 national lockdown, another cause of looting (Casale and Sheperd 2021). This contradicts interconnectedness, respect and dignity, collectivism and solidarity, communal enterprise and leadership legitimacy, which are the cornerstones of Ubuntu (Sotuku and Duku 2010).

In South Africa, overall, the size of the household that is unemployed is nearly double that of the employed household, which has on average more than five times the income that is disposal (Statistics South Africa 2019). The lack of disposable income for households that are unemployed requires their prioritization of expenses and concentration of their spending on transport, rent, utilities and food (Casale and Sheperd 2021). The effects of the COVID-19 pandemic and subsequent lockdown included an increase in the official unemployment to a record of 32 percent in the fourth quarter of 2020, an increase of 3 percent in three quarters, a loss of 2.2 million jobs and the contraction of the economy by 7.2 percent (Naidu 2021). The COVID-19 pandemic also negatively impacted all sectors, but closures of business were most prevalent in hospitality, trade, manufacturing and construction sectors culminating in unemployment that prompted tension in people, instigating looting (Bhorat et al. 2020). This is inconsistent with self-protection, in-group collectivism, consensus building and a 'being your brother's keeper' type of humane orientation that informs Ubuntu.

CONCLUSION

Unemployment since the attainment of democracy in South Africa requires the attention of the government. While households that are employed draw upon their bank savings and purchase food lavishly, unemployed families languish in poverty. The socioeconomic security of unemployed families is gravely affected. Unemployed families are forced to live in uncertainty, unsure of the source of their income, culminating in food insecurity and hunger. Residents of informal urban localities who are unemployed are the worst affected. Insufficient health care services and goods; limited basic infrastructure inclusive of sanitation, water and electricity; low-quality education and unemployment haunt them, instigating their looting. The dual economies, in which most livelihoods depend on sporadic informal earning, characterizes the South African community. Complete liberation is only realized when the dual economies are eliminated and a social revolution follows a national one. While a national democratic revolution was experienced, the socialist revolution that the working class backed was repudiated. The social transformation agenda succumbed to international monopoly capital interest during the negotiated transfer of political power in the 1990s. The dependence on the business sector to resolve social challenges has been unsuccessful, culminating in increased unemployment coupled with poverty, inequality and other social ills. The COVID-19 pandemic has exacerbated the moral standards of the country because of the denial of fundamental rights and freedom afforded to the least capable of the country. To mitigate looting, South Africa needs to implement national Black economic empowerment legislation and policies to realize human rights and social justice for all people regardless of their race.

REFERENCES

Alexander, Neville. 2003. *An ordinary country: Issues in the transition from apartheid to democracy in South Africa*. New York: Berghahn Books.

———. 2012. South Africa today: The moral responsibility of intellectuals. In *Enough is a feast: A tribute to Neville Alexander*, edited by H. Vally and M. Isaacson, 31–37 Johannesburg: Foundation for Human Rights.

———. 2013. *Thoughts on the new South Africa*. Johannesburg: Jacana Media.

Barnard-Naudé, Jaco. 2021. Anarchy in the Republic of South Africa: A spirit of revolt without revolution. *Daily Maverick*, 15 July. https://www.dailymaverick.co.za/opinionista/2021-07-15-anarchy-in-the-rsa-a-spirit-of-revolt-without-revolution/.

Béné, Christophe. 2020. Resilience of local food systems and links to food security: A review of some important concepts in the context of COVID-19 and other shocks. *Food security* 12, no. 4: 805–22.

Beresford, Alexander. 2015. Power, patronage, and gatekeeper politics in South Africa. *African Affairs* 114, no. 455: 226–48.

Bhorat, Haroon, Tim Köhler, Oosthuizen, Morné, Stanwix, Benjamin, Steenkamp, François, and Thornton, Amy. 2020. The economics of COVID-19 in South Africa: Early impressions. Cape Town: Policy Research Unit. http://www.dpru.uct.ac.za/sites/default/files/image_tool/images/36/Publications/ Policy Briefs/DPRU PB20_54.pdf.

Biko, Steven. 2004. *I write what I like*. Johannesburg: Picador.

Black, Sara, Spreen, Carol Anne, and Vally, Salim. 2020. Education, Covid-19 and care: Social inequality and social relations of value in South Africa and the United States. *Southern African Review of Education with Education with Production* 26, no. 1: 40–61.

Booysen, Susan. 2021. Time Bomb South Africa: the building blocks that triggered, facilitated and sustained the civil unrest. *Daily Maverick*, 15 July. https://www.dailymaverick.co.za/ opinionista/2021-07-15-time-bomb-south-africa-the-building-blocks-that-triggered-facilitated -and-sustained-the-civil-unrest/.

Broodryk, Johann. 2006. Ubuntu African life coping skills: Theory and practice. In *CCEAM Conference*, Lefkosia, Cyprus, p. 2.

Brown, Byron, and Shumba, Almon. 2011. Managing Africa's multiculturalism: Bringing the 'Madiba magic' into the African school curriculum. In *Handbook of African educational theories and practices: A generative teacher education curriculum*. 531–47. Bamenda, North West Region (Cameroon): Human Development Resource Centre (HDRC).

Buthelezi, L. 2021. *SA Lost R1.5 trillion to corruption in five years and continues to bleed report.* News24, 23 June. https://www.news24.com/fin24/economy/south-africa/sa-lost-r15-trillion-to-corrupion-in-five-years-and-continues-to-bleed-report-20210623.

Calland, R. 2021. *Historic moment as constitutional court finds Zuma guilty and sentences him to jail.* The Conversation, 29 June. https://theconversation.com/historic-moment-as-constitutional-court-finds-zuma-guilty-and-sentences-him-to-jail -163612.

Casale, Daniela, and Shepherd, Debra. 2021. The gendered effects of the COVID-19 crisis and ongoing lockdown in South Africa: Evidence from NIDS-CRAM waves 1–3. National Income Dynamics Study–Coronavirus Rapid Mobile Survey (NIDS-CRAM) Working Paper. https://cramsurvey.org/wp-content/uploads/2021/05/4.-Casale-D.

Cloete, Michael. 2014. Neville Alexander: Towards overcoming the legacy of racial capitalism in post-apartheid South Africa. *Transformation: Critical Perspectives on Southern Africa* 86, no. 1: 30–47.

Department of Planning, Monitoring and Evaluation. 2018. *Overcoming poverty and inequality in South Africa: an assessment of drivers, constraints and opportunities*. Pretoria: Department of Planning, Monitoring and Evaluation, Statistics South Africa, and World Bank Group. http://documents.worldbank.org/curated/en/530481521735906534/pdf/124521-REV-OUO-South-Africa-Poverty-and-Inequality -Assessment-Report-2018-FINAL-WEB.

Francis, David, Valodia, Imraan, and Ramburuth-Hurt, Kamal. 2020. Covid-19: The full economic impact will only be known later. *Wits. ac. za* 22. https://www.wits.ac.za/covid19/covid19-news/latest/covid-19-the-full -economic-impact-will-only-be-known-later.html.

Gaxamba, L. 2021. Social unrest will continue as long as high levels of poverty, inequality exist. *IOL*, 20 July. https://www.iol.co.za/business-report/opinion/social-unrest-will-continue-as-long-as-high-levels-of-poverty-inequality-exist-961cad42-3b80-4474-99e9-1155b89c2821.

Grobler, R. 2020. Lockdown: One in three adults in South Africa goes to bed hungry, according to latest research. News 24.com, 20 May. https://www.news24.com/news24/southafrica/news/lockdown -one-in-three-adults-in-sa-goes-to-bed-hungry-according-to-latest-research-20200520.

Habib, A. 2021. South Africa's rebellion and looting: Political courage needed to address security dilemma, to avoid being held hostage by rogues. *Daily Maverick*, 23 July. https://www.dailymaverick.co.za/opinionista/2021-07-23-south-africas

-rebellion-and-looting-political-courage-needed-to-address-security-dilemma-to-avoid-being-held-hostage-by-rogue.

Kalina, Marc. 2021. As South Africa's cities burn: We can clean-up, but we cannot sweep away inequality. *Local Environment* 26(10): 1186–91.

Khambule, Isaac. 2020. The effects of COVID-19 on the South African informal economy: Limits and pitfalls of government's response. *Loyola Journal of Social Sciences* 34(1): 95–109.

Khoza, R. J. 2004. Challenges facing African leadership. *Business in Africa.* http://www.businessinafrica.net/thoughtleadership (accessed on 11 May 2022).

Klasen, Stephan. 1997. "Poverty, inequality and deprivation in South Africa: An analysis of the 1993 SALDRU survey." *Social Indicators Research* 41, no. 1: 51–94.

Kunene, Z. 2009. *Ubuntu.* Keynote address on behalf of Zandile Kunene in the Gauteng Department of Education Conference in September 2009.

Letseka, Moeketsi. 2013. Educating for ubuntu/botho: Lessons from Basotho indigenous education. *Open Journal of Philosophy* 3(2): 337.

Levy, B., Hirsch, A., Naidoo, V., and Nxele, M. 2021. *South Africa: When strong institutions and massive inequalities collide*. Cape Town: Carnegie Endowment for International Peace. https://carnegieendowment.org/files/202103-Levy_etal_SouthAfrica.pdf.

Majoko, T. 2020. An Afrocentric perspective on Inclusion and Ubuntu. In *Autism: Perspectives from Africa*, edited by Dikeledi Mahlo, Mary G. Clasquin-Johnson, and Michael Clasquin Johnson, 1:7–15. Pretoria: University of South Africa Press.

Maringira, G. 2020. COVID-19: Social distancing and lockdown in black townships in South Africa. *Kujenga Amani* 7. https://kujenga-amani.ssrc.org/2020/05/07/covid-19social-distancing-and-lockdown-in-black-townships-in-south-africa.

Martin, G. 2021. *900 Service delivery protests in South Africa over six months*. Defence Web, 20 April. https://www.defenceweb.co.za/featured/900-service-delivery-protests -in-south-Africa-over-six-months.

Mawere, Munyaradzi, and Mubaya, Tapuwa R. 2016. *African philosophy and thought systems: A search for a culture and philosophy of belonging*. Mankon, Bamenda: Langaa Research and Publishing.

McKinley, D. T. 2021.Unrest of understanding, representation and explanation. *Daily Maverick*, 20 July. https://www.dailymaverick.co.za/article/2021-07-20-unrest-in-kzn-and-gauteng-ofunderstanding-representation-and-explanation.

Mkhize, S., Dube, G., and Quazi, T. 2014. *Informal economy monitoring study: Waste pickers in Durban, South Africa*. Manchester, UK: WIEGO. https://www.researchgate.net/publication/293487845_Waste_pickers_in_Durban_South_Africa.

Naidu, S. 2021. The impact of COVID-19: The conundrum of South Africa's socio-economic landscape. Accord, 3 March. https://www.accord.org.za/analysis/the-impact-of -covid-19-the-conundrum-of-south-africas-socio-economic-landscape/.

Naik, S. 2021. It will take years for South Africa's economy to recover from ongoing violence and looting, warn economists. *IOL*, 17 July. https://www.iol.co.za/saturday-star/news/it-will -take-years-for-sas-economy-to-recover-from-ongoing-violence-and-looting-warn-economists -b3be76e5-b758-4e3c-822b-48e6e0f7a834.

Netshitenzhe, Joel. 2013. "Why inequality matters: South African trends and interventions." Mapungubwe Institute for Strategic Reflection. Available at: http://www.mistra.org.za/Library/ConferencePaper/Documents/Why20.

News24. 2021. Unrest fallout: N3 highway reopened. 16 July. https://www.news24.com/fin24/economy/south-africa/live-unrest-fallout-sa-may-face-bread-shortage-as-riots-hit-yeast-wheat-supplies-20210714.

Nussbaum, Barbara., and Wiechel, Kimberly. 2010. The spirit of Ubuntu. Available at: http://www. peacexpeace. org/2010/07/the-spirit-of-Ubuntu.

Nyoka, Bongani. 2020. *The social and political thought of Archie Mafeje*. Pretoria: Wits University Press.

Oppenheim, Claire E. 2012. Nelson Mandela and the power of Ubuntu. *Religions* 3(2): 369–88.

Orthofer, A. 2016. Wealth inequality in South Africa: Insights from survey and tax data. Working Paper 15. World Bank. https://thedocs.worldbank.org/en/doc/73151 1476914370714005002201 6/original/Weath in equality in SouthAfrica.pdf.

Patel, J. 2021. *Social cohesion hangs in the balance as South Africans feel economically insecure: Reflections from the South African reconciliation barometer*. Johannesburg: Institute for Justice and Reconciliation. https://media.africaportal.org/documents/Occassional-paper-7.pdf.

Pellerin, Marquita. 2012. Benefits of Afrocentricity in exploring social phenomena: Understanding Afrocentricity as a social science methodology. *The Journal of Pan African Studies* 5(4): 149–60.

Phasha, N. 2016. Understanding inclusive education from an Afrocentric perspective. In *Inclusive education: An African perspective*, 3–28. Oxford: Oxford University Press.

Reuters. 2021.Counting the costs: South Africa businesses wrecked by unrest. *IOL*, 15 July. https://www.iol.co.za/business-report/companies/counting-the-costs-sa-businesses-wrecked-by-unrest-e0e49e51-b86e-5619-8e6e-f9f69cc10fc5.

Reyers, Michelle. 2019. Financial capability and emergency savings among South Africans living above and below the poverty line. *International Journal of Consumer Studies* 43(4): 335–47.

Rogerson, Christian M., and Rogerson, Jayne M. 2020. COVID-19 tourism impacts in South Africa: Government and industry responses. *Geo Journal of Tourism and Geosites* 31, no. 3: 1083–91.

Seekings, J. 2021. Making sense of disorder: Seven days of anarchy and government inaction that changed South Africa. *Daily Maverick*, 20 July. https://www.dailymaverick.co.za/ article/2021-07-20-making-sense-of-disorder-seven-days-of-anarchy-and-government-inaction -that-changed-south-Africa/.

Segalo, Puleng. 2015.Gender, social cohesion and everyday struggles in South Africa. *Psychology in Society* 49: 70–82.

Socio-economic Rights Institute of South Africa (SERI). 2018. *Informal settlements and human rights in South Africa: Submission to the United Nations special rapporteur on adequate housing as a component of the right to an adequate standard of living.* Johannesburg: Socio-economic Rights Institute of South Africa. https://www.ohchr.org/Documents/Issues/Housing/InformalSettlements/ SERI.

Sidimba, L. 2021. Civil unrest death toll in KwaZulu-Natal, Gauteng rises to 276. *IOL*, 21 July. https://www.iol.co.za/news/politics/civil-unrest-death-toll-in-kzn-gauteng-rises-to-276-c6e81aa7-96bb-416d-8f4f-9d685d2d33c8.

Sotuku, N., and Duku, N. S. 2014. Indigenous African theories in multicultural education. In *Schooling, society and inclusive education*, 17–38. Oxford: Oxford University Press.

Spaull, Nic. 2015. Schooling in South Africa: How low-quality education becomes a poverty trap. *South African child gauge* 12, no. 1: 34–41.

Statistics South Africa. 2019. *Inequality trends in South Africa*. Pretoria: Statistics South Africa. http://www.statssa.gov.za/publications/Report-03-10-19/Report-03-10-192017.pdf.

Swanson, Dalene M. 2007. Ubuntu: An African contribution to (re) search for/with a 'humble togetherness'. *Journal of contemporary issues in education* 2, no. 2 : 53–67.

Teresi, M. 2021. Effects of COVID-19 on the South African economy. *Borgen Magazine*, 25 June. https://www.borgenmagazine.com/south-african-economy/.

Thomas, E. 2020. Why do protests turn violent? It's not just because people are desperate. The Conversation, 5 June. https://theconversation.com/why-do-protests-turn-violent-its -not-just-because-people-are-desperate-139968.

Tutu, D. 1999. *No future without forgiveness.* London: Rider.

Vally, Salim, and Motala, Enver. 2021. Neville Alexander's warning. *Education as Change* 25(1): 1–5.

Van der Burger, Ronelle, Servaas Van der Berg, Sarel Van Der Walt, and Derek Yu. 2017. "The long walk: Considering the enduring spatial and racial dimensions of deprivation two decades after the fall of apartheid." *Social Indicators Research* 130, no. 3 : 1101–23.

Visagie, J., and Turok, I. 2021a. Rural–urban inequalities amplified by COVID-19: Evidence from South Africa. *Area Development and Policy* 6(1): 50–62.

———. 2021b. *Driven further apart by the pandemic? Contrasting impacts of COVID-19 on people and places.* 8 July. Cape Town: National Income Dynamics Study. https://cramsurvey.org/wp-content/uploads/2021/07/12.-Turok-I.

Webster, E., and Francis, D. 2019. The paradox of inequality in South Africa: A challenge from the workplace. *Transformation: Critical Perspectives on Southern Africa* 101(1): 11–35. doi:10.1353/trn.2019.0035.

Chapter Six

An Appraisal of South Africa's July Civil Unrest through the Lens of Frustration-Aggression Theory

The Case of KwaZulu-Natal Province

Methembe Mdlalose

INTRODUCTION

Protest movements are on the rise worldwide amid deepening inequalities and job crises worsened by the coronavirus pandemic. Since the start of the COVID-19 outbreak, the number of major civil unrest events worldwide has risen sharply (Institute for Economics and Peace 2020). In 2020 alone, widespread COVID-19 lockdowns sparked protests in countries across the world, with millions marching through the streets demanding jobs, democratic freedoms, social justice and an end to corruption. But worsening economic conditions and government inaction to address the issues facing people will likely trigger more sporadic civil unrests. As such, the growth of such events presents complex research problems and requires interdisciplinary collaboration. To date, researchers have tried to understand better factors that cause social unrest by analysing direct relationships between social unrest and various economic and socioeconomic variables. In the context of this paper, civil unrest is a term that is characteristically used in law enforcement to describe disorders caused by a person or group of people (Schurink 1990). Accordingly, civil unrest involves a group of people that conduct mass protests, refusing to obey authority. There are typically two types of civil disorders, namely nonviolent and violent disorders. The former may include parades, boycotts and sit-ins. In contrast, the latter contains obstructions like rallies, marches, riots, and sabotage which often leads to damage to property or injury to other people (Sändig 2015). While typically intended to be a demonstration to the government, it can escalate into insurgency (Sändig 2015). Thus, civil unrest is typically a symptom of and a form of protest against a state's major socio-political or economic problems. Civil unrest can be attributed to myriad issues such as political grievances (including opposition to tyrannical governments), ethnic clashes, service delivery and corruption, and long-standing oppression (IMF 2020).

While there had not been any sizeable COVID-19-related protest recorded since 2020, in July of the following year, civil unrest in South Africa uncharacteristically ensued in two of the country's most populous provinces, which also account for nearly 50 percent of the country's Gross Domestic Product (GDP). Between the 9th and 18th of July 2021, the Gauteng and KwaZulu-Natal (KZN) provinces, were engulfed by protests which evolved into rioting and looting following the incarceration of South Africa's former president, Jacob Zuma for contempt of court (Vhumbunu 2021). Earlier in the year, the Constitutional Court of South Africa sentenced the former president to fifteen months imprisonment for defying its order to comply with the summons to appear before the Judicial Commission of Inquiry into Allegations of State Capture, Corruption and Fraud in the Public Sector (Constitutional Court of South Africa 2021). Interestingly, there has been wide-ranging debate across the country on whether the 'Free Zuma' protests, looting and socio-political unrest were caused by the imprisonment of Zuma or other underlying issues.

Using the Frustration-Aggression theory and data derived from secondary sources, this chapter sheds light on the factors leading to the July civil unrest in South Africa's KwaZulu-Natal province.

FRUSTRATION-AGGRESSION THEORY

The frustration-aggression hypothesis emerged from the work of a group of Yale University psychologists—John Dollard, Leonard Doob, Neal Miller, O. H. Mowrer, and Robert Sears—in a critical monograph, *Frustration and Aggression* (1939), in which they integrated ideas and findings from several disciplines, especially sociology, anthropology and psychology. Their work was notable for its eclectic use of psychoanalysis, behaviourism and Marxism. It became one of the most influential explanations of aggressive behaviour in social science history. The initial frustration-aggression formulation postulated that frustration (the blocking of a goal-response) was a necessary antecedent of aggression and that aggression was an inevitable consequence of frustration (Dollard et al. 1939; Miller 1941). In their book *Frustration and Aggression*, Dollard et al. (1939) succinctly summarized their theory using two bold assertions. First, they contend that the occurrence of aggressive behaviour always presupposes the existence of frustration. Secondly, they argue that the existence of frustration always leads to some form of aggression. In other words, aggression was always a consequence of frustration, and frustration was always followed by aggression. However, critics disparaged the idea that frustration always leads to aggression, as stated in the initial hypothesis. Generally, modern researchers reject the initial version of the theory in favour of Berkowitz's iteration or another aggression model, which contends that only some frustrations will lead to aggression (Fox and Spector 1999). As Miller (1941) and Berkowitz (1989) postulate, whether or not frustration produces an aggressive response depends upon several factors, including proximity of goal attainment and the potential for the punishment of aggressive behavioural responses. It is worth noting that Berkowitz's (1989) work has seen more success than Dollard's initial version of the frustration-aggression hypothesis and is used as a theoretical basis for most modern research (e.g., Breuer et al. 2015). To understand frustration-aggression Theory further, Berkowitz (1989) argues that there must be comprehension of the term *frustration*.

The frustration-aggression hypothesis states that aggression is a result of frustration. Frustration is any event or stimulus that prevents an individual from attaining a goal and its accompanying reinforcement quality (Dollard and Miller 1939). Moreover, frustration, as described by Berkowitz (1989), is an unpleasant, aversive stimulus which evokes negative affect by automatically eliciting cognitions that are associated with aggressive tendencies. Moreover, Hanratty et al. (1972) describe frustration as the withdrawal of an anticipated reinforcer (Breuer and Elson 2017). Historically, behaviourists in early psychology defined frustration as an event resulting from the termination of reinforcement that had previously maintained a behaviour. As such, the psychological explanation of aggressive behaviour stems from the frustration of goals. As such, Amsel (1962) correctly predicts that frustration occurs when the anticipated goal is unattainable, or the reward is reduced.

When our drive to reach a goal is blocked by external factors, we experience frustration which, in turn, creates an aggressive drive, which can lead to aggressive behaviour (Amsel 1962). When we express this aggression physically, verbally or by fantasizing, we experience catharsis, and our emotional tension is reduced. However, our aggression is not always expressed towards the legitimate target, as it could be too dangerous, and we risk punishment because this target is not available. Resultantly, we displace our aggressive response towards a less perilous target or one who just happens to be present (Breuer and Elson 2017). This condition is called displacement. Thus, the hypothesis is applied in studies of scapegoating and hate crimes, which indicate that as sources of frustration accumulate—during an economic crisis, for example—frustrated groups may unleash their aggression on a convenient social target, often a minority group (De Gaay Fortman 2005).

DETAILING THE JULY CIVIL UNREST IN KWAZULU-NATAL: POLITICAL INSURGENCE OR RESPONSE TO GOVERNMENT FAILURES?

There has been expansive discourse across academia, political circles and the general public on the factual circumstances surrounding the July 2021 protests and subsequent socio-political unrest. Shortly after the former president of South Africa, Jacob Zuma handed himself over at Estcourt Correctional Service Centre in KZN on 7 July 2021; pandemonium erupted in KwaZulu-Natal through widespread violent protests, rioting and looting of shops and businesses (The Presidency 2021). The arrest of Jacob Zuma came after a warrant of arrest was issued over his defiance of a court ruling compelling him to appear before the State Capture Commission, in which he was heavily implicated in corruption. The chaos spread to parts of Gauteng province from 9 to 17 July 2021. Zuma had been summoned to appear before the Commission between 18 and 22 January 2021 but continuously expressed reluctance to appear before the Commission, citing his treatment as an accused rather than as a witness and health concerns, and later, he unsuccessfully appealed for the recusal of the chairperson of the Commission. The Commission launched contempt of court proceedings at the Constitutional Court (South African Constitutional Court 2021). On 29 June 2021, the Constitutional Court sentenced Zuma to fifteen months in prison for failing to comply with the court order to testify before the Commission. His conduct constituted a 'reprehensible attack on the rule of law', and his contempt of court 'posed a severe risk that it would inspire others to undermine the administration of justice (South African Constitutional Court, 2021). The 'Free Zuma' protests resulted in extensive damage to the economy and businesses while threatening the lives and livelihoods of the people who were already reeling under the effects of COVID-19. Protesters blockaded and damaged parts of the main national highways, resultantly disrupting commercial traffic along the routes, which serve as strategic logistics arteries nationally and regionally (The Presidency 2021). More than 30 trucks were burnt and looted, mostly at Mooi River Town in KwaZulu-Natal (News24 2021). The 2,255 km national (N2) highway connects Cape Town with Durban, while the 579 km national (N3) highway connects Gauteng with KwaZulu-Natal. The latter is a strategic route in Southern Africa along the north-south corridor, as the route facilitates road transit freight and commercial cargo traffic from landlocked countries, such as Zimbabwe, Zambia and the Democratic Republic of the Congo. This corridor largely imports and exports to and from the strategic seaports of Durban (Africa's busiest port), Richards Bay and King Shaka International Airport.

On a national scale, SAPOA estimated that the damage was worth R50 billion, while the KZN province lost R20 billion, and in Durban alone, R1.5 billion of stock was lost by businesses (ACCORD 2021). In total, an estimated 40,000 businesses and 50,000 informal traders were affected, with 150,000 jobs put at risk, primarily due to business closures and the possibilities of delayed restocking and reopening (SA News 2021). A total of 161 malls were damaged countrywide, while 161 liquor outlets and distributors, 11 warehouses, and eight factories were extensively damaged (SA News 2021). Banking services were affected, as most banks in KZN and Gauteng closed their branches (ACCORD 2021). Shoprite Group Stores reported that out of its 1,189 supermarkets trading under different names, a total of 200 Shoprite Group Stores were looted, vandalized or burnt in KZN and Gauteng. The number includes sixty-nine Shoprite supermarkets, fifty-four Shoprite Liquor Shop outlets, forty-four Usave stores, thirty-five furniture stores, six Checkers supermarkets, one Checkers Hyper, and one Freshmark Distribution Centre. Massmart Holdings Limited reported that forty-one of its stores had been looted in KZN and Gauteng, with four facilities burnt and damaged (Moneyweb 2021). All this consequently led to food shortages and under-supply of essential commodities. In addition, it led to Communal violence and racial tensions that sparked as a result of vigilantism across KwaZulu-Natal, especially in the provinces' only metropolitan city, Durban. Business owners and armed civilians resorted to self-defence, self-protection, and community citizen policing. In Phoenix, a predominantly Indian suburb of Durban, the official death toll reached thirty-six people as allegations of racial profiling and 'race-targeted' attacks on suspected looters and pillagers surfaced (The Presidency 2021). South Africa's head of state Cyril Ramaphosa, in his national debrief on 16 July 2021, described the protests as 'nothing less than a deliberate, coordinated, and well-planned attack on the actions . . . intended to cripple the economy, cause social stability and severely weaken or even dislodge—the democratic state (The Presidency 2021). Following this view, some in support of President Ramaphosa hold the view that the unrest was led by disgruntled fellow African National Congress (ANC) members that sought to provoke a populist insurrection. The preceding view comes at the back of a long-standing culture of factionalism amongst leaders of the ANC, South Africa's ruling party (Booysen 2018). Today the most current and notable instalment of factional battles is between, on the one hand, staunch *CR17* supporters of current ANC president Cyril Ramaphosa and loyalists of former ANC president Jacob Zuma. Although the cracks between the two groups of supporters had been implicitly visible some few months before the ANC's fifty-fourth national electoral conference, tensions became amplified by the state capture commission, where supporters of Zuma's Radical Economic Transformation faction accused the State Capture Commission of using state resources to target political opponents (*IOL* 2022). The State Capture Commission was established in January 2018 by then president, Jacob Zuma, who appointed then deputy-chief Justice Raymond Zondo to chair, following the recommendations of then chief justice Mogoeng Mogoeng as the chairperson, in accordance with Section 84(2) of the Constitution. The state Capture commission followed the investigation and remedial action of the Public Protector concerning complaints and allegations of State Capture in the democratic dispensation (Madonsela 2016).

Notably, one may argue that there may be some merit in the argument that the July unrest was a planned insurgence by disgruntled Zuma supporters. However, it is equally plausible to argue that socioeconomic frustrations harboured by citizens sometimes trigger such opportunistic acts of rebellion. As such, this article advances the view that such violent behaviour can be understood within the theoretical framework of FAT and other similar deprivation theories. Crucially, as we now know, the theory holds that a group's relative disadvantage in relation to others, which may be manifested in income inequality or hierarchical class, results in frustration which breeds grievance and aggression (Beavers 2019). Accordingly, in line with the characterization of insurgencies and civil unrests, it is, therefore, crucial to appreciate the role of frustration, whether economic or socio-political. For instance, in line with the foregoing, the case of Boko Haram may be necessary to classify how frustration resorted to extremely violent behaviour. In a recent study, Olaniyi and Ikechukwu (2019) found that the prevailing unpleasant socio-material conditions pertaining to survival, economic deprivation, structural inequities, environmental degradation, governance deficits and many other deprivations were significant causes of Niger Delta militancy, Boko Haram terrorism and Fulani herdsmen attacks in Nigeria. Thus, applying the framework of the FAT, it is possible to argue that frustration over the government's economic failures compounded an increase in Boko Haraam's aggressive behaviour and proved to be a factor in mobilizing the Boko Haram insurgency. Noticeably, such trends have not only been seen in Africa but elsewhere as well. For instance, a series of high-profile social protests—the Arab Spring, Black Lives Matter, the Gilets Jaunes, and Occupy Wall Street were all mainly triggered by long-standing socioeconomic frustrations directed at respective governments.

As we are all aware, the COVID-19 pandemic has presented an unprecedented disruption to the global economy and world trade, as production and consumption are scaled back across the globe. As a result, global trade collapsed in 2020 owing to border closures and supply disruptions which interrupted the international provision of goods and services. KwaZulu as the key exporter both in South Africa and the SADC region, was one the most affected by the disruption (Metalbulletin 2021). Given the above, and alongside a chronically weak domestic economy, high levels of unemployment and poverty and generally poor service delivery, it must be said that there has been very little to insulate the province against triggers of socioeconomic crisis. Thus, it should be less of a surprise that an opportunistic "Free Zuma" campaign could singlehandedly trigger such country-wide pandemonium. More importantly, as we seek to test the veracity of the preceding assertion, it may be equally necessary to study the socioeconomic realities of KwaZulu-Natal before the unrest, where the unrest began.

To begin with, in 2021, South Africa's population eclipsed sixty million people, all this whilst the economy has persistency failed to grow beyond 2 percent, and unemployment hit a historic 35 percent in arguably the most unequal country in the world (Statistics South Africa 2021). Therefore, against this background, one can thus be tempted to entertain possibilities of the KZN July unrest falling outside a single constructed narrative but within several nuanced sequences of frustrations that have manifested within the province. Accordingly, in agreement with the FAT, what this analysis seeks to point out is the proposition that the unrest that was seen to have been inspired by the "Free Zuma" campaign may, in fact, be misplaced frustration. As discussed in the last section, the FAT implies that misplaced aggression occurs when thwarted goals trigger primitive impulses towards violence. Resultantly, this inhibits self-regulation and ultimately decreases compliance with social norms. Following this theory, the paper highlights below a list of potential precursors within KwaZulu-Natal that need not be ruled out as potential frustration triggers of the July 2021 civil unrest.

WEAK POLITICAL LEADERSHIP AND LOSS OF LEGITIMACY

According to Koontz and Donnell (1955), leadership is the activity of persuading people to cooperate in the achievement of a common objective. In general, leadership basically entails influencing other people's actions in a goal-directed cooperative effort. Conversely, poor leadership can be defined as leadership style, intents, and actions pushing an organization away from realizing the organisation's goals, mission and vision (Kumar 2022). Poor leadership in political parties has been noted as a critical factor associated with problems of socio-political and socioeconomic instability, social malaise and governance, as well as the general lack of respect for the rule of law (ACCORD 2007). Thus, to build a progressive society, it is advised that political leaders create robust frameworks built on competence, integrity and authentic contribution to the long-term welfare of citizens (Valgarðsson et al. 2020). The issue of political leadership and the desire to produce people who command national legitimacy has been challenging in all polities—and this dilemma is probably more critical in developing nations (Udogu 2008).

Interestingly, South Africa is an example of this. Since the beginning of the democratic dispensation, the country has experienced considerable leadership challenges, with its poor leadership record badly contributing to leadership challenges throughout the three spheres (Rotberg 2014). The propensity of the South African government to condone impunity, especially in the realm of political violence and corruption, has contributed not only to the ANC being perceived as weak and incompetent but also to being oblivious to crime in general (Cedras 2021). As has been widely documented in the literature, KwaZulu-Natal is considered the epicentre of political violence in South Africa (Johnston 1996). The province accounts for the majority of political violence that occurs in South Africa, especially around election time, as political assassinations increase (Krämer 2019). For a long time political intolerance has been seen between the ANC and Inkatha Freedom Party, the latter, KwaZulu-Natal's second-largest political party. Leading up to democracy and for a while after, power contestations between the two parties have often been mired by assaults and assassinations due to the lack of political tolerance (Höglund and Jarstad 2011). Today, intraparty factionalism has replaced interparty violence as the largest source of political intolerance and violence and, simultaneously, the biggest threat to political instability.

Kanyane (2021) calls factionalism an old age phenomenon. He argues that factionalism leads to havoc, conflicts, splits and instability. Typically, intraparty factions are meant to be inherently internal and private. However, of late, in KwaZulu-Natal and other provinces, to a certain extent, what has been witnessed is a growing culture of political divisions making it into the public realm. For instance, during one of Jacob Zuma's court appearances at the Pietermaritzburg High Court, Sihle Zikalala (former ANC KZN chairperson) and Mdumiseni Ntuli (former ANC KZN secretary general) were individually booed off the stage. They were branded Cyril Ramaphosa apologists after allegedly 'failing' to support Zuma (Times Live 2021). Given the above, it then becomes possible for one to reasonably deduce that the result of a fragmented ANC is likely to promote a further decline in public trust and confidence, inevitably leading to a gradual decline in legitimacy.

While it remains, albeit at a gradual decline, the most dominant political party in much of South Africa, the ANC in KwaZulu-Natal has been under the microscope following their dismal performance in the most recent local elections. On 1 November 2021, South Africa conducted its sixth local government election. Noticeably, the election results in KwaZulu-Natal portrayed an apparent decline in the dominance of the ANC in the province, with ANC only managing to secure 41 percent of the general vote leaving twenty-one municipalities in the province without a majority vote (*Mail and Guardian* 2021). The IFP was the biggest winner; although the party secured 24.29

percent of the overall vote, the IFP managed to claim several municipalities formerly controlled by the ANC or forced coalitions on hung municipalities previously controlled by the ANC (*Mail and Guardian* 2021). Notable reasons highlighted for a decline in the ANC vote at the local level include service delivery, corruption amongst ANC leaders in local government and the general unhappiness with the ANC's Provincial Executive Committee's inaction with the Zuma arrest (*IOL* 2021).

Notably, the decline of the ANC in KwaZulu-Natal's local elections indicates the demise of the public's trust levels towards the political party as a legitimate leader of society and demonstrates a further deterioration in the perceptions of legitimacy towards the ruling party in KZN. There is ample evidence pointing to the positive correlation between illegitimacy and violence (Schoon 2016). A decline in public legitimacy triggers instability and anarchy. Thus, in line with this interpretation, this reinforces the view that the civil unrest can be attributed in part to the frustration of Jacob Zuma's supporters, unhappy with the lack of action from the KZN ANC leadership following the Jacob Zuma unrest. For others, the subsequent anarchy and looting were a facade to mask the peoples' continued frustration with the province's government over political leadership's fundamental failure on socioeconomic policy and poor service delivery at the local level. Brought together, the gravity of these issues can only suggest that the rioting and mass looting were positioned as a stern indication of a call for change in the ANCs current leadership.

STATE OF THE ECONOMY

As highlighted in previous sections, the July report compiled by the South African government firmly postulates that the unrest, which almost brought the two largest provinces by GDP to their knees, was orchestrated, instigated and planned (The Presidency 2021). While there may be some merit in the preceding view, it is equally necessary to caution the following: to simplistically brand the riots as opportunistic or premeditated criminality is to ignore the broader existing social and economic issues both in KwaZulu-Natal and broader South Africa. However, this misguided narrative attempts to silence important messages contained in the rioting behaviour, especially from disenfranchised and deprived citizens. Notably, the correlation between economic deprivation and public violence has supported a positive relationship between poor economic performance and confrontational activism (Beavers 2019). Similar studies have supported primarily a relative deprivation theory–based explanation of why citizens choose to participate in violent protests. Initially, the relative deprivation theory presented by Gurr (1970) listed poor economic conditions, disappointment with economic policies, economic injustice, and a gap in personal economic expectations as driving factors for people to act rebellious. Previous studies on post-recession Europe (Kern et al. 2015; Quaranta 2015; Vassallo and Ding 2016) used relative deprivation theory to explain protest and highlight the relevance of economic scarcity as a grievance strong enough to convince more people to take to the streets. In the most extreme cases of economic collapse, in the so-called PIIGS countries (Portugal, Ireland, Italy, Greece and Spain), among others, levels of confrontational activism (street demonstrations, building occupations, damages to property or general strikes) spiked, with more than the usual citizens participating in forms of confrontational action (Verney and Bosco 2013; Calvo 2013; Kosmidis 2014; Accornero and Pinto 2015). Accordingly, findings in relation to the July unrest also seem to suggest the assertion that perceived deprivation at the individual level from lower income levels, growing inflation, limited public services and smaller social policy budgets were responsible for the general outrage. Moreover, the extent of the rioting in KwaZulu-Natal exposed South Africa's broader underlying economic concerns.

It is no secret that since the 2009 global financial crisis KwaZulu-Natal province, like most South African regions, has had to deal with several structural factors that have worsened the socioeconomic conditions (Treasury 2019). Notably, from an economic perspective, over the last few years KwaZulu-Natal has experienced persistent challenges of premature deindustrialization, obstinately low growth in important employment sectors (manufacturing, agriculture, tourism), a growing unemployed youth population, poverty and, importantly, unabated corruption in the province (Treasury 2019). Furthermore, in 2018, the province experienced a severe technical recession, contracting in the first and second quarters by -3.9 percent and -2.4 percent, respectively (Treasury 2019). The economic horror show continued into 2019; the country's economic growth contracted in the first, third and fourth quarters. Significantly, the province of KwaZulu-Natal fared worse due to its exposure to troubling sectors also contracting in the first, third and fourth quarters (Treasury 2019). Resultantly, KwaZulu-Natal's 2018 GDP growth stood at 0.8 percent, far below what is required to create jobs and tackle the high level of youth unemployment and poverty. The following year, the KwaZulu-Natal economy entered into another technical recession in the last half of 2019, following a 1.4 percent contraction of the economy in the fourth quarter, after the economy shrank by 0.8 percent in the third quarter. Notably, before the devastating COVID-19 pandemic, this was the country's and province's third recession since 1994, with the worst economic recession occurring during 2009–2010.

As has been noted in the above sections, KwaZulu-Natal is the second-largest contributor (approximately 16 percent) to the South African GDP after Gauteng, mainly owing to its high level of industrialization, diversified economic activities and superior export propensity, given its highly competitive advantage in capital-intensive manufacturing (Treasury 2019). KwaZulu-Natal further boasts a strong finance, agriculture, forestry and fishing sector (3.4%) that is the leading contributor to the national output in this sector (27%). However, even with all these achievements combined, KwaZulu-Natal has not been able to remove the fact that the province has been performing undesirably since the 2009 financial crisis that also impacted South Africa (Treasury 2019). Over the last few years, the province has seen a drastic decline in economic output in some of its major sectors, such as manufacturing and mining, which has resulted in the gradual de-industrialization of many towns such as Newcastle, Ladysmith, Pinetown, Durban and Mandeni (Treasury 2019). The economic structure in KwaZulu-Natal is based on a large manufacturing sector contributing 20 percent to the country's manufacturing gross value added, which is the second largest in the country after Gauteng and contributes a further 16 percent to the provincial GDP, which is a substantial 20percent of the provincial employment (Zhou and Gumbo 2021). However, it is generally agreed that South Africa's manufacturing sector has experienced limited development over the last two decades, with several indicators showing worrying signs of premature deindustrialization. Expectedly, KwaZulu-Natal, the country's second-largest employer in this sector, has suffered greatly from this trend. Resultantly, the shredding of jobs within the manufacturing sector has been seen across most industries. For example, in the oil and gas industry, it was recently announced that the major oil refineries in the province were set to suspend operations. Notably, this comes after South African Petroleum Refineries (SAPREF), and Engen announced they would suspend their Durban operations before the end of 2022 as they looked for a new buyer (*Engineering News* 2022). SAPREF, situated in Durban, is southern Africa's largest crude oil refinery. Despite employing eight hundred permanent staff, it is believed that more than two thousand workers are employed by its fifteen contractors.

For a while now, as has been argued extensively by researchers, KwaZulu-Natal has generally seen deteriorating levels of manufacturing contribution to GDP; gross fixed capital formation; foreign direct investment; manufacturing goods contribution to balance of payments; and employment in manufacturing (Zhou and Gumbo 2021). To be fair, it is important to note that manufacturing misfortunes in KwaZulu-Natal and the broader South Africa are in part historically an outcome of the country's overall industrial direction. South Africa's industrial policy has been criticized for being narrowly designed and entrenched in minerals extraction activities associated with the minerals energy complex

(Mdlalose and Taylor 2019). Although there were some achievements on the economic front, the biased approach to industrialization has entrenched a growth path characterized by capital-intensive production processes, a paucity of skilled labour and exceptionally high unemployment. Consequently, in 2007, the Industrial Development Zone programme, one of the industrial Policy Action Plan's (IPAP) key initiatives, was reviewed. It was agreed that the policy had to be revamped after its dismal performance (Mdlalose and Taylor 2019). By 2014, the ANC government had introduced the SEZ policy and the SEZ programme as a response to the challenges of the current IDZ programme (Mdlalose and Taylor 2019). According to the DTI, the SEZ policy provides a clear framework for the development, operations and management of SEZs, which is in turn meant to benefit sub-national economies through the provisioning of several incentives would be available to ensure SEZs growth, revenue generation, creation of jobs, the attraction of Foreign Direct Investment (FDI) and international competitiveness (DTI 2018). Unfortunately, the benefits of the upgraded SEZ programme remain to be seen in KwaZulu-Natal's Richards Bay IDZ and Dube Trade Port.

Importantly, we know now that South Africa's industrial policy has generally lacked coherence and alignment and that there has been "massive" fragmentation across government departments (Farole and Sharpe 2017; Mdlalose and Taylor 2019). Accordingly, the national government's Department of Trade, Industry and Competition has also summarized several factors that have led to the sector's relatively poor manufacturing performance in its various Industrial Policy Action Plans, namely: sub-optimal performance of state-owned companies; logistical bottlenecks; infrastructure constraints; volatility of South African exchange rate; monopoly pricing of key economic inputs, such as steel; skills deficiencies across the national economy; ageing capital equipment; and the rapid liberalization of the domestic economy to global trade in the late 1990s and early 2000s (Barnes 2019).

Tourism is a key driver of economic delivery and a priority sector for employment creation in the KwaZulu-Natal province. A recent report by the KwaZulu-Natal Tourism Department noted that KwaZulu-Natal remains one of the country's top three domestic tourism destinations, and statistics demonstrate that domestic and international leisure and business tourists continue to holiday, attend conferences and events and conduct business in this region (KwaZulu-Natal Department of Tourism 2020). This is mainly because KwaZulu-Natal receives domestic tourists from all provinces, with the primary sources of domestic tourists being Gauteng and KwaZulu-Natal, followed by Mpumalanga and Limpopo (KwaZulu-Natal Department of Tourism KwaZulu-Natal Department of Tourism 2020). However, while the sector has been immensely affected by the recent floods and global COVID-19 pandemic, which has wreaked havoc across the tourism sector worldwide, it is worth mentioning that the sector has been heavily embattled for a while, with trends reflecting a significant decline in productivity (KwaZulu-Natal Department of Tourism 2020). For example, overall domestic trips in the province have declined from the high of 5.2 million trips in 2014, although there has been a year-on-year increase since 2017 (KwaZulu-Natal Department of Tourism 2020). This is despite having experienced a 112 percent increase in 2019 in domestic tourist trips, which saw 6.2 million trips undertaken into and within the province. This is the most significant growth that the province has seen on the domestic front in the past seven years (KwaZulu-Natal Department of Tourism 2020). The tourist stats for KwaZulu-Natal as a whole give credence to the theory: In 2010, there were 956,550 tourists to KwaZulu-Natal, which decreased to 908,277 in 2011, and further reduced to 891,822 tourists in 2012, 847,146 in 2013, 768,228 in 2014 and 743,615 in 2015 (SAT). At the same time, the number of foreign tourists from Africa has decreased only slightly, from 393,017 in 2010 to 371,218 in 2015. The blame for declining tourist numbers in KwaZulu-Natal can be attributed directly to the decrease in road trips South Africans make to KZN. From a cruise perspective, Durban faced serious headwinds at the end of 2014–2015 when MSC Cruises decided to send only one ship (The MSC *Sinfonia*) to South Africa compared to the two during the previous season (The MSC *Sinfonia* & MSC *Opera*). This resulted in a fall of some fifty thousand cruise passengers (Although some of the drops were for Cape Town cruises). The Hospitality industry in KwaZulu-Natal was severely knocked during COVID-19, with a number of establishments closing due to the lockdowns. Notably, Durban's Hilton Hotel—an award-winning five-star establishment next to the International Convention Centre (ICC)—was forced to close indefinitely due to lockdown losses. The ICC has also suffered significant losses due to the cancellation of international conferences and other events (*Daily Maverick* 2021).

Although KwaZulu-Natal's agriculture, forestry and fishing sector is the leading contributor to the national output in this sector (27%), trailed only by the Western Cape, it is the smallest contributor to the provincial economy (3.4%) (KZN Treasury, 2019). The sector further plays a critical role in agricultural production and food processing capacity and connects South Africa's food system with the international community through the Port of Durban. Agriculture in KwaZulu-Natal is extremely diverse and is reflected in the patterns of its topography. Given the region's excellent and reliable rainfall and fertile soils, KwaZulu-Natal's agricultural sector has become highly productive and is known for its specialist capabilities. Across several types of farming, KwaZulu-Natal has a total of 6.5 million hectares of land for farming purposes, of which 82 percent is suitable for extensive livestock production, while 18 percent comprises arable land (KZN Treasury 2019). Meat and poultry are the highest contributors at 31 percent of the provincial GVA, followed by bakery and tortilla products at 16 percent and fruits and vegetables at 11 percent (KZN Treasury 2019). Estimates from the Bureau for Food and Agricultural Policy (BFAP) show that about 30 percent of South Africa's dairy herd is in KwaZulu-Natal, and significant volumes of chicken eggs and pigs are produced with a 12 percent share each (BFAP 2021). Moreover, almost 81 percent of the country's sugar is produced in the province, which, if not produced or transported, will have economic repercussions for the entire industry (*Mail and Guardian* 2022). However, in recent years, this sector has been tested by a multitude of issues ranging from droughts, intense rainfalls and government policy impacts to internal governance issues that have affected productivity.

For instance, Rainbow Chicken, the poultry farming giant, recently downsized their operations, selling its farms on the Durban-to-Pietermaritzburg N3 route due to the increased volumes of dumped chicken flooding the market, primarily from the European Union (*Daily News* 2017). The sale of fifteen broiler farms started in February 2017. The properties on which fifteen of the twenty-two broiler farms were located were sold to buyers who intended to develop them for commercial purposes other than farming (*Farmers Weekly* 2018). The farms have already been taken out of production, costing 1,350 people their jobs (*Daily News* 2017).

In the sugar industry, two of South Africa's biggest sugar producers, Illovo Sugar and Tongaat, have also been scaling down their operations, albeit for different reasons. In 2015, the former closed its uMzimkhulu mill for the year-long milling season. Illovo blamed significantly below-average rainfall in KwaZulu-Natal during the 2014 milling season and frost during the past winter, severely affecting cane supplies for the forthcoming season (*IOL* 2015). The other giant, Tongaat Hulett, has been through the wringer over the past few years following the discovery of accounting irregularities in 2019, which resulted in the company having to restate its results and being fined by the Johannesburg Stock Exchange (Business Insider 2019). The share price implosion has had the effect of rendering the company's balance sheet on the verge of being unsustainable. Its huge debt load of roughly R6.6 billion is now at risk, causing a minor panic among its bankers (Business Insider 2019). Tongaat produces about 43 percent of South Africa's sugar and is one of SA's biggest landowners. The sugar company recently closed Darnall Mill, leaving hundreds jobless (*The North Coast Courier* 2020). Established in 1846, the Darnall sugar mill has provided work and operated as a staple in the small sugar farming community for over a hundred years (*Farmers Weekly* 2020). Small-scale farmers, who are already struggling to stay afloat, face an even bleaker future as challenges in the industry deepen. According to The SA Farmers Development Association (SAFDA), there has been a significant decline in small-scale sugarcane farmers—from around fifty thousand in the early 2000s to below twenty thousand today (SAFDA 2019). The closure was expected to affect an estimated two hundred small-scale sugarcane growers who rely on the milling firm for their livelihoods (*Farmers Weekly* 2020). The "closures" of the Darnall and uMzimkhulu sugar mills pose serious negative consequences for affected sugar cane farmers, especially for the young, Black, small-scale and land reform growers who did not have ready access to finance and were often highly indebted (*Farmers Weekly* 2020). Given the foregoing factors, one can postulate using the deprivation principle found in the frustration-aggression theory that, aside from some criminal elements, KwaZulu-Natal citizens responded to the sharp economic decline in their daily lives with a strong opposition to their local and provincial leadership through violent protests.

SERVICE DELIVERY

The present South African government inherited service delivery backlogs from the apartheid era that serviced a white minority population and disenfranchised millions of citizens (Breakfast, Bradshaw and Nomarwayi 2019). Thus, the new democratic government was tasked with the monumental task of providing basic services for all citizens through the formation of a democratic and developmental local government (Breakfast et al. 2019). Basic services are the fundamental building blocks of improved quality of life, and adequate supplies of electricity, safe water and adequate sanitation are necessary for life, well-being and human dignity (Statistics South Africa 2016). As such, local government in South Africa is largely understood in terms of service delivery and the South African Constitution (Act No. 108 of 1996), which assigns municipalities the role of mobilizing economic resources toward improving the lives of all citizens. Municipalities are the country's most basic units of government and are tasked with providing basic services whilst fostering development in the regions they control (Republic of South Africa 1996). Since the inception of democratic local government, violent protests have been at a surge. Evidence confirms that most post-1994 regime protests in South Africa are closely related to the lack of service delivery or no delivery of services at all (Alexander 2010). Some of the causes of the protests include lack of service delivery, a lack of accountability by local councillors and municipal officials, lack of leadership, poor financial controls, corruption in the allocation of houses, lack of proper water and sanitation and lack of electricity (Shaidi 2013; Twala 2014).

From a political science view, it has generally been argued that more concrete transition benefits took place between capital and the new ANC elite, largely side-lining the poor, invoking the resurgence of resistance from the poor manifest through service delivery protests (Bond 2006; Madlingozi 2007). In predominantly poor areas, recipients of services generally perceive service delivery as being at a snail's pace and not visible enough to the majority of the people who still live in abject poverty (Statistics South Africa 2016). The provinces identified as grossly lagging in services were Limpopo, KwaZulu-Natal, Mpumalanga and the Eastern Cape (Statistics South Africa 2016). As such, leading up to the civil unrest in July 2022, it is vital to highlight the situational analysis of KZN below using the Statistics South Africa 2016 service delivery report to better understand the postulated correlation. Nationally, the total number of households increased from 14.5 million in 2011 to an estimated 16.9 million in 2016. Gauteng (29.3%) and KwaZulu-Natal (17.0%) contained the highest number of households in 2016.

Firstly, with respect to water, in 2016, 1.7 million households (8.8% of all households) in the country were without access to piped water. The lowest backlog was noted in Western Cape (1%), while KwaZulu-Natal (14.6%) was observed to have the third-highest backlog (Statistics South Africa 2016). The report further found that while a large percentage of households in Western Cape (99%), Gauteng (97.4%), and Free State (96.2%) had access to piped water as their source of income, in KwaZulu-Natal (7.6%) relied on unsafe sources of water (Statistics South Africa 2016). Furthermore, at least 40% of municipalities in which households had the lowest access to improved water sources were located in KwaZulu-Natal. While at least one-fifth of households mainly accessed drinking water from streams, rivers and rainwater, thirty-five municipalities were found in either Eastern Cape or KwaZulu-Natal (Statistics South Africa 2016). While KwaZulu-Natal's sanitation index was relatively good compared to some provinces, in numbers, it is crucial to note that161,535 households lacked any type of sanitation (Statistics South Africa 2016).

Moreover, while households in larger municipalities, particularly in the Western Cape, Gauteng and parts of Northern Cape, enjoyed near-universal access to improved sanitation, access in poor, predominantly rural municipalities in Eastern Cape, KwaZulu-Natal and Limpopo were much more basic (Statistics South Africa 2016). Concerning refuse, refuse removal services were most common in the metropolitan areas and some urban municipalities. Data suggests that virtually no refuse removal services exist across most of the rural municipalities in KwaZulu-Natal. Findings further revealed that households in Western Cape municipalities were generally most satisfied. In contrast, those in Eastern Cape, KwaZulu-Natal and a few Northwest municipalities were most dissatisfied with refuse removals (Statistics South Africa 2016). While electricity has become almost ubiquitous in South Africa, with 87.6% of households reportedly having access to electricity by 2016, access varied across municipalities, with Western Cape (92.7%), Free State (91.9%) and Limpopo (91.4%) having the highest, Eastern Cape (84.3%), Gauteng (85.6%) and KwaZulu-Natal (85.6%) lagged (Statistics South Africa 2016). For the household perception of electricity distribution, the lowest positive ratings were given in 60 percent of the twenty municipalities in which less than one-half of households rated the electricity services as 'good', and nine were in KwaZulu-Natal (Statistics South Africa 2016). Data show that approximately two-thirds (64.8%) of South African households were satisfied with the electricity they received. Households in Western Cape (72.7%) and Northern Cape (72.6%) were generally most satisfied with the electricity, while those in the more rural provinces of the Eastern Cape (56.5%) and KwaZulu-Natal (60.4%) were least satisfied. Finally, the data show that municipalities with the best service delivery scores were highly concentrated in the Western Cape province, Gauteng and Northern Cape and Free State (Statistics South Africa 2016). KwaZulu-Natal made the list of provinces that received the lowest service delivery scores, alongside the Eastern Cape and Limpopo (Statistics South Africa 2016).

EROSION OF UBUNTU FABRIC

KwaZulu-Natal is the second-most-populace province in South Africa after Gauteng province. While the province of KwaZulu-Natal has a diverse social culture, *the province of the Zulus*, as it is widely known, is also the home of the Zulu tribe. The Zulu tribe is the largest ethnic tribe in South Africa, and out of the eleven official languages, Isizulu (25.1%) is the most widely spoken language in South Africa, followed by English (16.6%) and IsiXhosa (12.8) (Statistics South Africa 2018). in KwaZulu Natal, approximately 78 percent of the population speak isiZulu as their home language. The Zulu tribe has a strong belief in cultural spirituality and customary traditions through the relations that exist between the community and traditional leadership. Mamdani (1996) argues that traditional leadership is an integral part of African society and is the oldest institution of governance on the continent. Traditional leadership in KwaZulu-Natal is highly respected as it is considered the custodian of such cultures, traditions, norms and values. The social structure of the Zulu tribe, predominantly rural parts of the province, is still premised on the concept of Ubuntu, which promotes the role of the community over individuality. Ubuntu, which is part of the Zulu phrase "umuntu umuntu ngabantu", which means that a person is a person through other people, is a Nguni concept rooted in African philosophy and generally advocates the idea of community as one of the building blocks of society. Ubuntu is a well-recognized African concept of humanness (Nyaumwe and Mkabela 2007). It gives expression to deeply held African ideals of one's personhood being rooted in one's interconnectedness with others. Gade (2012) found two distinct clusters of meaning. First, Ubuntu refers to the moral qualities of a person, notably features like generosity, empathy, forgiveness and considerateness. Second, Ubuntu refers to a pattern of interconnectedness between people in the form of a worldview or philosophy. Contemporary research shows that Ubuntu continues to play an essential role in African society. It is regarded as a critical cultural strength of families (Nkosi and Daniels 2007). Significantly, it can be argued that the ushering in of democracy without the important foundations of African customs such as Ubuntu in South Africa has in part contributed to the gradual demise of the social fabric in poor and working-class communities, which is and has been the breeding ground for the kind of social unrest witnessed after the incarceration of former President Jacob Zuma in July as well as extreme forms of violence and brutality against women and children, rising crime, gangsterism and substance abuse, xenophobic violence and pogroms.

Today, KwaZulu-Natal is arguably the most dangerous province in the country. The KwaZulu-Natal (KZN) crime statistics for the third quarter of 2021—October to December last year—reported that KwaZulu-Natal remains the murder capital of the country with a 17 percent increase from the same period during 2020. This while the Inanda and Umlazi SAPS stations are ranked first and third, respectively, in crimes of this nature countrywide. Attempted murder increased by 15.1 percent from the same period in 2020, while robbery with aggravating circumstances rose 5.2 percent from the third quarter of 2020 to reach 6,188 cases (South African Police Service 2021). Notably, as can be seen, the statistics above correspond with the growing recognition that the social fabric of KwaZulu-Natal has deteriorated. Notably, the central proposition made in this paper regarding the rapid decline of the social fibre in KwaZulu-Natal is that two of KwaZulu-Natal's most critical social institutions are collapsing. The death of the AmaZulu monarch, King Zwelithini ka Bhekuzulu, the longest-serving Zulu monarch, has left a gaping hole in the Zulu nation's social structure. According to KwaZulu-Natal Premier, Sihle Zikalala, AmaZulu King Goodwill Zwelithini was the Zulu nation's moral compass, pointing the way forward as a custodian of the Zulu culture and tradition (Eyewitness News 2021). Moreover, it has been argued that the previous Zulu monarch was a man who knew how to use his influence, especially for the preservation of his people, by presiding with peace and stability over the nation during some of the most tumultuous and challenging periods in history (City Press 2021). Following the monarch's death, there has been visible anxiety, social instability and uncertainty throughout the province caused by tensions in the royal house over the rightful successor of the Zulu throne.

Interestingly, the never-ending tussle for power that has fashioned social instability and uncertainty has not only been seen in the Zulu royal house but other groups of society as well. The Shembe Church, formally known as iBandla lamaNazaretha is one of the largest African religious movements in South Africa. Isiah Shembe founded this movement in 1910 to unite Africans and celebrate African ideas (Hausse 1996). He did this during a time when he felt orthodox Christianity had failed Africans. According to Hausse (1996), Shembe aimed to return to religious forms consistent with the cultural traditions of Africans. Isaiah Shembe, in his formation of the Shembe religion, sought to reconstitute a sense of community and collective identity among the African people in the province of Natal, neighbouring Zululand and Africa as a whole (Muller 1994). Shembe believed that Christianity should be taught to indigenous people in order to better their lives; however, he believed this should be done without breaking down "tribalism" and tradition. After his death, Johannes Galilee Shembe, one of his sons, took over the church. After Johannes's death in 1976, the church split into two factions; one led by Amos Shembe, one of Isaiah Shembe's younger sons, and the other was headed by Johannes Shembe's son Londa Shembe (Hausse 1996; Vilakazi, Mthethwa and Mpanza 1986). Every time a leader dies, the church is even more uncertain about who the next leader should be. As a result, this creates more tensions and conflict. Today there are more than four divisions within the church and an ongoing battle for leadership.

CONCLUSION

The riots, which were the worst since the end of apartheid and claimed 354 lives, led to heavy criticism of the ANC government and its ability to respond to political and socioeconomic issues. One of the key concerns raised by this chapter is the possibility of social unrest. The July 2021 riots in KwaZulu-Natal and parts of Gauteng not only caused billions of Rands in damage and significant damage to future investment in the country but it has also put to light the perils of a fragmented political sphere and socioeconomic inefficiencies of government. At the same time, the alleged orchestrators of the unrest have been named by the police ministry and are attending court. It remains to be seen if the state can prove that twelve individuals can take full responsibility for the unrest that took place across two of the largest provinces in the country. Thus, this chapter maintains that the protests were primarily driven and sustained by grievances over the government's perceived inability to address a variety of socioeconomic issues. In fact, for years, many have predicted that South Africa, the most unequal country on the planet, would be hit by mass unrest. The majority of people live in poverty; more than 30 percent of the labour force is unemployed, while basic services have collapsed in much of the country, and the government is inefficient and corrupt. In KwaZulu-Natal, the specific problems, including the state of the economy and poor services, have led to a general loss in optimism and a rise in the philosophy of individuality. In a province that is mainly rural and rooted in cultural principles of Ubuntu, the rise of individualism and deterioration of the social fabric has also been exacerbated not only by a weak political government but also by a frail traditional leadership institution that is meant to be the moral compass of most of the Zulu subjects. The July unrest and everything else combined have exposed the vulnerability of South Africa's resilience. Neither KwaZulu-Natal nor South Africa needs more resilience tests. While protests are common in South Africa and are not isolated to urban or rural areas, a growing pattern of frustration-led aggression has been observed, given the frequency and intensity of protests in recent events. Thus, if this is not addressed comprehensively, this chapter warns, an entire uprising triggered by even the slightest of events could be in the cards in the near future. Importantly, in light of the above, this chapter recommends the following economic and administrative considerations for KwaZulu-Natal. Firstly, better-quality industrial development and service delivery policy measures to prevent conflict from escalating or degenerating into avoidable crises. Secondly, and most important to note as the chapter concludes, is that rebuilding KwaZulu-Natal post-unrest and COVID-19 will, in addition, require a collaborative effort from all stakeholders to reconstruct KwaZulu-Natal's social fabric; this can be achieved precisely by forming solid and improved provincial leadership dynamics, ensuring that the issues confronting the embattled Zulu royal house and the Shembe church are resolved, and there is an active drive to produce enriched community-building mechanisms at the societal level through Ubuntu.

REFERENCES

ACCORD. 2007. Political leaders in Africa: Presidents, patrons or profiteers? Occasional Paper Series: 2(1).

———. 2021. *Conflict trends*. Issue 3.

Accornero, Guya and Pedro Ramos Pinto. 2015. "'Mild Mannered'? Protest and Mobilization in Portugal under Austerity, 2010–2013." *West European Politics* 38 (3): 491–515

Alexander, Peter. 2010. Rebellion of the poor: South Africa's service delivery protests-a preliminary analysis. *Review of African Political Economy* 37(123): 25–40.

Amsel, Abram. 1962. Frustrative nonreward in partial reinforcement and discrimination learning: Some recent history and a theoretical extension. *Psychological Review,* 69(4), 306–28. doi:10.1037/ h0046200.

Barnes, Justin. 2019. *Developing manufacturing leadership in South Africa (and regionally): The role of Monozukuri*. Paper presented at the South Africa-Japan University Forum Conference, Pretoria.

Beavers, Larissa. 2019. Boko Haram and frustration-aggression theory: A potential explanation. *Modern Diplomacy*, 2 July. https://moderndiplomacy.eu/2019/07/02/boko-haram-and- frustration-aggression-theory-a-potential-explanation/.

Berkowitz, Leonard. 1989. Frustration-aggression hypothesis: Examination and reformulation. *Psychological Bulletin*, 106(1), 59–73. doi:10.1037/0033-2909.106.1.59.

Bond, Patrick. 2006. *Elite transition: From apartheid to neo-liberalism in South Africa*. Pietermaritzburg: University of Natal Press.

Booysen, Susan. 2018. Hegemonic struggles of the African National Congress: From cacophony of morbid symptoms to strained renewal. *Africa Spectrum* 53(2): 5–35.

Breakfast, Ntsikelelo, Bradshaw, Gavin, and Nomarwayi, Thandolwethu. 2019. Violent Service Delivery Protests In The Nelson Mandela Bay Municipality (Nmbm): A Case Study Of Walmer Township (2012–2019). *African Journal of Public Affairs.* 11 (1).

Breuer, Johannes, and Elson, Malte. 2017. Frustration-aggression theory. In *The Wiley handbook of violence and aggression*, edited by P. Sturmey, 1–12. Chichester: Wiley Blackwell.

Breuer, Johannes., Vogelgesang, Jens., Quandt, Thorsten., and Festl, Ruth. 2015. Violent video games and physical aggression: Evidence for a selection effect among adolescents. *Psychology of Popular Media Culture*, 4(4), 305–28. https://doi.org/10.1037/ppm0000035.

The Bureau for Food and Agricultural Policy (BFAP). 2021. *BFAP baseline agricultural outlook 2021–2030.*

Business Insider. 2019. Tongaat Hulett's listing has been suspended—here's what we know about the crisis at the sugar giant. https://www.businessinsider.co.za/tongaat-hulett-jse-2019-6.

Calvo, Kerman. 2013. "Fighting for a Voice: The Spanish 15-M/Indignados Movement". 236–53 in *Understanding European Movements: New Social Movements, Global Justice struggles, Anti-Austerity Protest*, edited by Cristina Flesher Fominaya and Laurence Cox. London: Routledge.

Cedras, Jody Paul. 2021. The ANC-led alliance in government: A question of legitimacy and trust. *African Journal of Public Affairs* 12(1).

City Press. 2021. Zwelithini played a critical role for peace and stability in KwaZulu-Natal—Ramaphosa. News24. https://www.news24.com/citypress/news/zwelithini-played-a-critical-role-for-peace-and-stability-in-kwazulu-natal-ramaphosa-20210318.

Constitutional Court of South Africa. 2021. Secretary of the Judicial Commission of inquiry into allegation of state capture, corruption and fraud in the public sector including Organ of State v. Jacob Gedleyihlekisa Zuma: CCT52/21 [2021] ZACC 18. 21 [Accessed 31 March 2022].

Daily Maverick. 2021. KwaZulu-Natal's battered and bruised tourism sector prays for a bumper festive season. https://www.dailymaverick.co.za/article/2021-12-15-kwazulu-natals-battered-and-bruised-tourism-sector-prays-for-a-bumper-festive-season/.

Daily News. 2017. End of the rainbow? Poultry giant selling off farms in KZN. https://www.pressreader.com/south-africa/daily-news-south-africa/20170324/281479276242386.

De Gaay Fortman, Bas. 2005. Violence among peoples in the light of human frustration and aggression. *European Journal of Pharmacology* 526(1–3), 2–8. doi:10.1016/j.ejphar.2005.09.035.

Department of Trade and Industry (DTI) 2018. *Industrial policy action plan, 2018/19–2020/21*. https://www.gov.za/sites/default/files/gcis_document/201805/industrial-policy-action-plan.pdf.

Dollard, John., Doob, Leonard. W., Miller, Neal. E., Mowrer, Hobart, O., and Sears, Robert. R. 1939. *Frustration and aggression*. New Haven, CT: Yale University Press. http://dx.doi.org/10.1037/10022-000.

Engineering News. 2022. Sapref to halt operations by end-March. https://www.engineeringnews.co.za/article/sapref-to-halt-operations-by-end-march-2022-02-10.

Evans, Olaniyi, and Ikechukwu. Kelikume. 2019. The Impact of Poverty, Unemployment, Inequality, Corruption and Poor Governance on Niger Delta Militancy, Boko Haram Terrorism and Fulani Herdsmen Attacks in Nigeria. *International Journal of Management, Economics and Social Sciences*, Vol. 8(2), pp. 58–80.

Eyewitness News. 2021. Zikalala: King Goodwill Zwelithini was a shining symbol of hope and unity. https://ewn.co.za/2021/03/12/zikalala-king-goodwill-zwelithini-was-a-shining-symbol-of-hope-and-unity.

Farmers Weekly. 2020. Another sugar mill shuts operations for the 2020/2021 season. https://www.farmersweekly.co.za/agri-news/south-africa/another-sugar-mill-shuts-operations-for-the-2020-2021-season/.

Farole, Thomas, and Sharpe, Mathew. 2017. Spatial industrial policy, Special economic zones, and cities. Paper presented for the Urbanization Review of South Africa.

Fox, Suzy., and Spector, Paul. E. 1999. A model of work frustration–aggression. *Journal of Organizational Behavior*, 20(6), 915–31. doi:10.1002/(SICI)1099-1379(199911)20:6 < 915::AID-JOB918>3.3.CO;2-Y.

Gade, Christian B. N. 2012. What is Ubuntu? Different interpretations among South Africans of African descent. *South African Journal of Philosophy* 31: 484–503. doi: 10.1080/02580136.2012.10751789.

Gurr, Ted, R. 1970. *Why men rebel*. Princeton, NJ: Princeton University Press.

Hanratty, Margaret. A., O'Neal, Edgar., and Sulzer, Jefferson. L. 1972. Effect of frustration upon imitation of aggression. *Journal of Personality and Social Psychology*, 21(1), 30–34. doi:10.1037/h0031903.

Höglund, Kristine, and Jarstad, Anna, K. 2011. Toward electoral security: Experiences from KwaZulu-Natal. *Africa Spectrum* 46(1): 33–59.

Institute for Economics and Peace. 2020. *Global peace index 2020: Measuring peace in a complex world*, Sydney, June 2020.

International Monetary Fund (IMF). 2020. *Measuring social unrest using media reports*. IMF Working paper. Research and Middle East and Central Asia Departments.

IOL. 2015. Drought closes KZN sugar mill. https://www.iol.co.za/business-report/companies/drought-closes-kzn-sugar-mill-1806304.

———. 2021. Voters punish the ANC in KZN: ANC's poor handling of Zulu king's succession issue and arrest of Zuma cost it support, say political analysts. https://www.iol.co.za/dailynews/news/kwazulu-natal/voters-punish-the-anc-in-kzn-ancs-poor-handling-of-zulu-kings-succession-issue-and-arrest-of-zuma-cost-it-support-say-political-analysts-057d6f5c-9724-4978-a1b5-507ae7240241

———. 2022. Radical Economic Transformation group rejects Raymond Zondo's state capture commission report as a 'gimmick'. https://www.iol.co.za/dailynews/news/kwazulu-natal/radical-economic-transformation-group-rejects-raymond-zondos-state-capture-commission-report-as-a-gimmick-1df604e9-a842-44d1-a56b-ec4fcb87a9ac.

Johnston, Alexander. 1996 Politics and violence in KwaZulu□Natal. *Terrorism and Political Violence*8(4): 78–107, DOI: 10.1080/09546559608427373.

Kanyane, Modimowabarwa. 2021. Factions and factionalism in South African party politics: Appraising (de)merits. *Politikon* 48(4): 572–88, DOI: 10.1080/02589346.2021.1913553.

Kern, Anna, Sofie Marien, and Marc Hooghe. 2015. "Economic Crisis and Levels of Political Participation in Europe (2002–2010): The Role of Resources and Grievances." *West European Politics* 38(3): 465–90.

Koontz, Harold, and O'Donnell, Cyril 1955. *Principles of management: An analysis of managerial functions.* New York: McGraw-Hill

Kosmidis, S. 2014. Government Constraints and Accountability: Economic Voting in Greece Before and During the IMF Intervention. *West European Politics* 37(5): 1136–55.

Krämer, Mario. 2019. Violence, autochthony, and identity politics in KwaZulu-Natal (South Africa): A processual perspective on local political dynamics. *African Studies Review* 63(3): 540–59.

Kumar, Ramesh. 2022. Cost of poor leadership. *Global Journal of Business and Integral Security*. Retrieved from https://www.gbis.ch/index.php/gbis/article/view/71.

KwaZulu-Natal Department of Tourism. 2020. *Tourism KwaZulu-Natal annual report 2019/20.*

La Hausse, Paul. 1996. "Isaiah Shembe's Church." *Journal of African History.* 37(2), 332–34.

Madlingozi, Tshepo. 2007. Post-apartheid social movements and the quest for the elusive 'new' South Africa. *Journal of Law and Society* 34: 77–98. https://doi.org/10.1111/jols.2007.34.issue-1.

Mail and Guardian, 2021. KZN's ANC premier calls for peaceful post-election transition. https://mg.co.za/politics/2021-11-08-kzns-anc-premier-calls-for-peaceful-post-election-transition/.

———. 2022. KwaZulu-Natal's agriculture and food production in this time of floods. https://mg.co.za/opinion/2022-04-19-kwazulu-natals-agriculture-and-food-production-in-this-time-of-floods.

Mamdani, Mahmood. 1996. *Citizens and subjects: Contemporary Africa and the legacy of late colonialism.* Princeton, NJ: Princeton University Press.

Mdlalose, Methembe, and Taylor, Simon 2019. *Concept for coastal regional development in South Africa, with refence to special economic zones.* WIT-Transactions on the Built Environment.

Metalbulletin. 2021. Riots, looting trigger force majeure at South African ports. https://www.metalbulletin.com/Article/3998453/Riots-looting-trigger-force-majeure-at-South-African-ports.html.

Miller, Neal. E. 1941. The frustration-aggression hypothesis. *Psychological Review*, 48(4), 337–42.

Moneyweb. 2021. Over 200 Shoprite group stores looted in last week's unrest. https://www.moneyweb.co.za/news/companies-and-deals/over-200-shoprite-group-stores-looted-in-last-weeks-unrest/

Muller, Carol. A. 1994. *Nazarites song, dance, and dreams: the sacralization of time, space and the female body in South Africa.* UMI Dissertation Services: A Bell and Howell Company.

News24. 2021. More than 30 trucks torched during protests across KZN. https://www.news24.com/witness/news/kzn/more-than-30-trucks-torched-during-protests-across-kzn-20210710.

Nkosi, Busisiwe. and Daniels, Priscilla. 2007. Family strengths: South Africa. *Marriage & Family Review*, 41:11–26.

The North Coast Courier. 2020. *Tongaat Hulett to close Darnall Mill leaving hundreds jobless.* https://northcoastcourier.co.za/148759/tongaat-hulett-close-darnall-mill-leaving-hundreds-jobless/.

Nyaumwe, Lovemore J., and Mkabela, Queeneth. 2007. Revisiting the traditional African cultural framework of Ubuntuism: A theoretical perspective. *Indilinga: African Journal of Indigenous Knowledge Systems* 6:152–63.

The Presidency. 2021. Update by President Cyril Ramaphosa on security situation in the country. 16 July. http://www.thepresidency.gov.za/speeches/update-president-cyril-ramaphosa-security-situation-country [Accessed 10 August 2021].

Quaranta, Mario. 2015. "Protesting in 'hard times': Evidence from a comparative analysis of Europe, 2000–2014." *Current Sociology*. DOI: 10.1177/0011392115602937.

Republic of South Africa (RSA). 1996. Constitution of the Republic of South Africa 1996. (Act 108 of 1996). Pretoria: Government Printers.

Rotberg, Robert. I. 2014. The need for strengthened political leadership. *The Annals of the American Academy of Political and Social Science*, 652: 238–56. http://www.jstor.org/stable/24541726.

SA Farmers Development Association (SAFDA). 2019. Transformation of the South African sugar industry. https://sa-fda.org.za/2019/01/22/transformation-in-the-south-african-sugar-industry/.

SA News. 2021. Thousands of jobs at risk as government consolidates relief proposals. https://www.sanews.gov.za/south-africa/thousands-jobs-risk-government-consolidates-relief-proposals.

Sändig, Jan. 2015. Framing protest and insurgency: Boko Haram and MASSOB in Nigeria. *Civil Wars*, 17(2): 141–60, DOI: 10.1080/13698249.2015.1070450.

Schoon, Eric W. 2016. Rethinking legitimacy and illegitimacy in violent political conflict. *Sociology Compass* 10(2): 143–52.

Schurink, Willem. J. 1990. *Victimization: Nature and trends*. Johannesburg: Human Sciences Research Council.

South African Police Service. 2021. *Police recorded crime statistics. Third quarter of 2021/2022 financial year (October to December 2021).* Republic of South Africa.

Statistics South Africa. 2016. *The state of basic service delivery in South Africa: In-depth analysis of the Community Survey 2016 data*. Pretoria: Statistics South Africa.

———. 2019: *General household survey 2018*. http://www.statssa.gov.za/publications/P0318/P03182018.pdf. [Accessed October 2019].

———. 2021. GDP rises in the first quarter of 2021. 8 June, http://www.statssa.gov.za/?p=14423 [Accessed 7 March 2022].

Times Live. 2021. They are brought in carrier bags to destabilize KZN—ANC's Mdumiseni Ntuli on being booed outside court. https://www.timeslive.co.za/politics/2021-05-17-listen-they-are-brought-in-carrier-bags-to-destabilise-kzn-ancs-mdumiseni-ntuli-on-being-booed-outside-court/.

Treasury. 2019. *Province of KwaZulu-Natal: Socio-Economic Review and Outlook 2019/2020*. KwaZulu-Natal Government.

Twala, Chitja. 2014. The Causes and Socio-political Impact of the Service Delivery Protests to the South African Citizenry: A Real Public Discourse. *Journal of Social Sciences,* 39:2, 159–67, DOI: 10.1080/09718923.2014.11893279.

Udogu, E. Ike. 2008. The issue of political leadership in the third world: What is to be done? *Journal of Third World Studies* 25(1): 13–23. http://www.jstor.org/stable/45194435.

Valgarðsson, Viktori. O., Clarke, Nick., Jennings, Will., and Stoker, Gerry. 2021). The Good Politician and Political Trust: An Authenticity Gap in British Politics? *Political Studies* 69(4): 858–80. https://doi.org/10.1177/0032321720928257.

Vassallo, Francesca and Ding, Pauline. 2016. "Explaining protest in the aftermath of the Great Recession in Europe. The relevance of different economic indicators." *Partecipazione e Conflitto* 9 (1): 101–26.

Verney, Susannah. and Bosco, Anna. 2013. Living Parallel Lives: Italy and Greece in an Age of Austerity. *South European Society and Politics* 18(4): 397–426.

Vhumbunu, Clayton. H. 2021. The July 2021 protests and socio-political unrest in South Africa: Reflecting on the causes, consequences and future lessons. ACCORD. https://www.accord.org.za/conflict-trends/the-july-2021-protests-and-socio-political-unrest-in-south-africa/.

Vilakazi, Absolom; Mthethwa, Bongani and Mpanza, Mthembeni. 1986. *Shembe.The Revitalization of African Society*. Skotaville: Johannesburg.

Zhou, Helper, and Gumbo, Victor. 2021. Rural-urban comparison of manufacturing SMMEs performance in KwaZulu Natal Province, South Africa. *African Journal of Development Studies* 11(1) published online.

Chapter Seven

Looting and Unrest after Former President Zuma's Incarceration

Politics of Belonging and Entitlement to Property Ownership in South Africa

Sifiso Ndlovu

INTRODUCTION

The chaos and unrest that South Africa plunged into following the incarceration of former president Jacob Zuma attracted global gaze and triggered reflections from the state, various sectors of the society and academic circles. These reflections revolved around naming what was happening. Some like President Cyril Ramaphosa used the 'ethnic mobilisation' narrative when he addressed the nation on Sunday, 11 July 2021, on the developments that were underway in different parts of the country. This narrative was however disputed by the facts on the ground because the unrest that engulfed the country transcended the Zulu identity and did not spare other parts of South Africa such as Gauteng, Mpumalanga and Northwest provinces for example. Despite the differences in magnitude of the looting and unrest in other provinces beyond KwaZulu Natal, the eruption of unrest in those other provinces pushed to visibility the weakness of the narrative of ethnic mobilisation as the cause of unrest. Some pointed to the insurgency thesis, wherein it was argued that the unrest was almost an expression of an attempt to stage a coup. Arguments on the insurgency thesis revolved around the weaknesses of the security sector. Some reflections and interpretations of the unrest highlighted that the outbreak of the COVID-19 pandemic, lockdowns and the concomitant loss of jobs exacerbated economic hardships, inequalities and poverty. Some saw the outbreak of unrest as a manifestation of internal factionalism within the ruling ANC party, which ended up affecting the South African state. All these are some of the interpretations of the unrest that engulfed KwaZulu-Natal province and beyond and these interpretations pushed to visibility the fragility of the idea of South Africa and rendered a big question mark. These various interpretations further clouded the visibility of a singular linear explanation of what exactly the crisis of the South African society is. This chapter takes this background as a point of departure to offer a long durée historical analysis that slices right through the imperial and colonial encounters to the present day politics of property ownership and entitlement in South Africa as one of the hotly contested arenas around which the social unrest that was expressed after Zuma's incarceration can be understood. The argument is that such an approach can offer a focused lens that unveils long-standing politics of belonging and how this ties in with the systemic socioeconomic and political challenges of property ownership and skewed access to economic benefits. Such an approach can enrich academic readings and interpretation of the unrest and looting in South Africa that have always been at the centre of the politics of belonging and contested and shifting meanings of the idea of South Africa.

The unrest and looting that was witnessed in South Africa can be traced to the advent and unfolding of a Eurocentric modern world system and the genealogy of South Africa as a geo-social construct. If the idea of South Africa is traced to the unfolding of the Eurocentric modern world system that came into being after the 'voyages of discovery', it can be traced back to 1488 when Bartholomew Diaz travelled to the Cape. Seen in this way, the idea of South Africa emerges concurrently with the idea of the Americas, which is traceable to the arrival of Christopher Columbus as one of the key figures in the 'voyages of discovery' and so called 'New World' in 1492. So, 1492 is important insofar as it enables us to understand when Euro–North American modernity began. This background is a vantage point that enables one to place the idea of South Africa as a question of the genealogy of South African modernity and the contested question of who is the 'authentic' South African and who is entitled to resources and property ownership as key in understanding the unrest and looting that happened in July 2021. In other words, this becomes a tale of South Africa's insertion into the modern capitalist system and what we learn from Keegan's (1996) works about the 'origins of the racial order' and the entanglement of South Africa in what Grosfoguel (2013, 85) describes as a 'modern/colonial, capitalist/patriarchal' power structure.

But more than a mere question of South African modernity, the long durée historical analysis of the idea of South Africa and property ownership requires us to unpack it as a multifaceted phenomenon and how it was translated from a mere figurative expression describing the southern tip of Africa to an identity of the people. Tied to the identity of the people is the contested idea of property ownership and skewed economic policies that have benefited some segments of the South African population at the expense of other segments. This has led to various forms of looting of resources across time and space such that even after the incarceration of the former president of South Africa, the previously marginalised Black population engaged in looting activities which can be articulated as a predication of the South African socioeconomic system on the politics of the contested 'authentic' subject of South Africa who is entitled to resources. As will be shown in this chapter, the contested, complex and shifting meanings of being South African across time and space has always been tied to the ownership of property in ways that are richly telling of power struggles and racial antagonisms that have occasionally invoked protests and looting of resources like the one that were seen in July 2021.

COLONIAL ENCOUNTERS AND THE 'EMPTY LAND' THESIS

Drilling deeper into the specificity of how the translation of a mere figurative expression into an identity of a people is useful insofar as it sheds light on how the politics of belonging and debates about ownership of resources was shaped. We learn from Marks and Trapido's (1987, 3) work that:

> In the 1870s at the beginning of the mineral revolution, South Africa was a geographical expression. Precapitalist and capitalist modes of production existed side by side, as did state forms of varying size with their own ruling groups and systems of exploitation. There were two British colonies, two ostensibly politically independent republics and numerous still autonomous African polities. All these were multi-ethnic and multilingual, although not all languages and ethnicities were equal. Colonists of British and European descent lived side by side in the colonies with large numbers of indigenous peoples, and in Natal with indentured labourers from the Indian subcontinent, African kingdoms were equally heterogenous entities, composed of peoples of different origins.. . .

What we learn from Marks and Trapido is that is that even as late as the 1870s, South Africa was still a mere geographical expression. The translation of a mere figurative expression that described the Southern tip of Africa to an identity of a people coalesced various configurations of power and initiatives to inscribe and naturalise particular forms of domination that shaped entitlement to resources.

To the imperialists and colonialists, the idea was about the subjugation, occupation, annexation, dispossession and subordination of weaker groups to the will of the powerful. From Ndlovu-Gatsheni's (2012) work we learn that race was used as the organizing principle that not only shaped the contested and shifting meanings of South Africa but also shaped the politics of entitlement to resources such as land within the imperial discourses of domination and exploitation. Neatly feeding into the colonial discourse of domination was also the idea of South Africa as an empty land, which is explained by Blaut (1993, 15). He had this to say:

> This proposition makes a series of claims, each layered upon the others: (i) a non-European region is empty or nearly empty of people (hence settlement by Europeans does not displace any native peoples). (ii) The region is empty of settled population: the inhabitants are mobile, nomadic, wanderers (hence European settlement violates no political sovereignty, since wanderers make no claim to territory). (iii) The cultures of this region do not possess an understanding of private property—that is, the region is empty of property rights and claims (hence colonial occupiers can freely give land to settlers since no one owns it). The final layer, applied to all of the Outside sector, is an emptiness of intellectual creativity and spiritual values, sometimes described by Europeans . . . as an absence of 'rationality.'

Historians like Shula Marks (1980) and Etherington (2004) have however argued against and falsified the 'empty land' discourse. It is a discourse that has continued to shape the competition of ownership of resources even in post-apartheid South Africa. Such has been expressed by utterances of Pieter Mulder—the leader of the Freedom Front Plus (FPP) who responded to the then president of South Africa, Jacob Zuma's State of the Nation address by saying:

> Africans in particular never in the past lived in the whole of South Africa. The Bantu speaking people moved from the Equator down south while white people moved from the Cape to meet each other at the Kei River. There is sufficient proof that there were no Bantu speaking people in the Western Cape and North-western Cape. These parts form 40% of South Africa's land surface. (Mulder 2012)

Mulder was particularly responding to the former president's emphasis for the need of land reform, as land has been one of the main resources that has continued to shape the contested entitlement of resources and articulations of the national question in the idea of South Africa across time and space. At the centre of contestations about belonging to South Africa, which Pillay (2004 215) rightly sees as "a political and legal construct [that] underwent shifting understanding", has been initiatives to inscribe forms of domination that will consequently structure access and entitlement to resources. Deeply rooted in white settler historiography, colonial discourse vehemently holds the myth of empty lands and Black and white people being migrants from elsewhere.

Scholars like Saunders (1988) and Bank (1997)—to mention just two—have been among those who have written on South African historiography and orchestrated the discourse of empty land in ways that have gone a long way in neatly feeding into the colonial narrative of constructing 'natives' and 'settlers' as identities that mattered politically. The common logic behind the 'empty land' thesis usually revolves around ideas of Bantu migration and *Mfecane*.[1] Although the historian Julian Cobbing (1988) has expressed that *Mfecane* was just a myth that served the apartheid regime's racist ideology to justify separate development and inequalities in land ownership and distribution, white settlers claimed to have occupied empty spaces that resulted from dispersal of population caused by Black-on Black violence and destruction of the *Mfecane* era in precolonial times. Arguments on Mfecane continued to feed into the 'empty land' thesis to the extent that it became instrumental in justifying the naturalization of domination by white settlers who had found empty lands and did not dispossess anyone's land.

Ideas of Bantu migration were equally instrumental in pushing the 'empty land' thesis where it was claimed that:

> The land of Southern Africa was empty, . . . and was peopled almost simultaneously by 'Bantu' from the north who moved south, and Europeans who were making their way north from the southernmost point of Africa, the Cape. The 'empty land' thesis, a thesis about mobility, thus suggests that no prior right to a connection with the land could be claimed by Africans and that colonial settlement therefore did not involve 'displacement', for in order to be displaced one has to be there already (Pillay 2004, 216)

The migratory thesis hinges on the idea that Europeans and Bantu (Africans) arrived in South Africa at the same time in the seventeenth century. Theal (1964), who claimed that Black and white people of South Africa were migrants, had this to say:

> In reality this country was not the Bantu's originally any more than it was the white man's because the Bantus were immigrants . . . most of their ancestors migrated to South Africa in comparatively recent times.

Even though the idea of migration was disputed by rich archaeological evidence, framing the Bantu as immigrants rendered the Afrikaners as natives who deserved entitlement to land ownership. The native-settler question which mediated the politics of belonging fed into the invented 'empty land' thesis in richly rewarding ways for the colonisers, as Pillay (2004 221) notes that "the settler was recast as ' belonging' and the native came to be recast as 'foreign'." 'Settlers' and 'natives' were produced as political identities as part of naturalizing domination that was rooted in white settler historiography to hold on to the claim that whites and the Black people of South Africa were migrants. So, the driving logic became that of justifying whites' occupation without dispossessing anyone and this interpretation of entitlement to resources resulted in skewed policies that benefitted white people and marginalised a majority of the Black population's access to resources. The failure by the ruling African National Congress (ANC) to reverse such interpretations of entitlement to resources have witnessed rising levels of frustrations of Black South Africans who experience various forms of hardships, resulting in them engaging in unrest and looting from time to time, such as the ones that happened after the incarceration of Jacob Zuma.

THE APARTHEID PERIOD AND SEGREGATION POLICIES

The foreign minority's burden of ruling the indigenous majority was also articulated as the 'native question' that further shaped the politics of property ownership and colonial discourses of domination and exploitation (Mamdani 1996). This was the segregation period when the apartheid state committed to protecting white dominance through a series of segregationist policies that turned Africans into providers of cheap labour through proletarianization either as urban-based or migrant workers. According to scholars like Dubow (1989), Bonner, Delius and Posel (1993), Posel (1993), Worden (1994) and Brown (1998), just to mention a few, in this period, apartheid state's enduring rationality was to ensure privileged access to political and socio-economic resources for the white population through administrative and legislative practices, with divide-and-rule and separate development as the guiding rationale. Through a modernist Marxist-inspired framework, Wolpe (1972) highlighted that a sustainable system of cheap labour power was the anchor on which the functionality of the apartheid system and South African capitalism hinged on. Ndlovu-Gatsheni (2012, 416) succinctly summarises:

> Apartheid's survival strategy consisted of four pillars. The first was restriction of franchise for Africans while monopolising and centralizing state power in the hands of Afrikaners. The second was racial spatialization of cities involving confining blacks to separate townships and homelands. The third included enforcing regulation that ensured supply of cheap African labour to the mines, industries, farms and white domestic households. Finally, the apartheid state actively and directly intervened in spheres of employment, education, health and other daily life human activities in favour of the Afrikaner community.

One of the major changes that happened during colonial encounter was ownership and regulation of land as the legal property of the colonial state, and this severely undermined the role of the traditional authority who previously held the land on behalf of the people (Ntsebeza 2010). The Natives Land Act of 1913 which restricted Africans to the reserves where they could have access to land especially in rural areas but not own it laid the basis for territorial segregation. According to Pillay (2004, 222):

> a total of 13 per cent of the land would be designated for Natives, governed by the Governor General who would act as 'Supreme Chief'. The designation of Native was not only a descriptive one, but also a legal one: to be classified as Native was to have spatially circumscribed implication in relation to movement and particularly regarding land ownership, employment opportunities and land tenure practices.

The debate on land reform in South Africa has been one of the most heated policy debates of recent times. Often termed 'the land question' or even 'the national question' this debate has been a long-standing feature of the contestations around entitlement and ownership of resources in South African politics, with the debates escalating to making a call to amend Section 25 of the Constitution. The suggestions to amend the section of the Constitution were mainly made to allow the state to expropriate land without compensation so as to accelerate the land reform policy, as areas of land reform vis-à-vis land restitution, land redistribution and security of land tenure have attracted heavy contestations. Youth-dominated parties like the Economic Freedom Fighters have made the loudest calls for land expropriation without compensation as part of debates on the politics of ownership of resources and the contested entitlement in the idea of South Africa. Revolving at the centre of the land debates is reversing the conquest and land dispossessions that took place in the nineteenth century and structurally altered African lives and property ownership.

As part of the contested politics of property ownership, the colonial state prevented the coalescence of the Black population by reinforcing tribal identities as part of divide and rule. Schutte (2000, 211) has it that Blacks and other groups were ideologically defined as 'ethnic peoples' and by extension reduced the minorities to the status of a discrete nation. Similarly, Ndlovu-Gatsheni (2012, 411) elaborated that, "the apartheid regime invented and recreated African ethnic fragmentations through legal codification to prevent the possibilities of coalescence of multiple ethnic African identities into a singular national identity." Thus, a unified concerted resistance by the majority of non-whites was something the apartheid state wanted to avoid at seemingly all possible costs, hence "it suppressed and distorted identity to the extent that it excluded and suppressed all constituents of identity except race and ethnicity" (Zegeye, Liebenberg and Houston 2000). From the 1950s, segregation was thus perceived to be a necessary undertaking in light of the influence of the South African Bureau

Racial Affairs (SABRA), a group of intellectuals who argued that South Africa is composed of cultural groups that seek expression in their own territories.

What apartheid South Africa did was reinvent and reify identities and construct 'foreign natives' out of Black indigenous people and 'native foreigners' out of white settlers (Neocosmos 2010), and this consequently structured their participation within the state and their entitlement to resources. The question of ruling an indigenous majority as a foreign minority constituted the driving logic of many of the segregationist policies that led to what is aptly captured in Mamdani's (1996) work. We learn through Mamdani's work that the colonial state constructed a deliberately bifurcated state of the colonised, who were deprived of all rights and citizenship, and the colonisers, who were accorded full legal rights and entitlement to resources. In using the theoretical handle of a 'bifurcated state', Mamdani explains how colonial rule worked at the level of lived reality and everyday ongoing subjugation by noting that law was used as a basis for classifying the population as citizens and subjects and consequently structuring their participation within the state. According to Mamdani, institutional segregation consisted of direct and indirect rule. Direct rule was a form of urban civil power and was about the exclusion of natives from civil freedoms granted to citizens. Colonised natives were profiled as belonging to ethnicities and were according to civil law excluded from racial category. Colonised natives were governed indirectly through traditional authorities and the customary mode of rule and cultural differences were transformed into a form of difference that mattered politically (Mamdani, 1996). The segregation that was consolidated after the coming into power of the National Party in 1948 not only recast "the settler as 'belonging' and the native as 'settler'" as Pillay (2004, 221) rightly argues, but it also shaped the politics of entitlement and ownership of resources. This politicisation of differences has remained lingering and continues to raise its ugly head as a nodal point in the context of post-apartheid South Africa. It shapes economic benefits and the looting of resources that were seen erupting to magnitudes that caught media attention soon after the incarceration of the former president Jacob Zuma.

The complex historical interactions and coalescence of diverse people as a dominant feature of South African history across various epochs has provoked various forms of contestations on the ownership and entitlement to property. For instance, the racial separation of people and reduction of Black people into sources of cheap labour during apartheid provoked African imaginations of the South African nation born out of resisting imperial, colonial and apartheid imaginations that excluded and marginalised Africans from property ownership.

POLITICS OF BELONGING AND AFRICAN NATIONALISM

Under African nationalisms, the idea of South Africa and imaginations of the authentic 'South African' entitled to resources and citizenship found different interpretations. For instance, the ANC Youth League of the 1940s advocated for radical Africanism and liberation of South Africa as a Black republic. According to Anthony Lembede (1973, 317), "Africa is a black man's country." The Pan-Africanist Congress (PAC) led by founding president Robert Sobukwe advocated for national struggle that would lead to the complete overthrow of white domination (Ndlovu-Gatsheni 2012), whereas the African National Congress (ANC) articulated the idea of South Africa through inclusivist terms of a multiracial society by adopting the Freedom Charter in 1956. The South African Communist Party (SACP) took a Marxist bent to articulate South Africa in class terms through the concept of a National Democratic Revolution (NDR), which put workers as key. The emphasis on inclusivity and democracy and the logic of reversing racism by articulating the idea of South Africa as non-racial that was emphasised by the ANC gained support ahead of other ideas of South Africa propagated by the Youth League, PAC and SAPC.

But by refusing to fall into another system of exclusion and difference that had haunted the idea of South Africa since the time of colonial encounters and introducing rainbowism, which emphasized inclusivity and celebration, the ANC did not address issues of competition for resources and the politics of property ownership. The ANC as a former liberation movement failed to deliver economic freedom and interpret the idea of South Africa in ways that address the questions of who the 'authentic' subject of the nation is, who deserves ownership of resources and property. Ownership of resources and property has been caught up in the broader idea of South Africa that had been dominated and shaped through contested, complex and shifting meanings of discursive-ideological frameworks across time and space. Colonial encounters and apartheid policies were skewed and predicated on racial separation of people and the reduction of Black people to sources of cheap labour. The failure to deliver economic freedom has frustrated a majority of the previously marginalised South Africans and provoked political contestation from youth-dominated political parties like Economic Freedom Fighters (EFF). For instance, the ANC Youth League has been pushing for nationalisation of mines since 2010.

The ANC's failure to deliver economic freedom and white South Africans' and transnational corporations' refusal to shed part of the benefits of resources and property gained from skewed apartheid policies has provoked struggles from below—especially by those experiencing economic hardships—that manifest as service delivery protests and looting. Taking a long durée historical analysis of the idea of South Africa thus places the chaos and unrest that South Africa plunged into following the incarceration of the former president into the context of the question of property ownership and lack of resources that has always been at the centre of who the 'authentic' subject of the nation and entitlement is. The idea of who belongs to South Africa has been a contested question since the time of complex and colonial encounters and was well understood by scholars such as Calpin who in 1941 argued that "the worst of South Africa is that you never come across a South African". It is the unresolved complexities of the idea of South Africa that led Chipkin (2007) to ask: *Do South Africans exist?* At the centre of analysis of Chipkin's work is the question of what constitutes South African-ness. Chipkin reflected on the contested idea of South Africa by drawing attention to how an 'African people' as a collectivity organised in pursuit of a political agenda came into being. In his elaboration, Chipkin traced the genealogy of a national identity called South African to the period of the African nationalist struggle and the post-apartheid period.

Partly constituting Chipkin's (2007, 2) concerns was to correct a false idea common within existing narratives of resistance, oppression, exploitation and popular nationalist discourses whereby 'the people' were viewed as 'existing' prior to the period of the nationalist struggle. Chipkin's intervention was a robust and intellectual one on the subject of the contested idea of South Africa, identity and nation-building and a useful one in understanding the making of people and nations in postcolonial Africa in general and post-apartheid South Africa in particular. His work also provides invaluable insights and a compass through which to read through the various interpretations of the idea of South Africa. The fundamental question of how South Africa has been conceived and imagined across three phases of South African history, namely, the colonial, anti-colonial and post-apartheid periods are in inextricably intertwined with complex interpretations of entitlement and ownership of resources. Reading the complex politics of entitlement and ownership resources through the perennial questions of the idea of South Africa and belonging opens a window of opportunity for us to see the looting and unrest that engulfed South Africa in July 2021 as tied to the intractable question of the meaning of South Africa. The unrest and looting can be read as an expression of frustrations about access to power and economic and social justice by most of the formally marginalised black population which in many ways is tied to the complex interpretations of belonging to South Africa and the 'authentic' subject of the nation entitled to resources.

CONCLUSION

Through an analysis of the various interpretations of the idea of South Africa and the imaginations of nationhood across different phases of South African history, the chapter argues that the unrest and looting that followed former president Jacob Zuma's incarceration relate to different interpretations of belonging in complex ways. Entitlement and ownership of resources has acquired complex and shifting meanings such that the resolution of economic inequalities has concomitantly been at the centre of the idea of South Africa in ways that provoke the Black majority who face economic hardships to engage in looting from time to time. In a nutshell, this chapter has tried, through a historically grounded reflection on the highly contested question of the idea of South Africa, to render transparent how issues of entitlement to resources have been entangled in broader discourses of domination, exploitation and resistance that invariably shape the politics of ownership of property.

NOTE

1. The term *Mfecane* was coined by E. A Walker in 1928 to refer to the myth of a cataclysmic period of Black-on-Black destruction in the times of the Zulu King Shaka between 1810 and 1830. However, Julian Cobbing convincingly dismisses Mfecane as a myth, arguing that the term itself is problematic and that it was used instead to justify white settlement by blaming Zulu people and their King Shaka for depopulating and devastating vast territories.

REFERENCES

Bank, Andrew. 1997. "The Great Debate and the Origins of South African Historiography." *Journal of African History.* 38:2. 261–81.

Blaut, James. 1993. *The colonizer's model of the world: Geographical diffusion and Eurocentric History*. New York: The Guilford Press.

Bonner, Philip, Delius, Peter, and Posel, Deborah (eds). 1993. *Apartheid's genesis 1935–1962*. Johannesburg: Ravan/Wits University Press,

Brown, Andrew. 1998. *Apartheid and the Conceptualisation of Race*. Skotaville Publishers. Johannesburg.

Calpin, G. H. 1941. *There are no South Africans*. London: Thomas Nelson and Sons.

Chipkin, Ivor. 2007. *Do South Africans exist? Nationalism, democracy and the identity of the 'people'.* Johannesburg: Wits University Press

Dubow, Saul. 2007. Thoughts on South Africa: Some preliminary ideas. In *History making and present-day politics*, edited by H. Erik Stolten, 51–72. Uppsala, Sweden: Nordic Africa Institute.

Etherington, Norman. 2004. A false emptiness: How historians may have been misled by early nineteenth-century maps of south-eastern Africa. *Imago mundi* 56(1): 67–86.

Grosfoguel, Ramon. 2013. The structure of knowledge in Westernized universities, Epistemic racism/sexism and the four genocides/epistimicides of the long 16th century. *Human Architecture: Journal of Sociology of Self-Knowledge* 11(1): 73–90.

Keegan, Timothy. 1996. *Colonial South Africa and the Origins of the racial order*. Cape Town: David Philip.

Lembede, Anthony. 1973. Policy of the congress youth league [1946]. In *From protest to challenge, Vol. 2, Hope and Challenge 1935–1952*, edited by T. Karis and G. M. Carter, 319–17. Stanford, CA: Stanford University Press.

Mamdani, Mahmood. 1996 *Citizen and Subject: Contemporary Africa and the legacy of late colonialism*. Princeton, NJ: Princeton University Press.

Marks, Shula. 1980. South Africa: The myth of the empty land. *History Today*, 7–12 January.

Marks, Shula, and Trapido, Stanely. 1987. 'The Politics of Race, Class and Nationalism.' In *The Politics of Race, Class and Nationalism in Twentieth-Century South Africa*, edited by S. Marks and S. Trapido. London : Routledge.

Mulder, Pieter. 2012. Are Sexwale and Ramaphosa really white land owners? Politicsweb. https://www.politicsweb.co.za/politics/are-sexwale--ramaphosa-really-white-land-owners--p.

Ndlovu-Gatsheni, Sabelo. 2012. Racialised Ethnicities and Ethnicised Races: Reflections on the Making of South Africanism. *African Identities* 10(4): 1–16.

Neocosmos, Michael. 2010. *From 'Foreign Natives' to 'Native Foreigners': Explaining Xenophobia in Post-Apartheid South Africa: Citizenship and Nationalism, Identity and Politics*. Dakar: CODESRIA Book Series.

Ntsebeza, Lungisile. 2010. "Reconciliation and the Land Question." *The Balance: South Africans Debate Reconciliation*. Jacana Media. 85–92.

Pillay, Suren. 2004. Where do you belong? Natives, foreigners and apartheid South Africa. *African Identities* 2(2): 215–32.

Posel, Deborah. 1997 *The making of apartheid, 1948–1961: Conflict and compromise*. Oxford: Clarendon Press.

Saunders, Cristopher. 1988. *The Making of the South African Past: Major Historians on Race and Class*. Totowa, New Jersey: Barnes and Noble Books.

Schutte, Gerhard. 2000. "Being African in South Africa: The Dynamics of Exclusion and Inclusion." *Social Identities*. 6. 207–22.

Theal, George. 1964. *History of South Africa*. Cape Town: Struik.

Wolpe, Harold. 1972. 'Capitalism and cheap labour power in South Africa: From Segregation to Apartheid'. *Economy and Society* 1(4): 425–56.

Worden, Nigel. 1994. *Breaking the Chains: Slavery and emancipation in the nineteenth-century Cape Colony*. Johannesburg: University of the Witwatersrand Press.

Zegeye, Abebe, Liebenberg, Ian and Houston, Gregory. 2000. Resisting ethnicity from above: Social identities and democracy in South Africa. In *Democracy and Governance Review: Mandela's Legacy, 1994–1999*, edited by Y. Muthien, M. M. Khosa, and B. M. Magubane. Pretoria: HSRC Publishers.

Chapter Eight

A Critical Reflection on Inequalities and Poverty as an Instigator of Looting in South Africa

Mfaniseni Wiseman Mbatha, Mandla A. Mubecua, Victor H. Mlambo and Philangani Sibiya

INTRODUCTION

The issues of poverty and inequality remain evident in most countries, affecting severely, the underdeveloped and developing countries. This is the concern of every government as these issues are persisting and a lot still needs to be done in countries such as South Africa where poverty and inequality have shown to be stubborn. This is because there is still a high level of inequality in South Africa, which is attributed to the legacy of apartheid, as the majority of people are excluded and struggling to participate in economic growth (Parnell 2005; Tshishonga 2019). As a result of poor service delivery in South Africa, there has been a drastic increase in protest and socio-political unrest (Breakfast, Bradshaw and Nomarwayi 2019) that saw citizens (mostly the poor) expressing their frustration by engaging in criminal activities such as looting because of the persistence of poverty and economic inequalities.

> The report by the chairperson of the National Council of Provinces Committee, Yunus Ismail Carrim in August 2021 reveals that heated debates have emerged over the causes of social unrest (referring to the unrest that took place in Kwa-Zulu Natal and Gauteng) that took place in South Africa. Some reflections show that the main cause of unrest that resulted in looting was related to political agendas and poor service delivery while other reflections associated it with poverty as well. In his report, Ismail posits that: "In order to ensure social unrest does not occur again, structural inequalities need to be addressed."

It became significant, therefore, to provide an Afrocentric perspective on how the nexus of poverty and inequality are perpetuating looting during the violent unrest. The objective that is addressed in this book chapter is based on how economic inequality and poverty are contributing to the looting and how the looting (itself) is contributing to inequality and poverty in South Africa. This book chapter relies extensively on secondary data and qualitative content analysis to meet the objective of this study and finds that the looting during the social or political unrest truly reflects the depths of poverty and inequality faced by South Africans, which can be traced back as consequences of the apartheid. The high level of inequality that exists in South Africa is confirmed in the report by Oxfam South Africa (2020), which reveals that the World Bank has ranked South Africa as the most unequal society in the world, with the majority of the wealth is owned by the only 10 percent of the population. As a result, the people are collectively expressing their frustrations grounded in the historical experiences of poverty and inequality, which is affecting almost all African people as reflected by Lateef (2015) in his study on Afrocentricity.

Some findings emerging in this book chapter show that the looting during protests and socio-political unrest is rooted around the failure of the State to overcome several challenges including poverty and inequality (itself) as the consequences of the high unemployment rate. It appears that these challenges have resulted in some economic exclusions, desperation and marginalisation among people in society. In that sense, the poor are driven by the common unjust act and mutual bonds as they gain a motivation to participate in looting for their survival, which is characterised by actions of violence. It can be noted, however, that looting has a negative impact, as it cripples the economy, causing social instability and harshly weakening or threatening the democracy of the country. It further comes with violence, torching and vandalizing of public infrastructure as looters attempt to access manufacturing companies, supermarkets and other food sources in the supply chain. As a result, the looting has long-term implications for the country's economy. The government should draw critical lessons from the recent unrest and looting, such as prioritizing the needs of the poor when rendering public services; this can help to prevent and manage any violent unrest and looting in the future.

A LITERATURE REVIEW ON POVERTY AND INEQUALITY

The issues of poverty and inequality are persisting in the majority of developing countries worldwide and Africa in particular. Drawing from the work of Aryeetey et al., (2012) it can be noted that poverty and inequality are hitting harder in the Southern African region where there are intolerably high levels of employment. In the context of South Africa, there has been debate revolving around economic growth and its impact on poverty and inequality. In this sense, Niyimbanira (2017) posits that the general consensus is that these two development issues are persisting in South Africa. The author goes on to regard poverty and income inequality as the outcomes of the apartheid system. The policies and laws introduced by the apartheid government have restricted Black people from participating in the economy (Lephakga 2017) and segregated them in places where there is no water, electricity, shelter, access to education facilities and other basic needs. According to Spaull (2013), the apartheid system remains the creator of the existing inequalities in South Africa. This was also confirmed by Schneider (2003, 24), who posits that: "South Africa is still in danger of widespread unrest brought on by the continued presence of economic inequality along racial lines." Schneider goes on to provide that such economic inequalities emerged during the apartheid era as the system of racial capitalism started to exist. This is where economic activities for Black people were brutally restricted, and their wages or salaries were kept low while white economic activities and workers flourished (Schneider 2003). As a result, the poor class became vulnerable and suffered from widespread malnutrition, diseases and poverty (McKenna, 2010). This is evidence that inequality is the main contributor to the increasing poverty rate, and it cannot be neglected in the fight against poverty. In their work, Ben Amar and Zghidi (2016) concur that inequality is strongly contributing to human underdevelopment since it affects economic growth, suggesting a need for the poor to participate in the economy. Hence, inequality is affecting poverty because it directly or indirectly regulates the distribution of income or wealth among people. The changes in inequality through economic growth are fundamental to addressing the level of poverty (Ben Amar and Zghidi 2016). This is because economic growth can play a crucial role by providing more opportunities for a better living environment that can possibly benefit all people including those who are poor.

> In democratic South Africa, a commitment to address issues of poverty and inequality has been a priority on the agenda of the government. This forms part of the National Development Plan vision for 2030 with a guiding principle that says, "No political democracy can survive and flourish if the mass of our people remains in poverty, without land, without tangible prospects for a better life. Attacking poverty and deprivation must be the first priority of a democratic government" (p. 14).

The National Development Plan postulates that addressing issues of poverty and inequality will require the involvement of different mechanisms and interventions including an increase in employment opportunities, incomes, productivity, social protection, and improved services delivery. Successful attainment of these mechanisms will be measured when the living standards of the poor are improving. In their work Leibbrandt, Wegner and Finn (2011) have revealed that poverty has decreased in South Africa while the level of inequality appears to be increasing. However, the nature of inequality in democratic South Africa is no longer strongly associated with racial makeup as it happened during the apartheid era. The literature shows that social policies developed by the government are well-targeted toward addressing racial inequalities and poverty amongst the poor. The special reference has been made based on a number of social grants introduced by the South African government to lift people out of poverty (Leibbrandt, Wegner and Finn 2011).

However, the above-mentioned effort of the government toward fighting poverty has failed to reverse the trends of inequality and provide equal opportunities for citizens. In his opinion piece with *Daily Maverick*, Motsohi (2017) concurs that South Africa remains an unequal society, and the majority of people are still suffering from poverty with only the minority having access to employment. The nature of inequality in South Africa has developed various motion forces that keep individuals, groups, and households in the poverty trap. Lamb (2021) posits that the ongoing crisis of inequality, poverty and unemployment have resulted in looting, especially in South Africa started during the apartheid. The looting is continuing to take place in democratic South Africa. As a result, the current chapter provides new knowledge on how inequality and poverty are contributing to the looting in South Africa.

METHODOLOGICAL ISSUES

This chapter is positioned within the Afrocentricity perspective to offer a content analysis of poverty and inequality as the instigators of looting in South Africa and how looting (itself) is worsening poverty and inequality in South Africa. As a methodology, Chawane (2016, 80) offers that Afrocentricity stands "as an answer to the intellectual colonialism that undergirds and serves to validate political and economic colonialism." Afrocentricity (as a theory) is used to position South African people at the centre of analysis as this book chapter critically reflects on how they behave and react to poverty and inequality, especially during the incidences of socio-political unrest. Chukwuokolo (2009) maintain that Africans have a right to provide their perspectives on the African experience, which involves ensuring that Afrocentricity is used as an exercise in self-knowledge.

This chapter uses qualitative research to gain an understanding of how poverty and inequality are contributing to looting. This research approach is recommended by Creswell and Creswell (2018), who posit that it is most fitting in studies that are aimed at exploring a phenomenon that is not extensively researched, such as how poverty and inequality are contributing to looting in South Africa. In order to successfully execute the qualitative approach, this book chapter adopts content analysis as a crucial tool to guide the mapping of data and analysis towards achieving its purpose. In their work, Elo and Kyngäs (2008) recommend that content analysis is a most fitting tool for qualitative studies that intend to analyse existing verbal, documented and visual data or communications. Williams (2007) maintains that content analysis in qualitative studies can be conducted with any written materials, newspapers or media products.

As a result, this chapter relies chiefly on secondary data, which included recent newspaper articles and peer-reviewed academic journals that delineate inequalities, poverty, and looting. Sources from Web of Science, Google Scholar, Sabinet African Journals, and Scopus databases were used to collect data for the current study. South African trustworthy online sources including *Mail and Guardian*, News24 and *Daily Maverick* were solicited to draw incidences of reports related to looting in South Africa. Keywords or themes such as *inequality*, *poverty* and *looting* were used to search for information related to the aim of the study. The articles retrieved were further limited by the term *South Africa* to ensure the relevance of the study, as a number of articles were received from online sources and search engines.

POVERTY, INEQUALITY AND LOOTING: SOME EVIDENCE FROM SOUTH AFRICA

The significance of this section is to understand the dilemma of looting and how poverty and inequality are exacerbating this violent exercise in South Africa. There have been many cases of looting during protests and unrest, but this chapter makes reference only to recent violent unrest that happened in the period of 9–17 July 2021. In his reflection, Cotterill (2021b) regards this unrest as extraordinary and the most severe unrest to take place since the apartheid. This is because the outcomes of the unrest were undesirable, as they resulted in the loss of employment, properties, business stock, livelihoods, food distribution and essential services from medical centres, hospitals and clinics.

THE NEXUS OF UNREST AND LOOTING: IMPACT AND IMPLICATION ON THE ECONOMY

Some debates have emerged around the main cause of the protests, socio-political unrest and looting that took place in July 2021, as some people believe that the jailing of the former president of the Republic of South Africa, Jacob Zuma, was the main cause. This is because the protests and unrest commenced after the former president was sentenced to fifteen months in jail. The jailing of the former president came after the judicial commission of inquiry, led by Deputy Chief Justice Raymond Zondo, filed for the concept of court charge since Zuma ignored multiple subpoenas; subsequently, the court found the former president guilty (Ndou 2021).

There were concerns relating to jailing the former president, considering his popularity, being known as the people's president, the fact that since the consolidation of democracy in South Africa, no president had been jailed and the fact that he was from the ANC's biggest voting region would likely lead to the resentment of the ANC and to societal conflict. However, Isike (2019) argued that the removal of the former president coincided with growing factionalism within the ANC. The author further contends that in South Africa, post-2008, unemployment, poverty, rising inequality, corruption, and maladministration at the local government level and the fragmentation of effective service delivery are other factors that were brewing in the background ready to explode. As a result, when the former president was jailed, societal discontent under the guise of #FreeZuma erupted and resulted in immense protests and unrest, causing considerable damage to the economy of the country.

The violent riots broke out in the provinces of KwaZulu Natal (Zuma's home province, where he still enjoys the support of the masses) and Gauteng, South Africa's economic hub. In KZN, the South African Property Owners Association (SAPOA) indicated that the cost of the unrest is estimated to exceed R20 billion, with a staggering "129,000 jobs" at risk following the looting of malls, factories, and certain industries. "A large portion of those workers" were likely to be added to the country's skyrocketing unemployment figures (Khumalo 2021). This adds a significant increase to the persistent poverty and high level of inequality faced by the country at large. In his public communication on the impact of unrest and riot, Premier Sihle Zikalala raised a concern that the police in KwaZulu Natal Province did not have sufficient resources to control and handle the unrest. While the premier of Gauteng, David Makhura, asserted that the financial cost of the unrest and looting in Gauteng is R3.5 billion and Gauteng businesses lost R5 billion because of the violent unrest and looting.

South Africa has experienced challenges with regard to consistent levels of economic growth, which has a direct impact on poverty and inequality. Hence, the lack of economic acclivity because of the looting and compounded by the COVID-19 pandemic has escalated the concern over the livelihood of the poor and the country's economy. For example, the number of unemployed people rose by 2.2 million to 6.5 million between the second and third quarters of 2020 (Payi 2020). Thus, the jailing of the former president may have been a factor in the July riots, but there were already other factors that were neglected for a long time and that consolidated societal discontent. The jailing of Zuma may also have been used to achieve the goals of certain individuals in the ANC, considering its fractured structure. This is the main concerning factor, as the leadership of the country neglected to directly deal with issues of poverty and inequality faced by the citizens and commited themselves and state resources instead to fighting their personal battles (Martin and Solomon 2016).

THE AFTERMATH OF LOOTING AND ITS IMPLICATIONS FOR POVERTY AND EQUALITY

The severe outcomes of the looting during the protest and violence had negative outcomes on people's daily livelihoods, and the poor were the main victims. The evidence shows a drastic increase in poverty and inequality as a result of economic stagnation. The people in the country's majority lost their jobs and became economically inactive with no purchasing power.

The president of the Republic of South Africa was convinced that they are people who took advantage of the social and economic conditions under which the majority of people in South Africa live to provoke South Africans, especially the poor, to participate in opportunistic acts of violent unrest and looting. Furthermore, such actions were aimed to invoke the frustrations of those who are most affected by poverty and inequality with an intention to sabotage the economy. Evidence of this is the disruption of businesses through looting, burning and vandalism of business properties, causing significant infrastructural and financial losses.

THE IMPACT OF LOOTING ON FOOD SECURITY IN SOUTH AFRICA

In an opinion piece, Sihlobo (2021) acknowledges that South Africa is food secure at the national level. However, there is a high level of food insecurity experienced at the household level as people, particularly the poor, are unable to have access to adequate food. Bowden (2019) is of the view that there is an existence of inequality regarding access to food in South Africa and relates that the country is able to produce enough food to feed the entire population but the poorer of the poor are unable to afford to buy it. This is confirmed in a report by Statistics South Africa (2021), which maintains that there is sufficient food available for everyone through domestic means of food production and food imports. The accessibility of such food, nonetheless, stands as the main problem at the household level because of the stubbornness of high income inequality.

The unrest and looting that surfaced in the country in July 2021 came at a time when the country was still faced with challenges of hunger and food inadequacy. The majority of households were lacking money and power to buy food due to their inability to generate income. The looting caused further suffering, especially in KwaZulu Natal and Gauteng provinces, from a shortage of food due to the interruption of the food supply chain. This is confirmed by the findings of Van der Merwe (2021) who states that the unrest and looting have caused significant troubles in the price and transportation of food and agricultural activities, which saw the prices attached to food items drastically increase, and the majority of citizens were left hungry. This is because food supply chains were disrupted not only in KwaZulu Natal and Gauteng provinces, but in the country overall for the foreseeable future. According to Cokayne (2021), the looting has caused a huge demand for logistic networks and storage, which causes drastic delays and challenges in food delivery.

The industries, on the other hand, have reported their concerns over the issues of unrest and looting in relation to food security. The report by Heiberg (2021) on New24 reveals that farmers in South Africa were also the victims of the unrest and looting. This is due to the sad reality that trucks were prevented from carrying produce from farms and the manufacturing sector, threatening the food supply. The consequences were immediately felt. Farmers from the South African Agricultural Industry Association have reported the loss of about R3 million worth of fresh produce that they did not transport because of the riot and people hijacking trucks that were carrying food.

THE IMPACT OF LOOTING AND UNREST ON THE HEALTH CARE SYSTEM

It can be noted that access to quality health care is set as a human right and provisioned within section 27 of the Constitution of the Republic of South

Africa. To bring this constitutional obligation into existence, the South African government has introduced several developmental programmes that are aimed at improving the safety, efficiency, quality delivery, and accessibility of health care services by citizens, including the poorest of the poor (Maphumulo 2019). Despite the efforts of the government toward improving service delivery in the health care system, the institutions of health are struggling to meet the standard of care people require. This is because of the inequality experienced within the country as some people, particularly the poor, are unable to access health services (Henning-Smith, 2020). This is confirmed by de Villiers (2021) who posits that health care in South Africa remains the responsibility of the government due to the stubbornness of poverty, high levels of unemployment, and inequality that exists between private and public health care centres. The public health care system is overburdened because it has to accommodate the majority of people, who cannot afford private sector health care.

Smit (2021) reports that the unrest has increased the workload on the health sector, which had already suffered from the great pressure of the coronavirus pandemic. Smit further states that "the unrest has also had an impact on access to other types of chronic and lifesaving medication for TB, HIV, and diabetes." Meanwhile, the looting put staff and patients in a vulnerable position as the pandemic was escalating at a high rate. In her report with the *Round-Up*, Majola (2021) maintains that the unrest and looting had a negative impact on the health care system, as the ambulances needed to transport medical services and patients were torched by the looters.

The unrest and looting only worsened the poverty and inequality as the health care services were interrupted and the poor from the most affected provinces were no longer able to access health facilities. In addition, the government's program of coronavirus vaccination roll-out was tragically interrupted as a number of vaccine doses were lost during the unrest (*BusinessTech* Staff Writer 2021a). Expanding on this, Malan (2021) points out that the shutdown of medical centres has left the majority of people as unable to collect essential medicines, which affected those who are living with chronic illnesses worst.

The above reveals the extent to which poverty and inequality continue to strike in South Africa. The two concerning challenges (poverty and inequality) have been shown to reproduce themselves and to push people to engage in violent activities and looting while putting in jeopardy the lives of those who rely on medications to survive. The sad reality is that violent unrest and looting backfires on those who engage in it, as evidenced by the reflections presented above.

DEFINING THE LONG-TERM EFFECT OF LOOTING ON A COUNTRY'S ECONOMY

According to Vhumbunu (2021), the recent unrest in South Africa has negative consequences for the country's economy and business while worsening poverty and jeopardizing the livelihoods of the poor, which were already under threat because of the coronavirus.

The looting resulted in massive job losses, and South Africa's GDP shrank by 1.5 percent as lockdowns and the results of looting bore down on economic growth. The twin pressures of tighter COVID-19 lockdown restrictions and the civil disorder in July led to the economy contracting in the third quarter of 2021 (*BusinessTech* Staff Writer 2021b). Looting brought millions of South Africans into deeper poverty, unemployment and economic misery. With the election of current president Cyril Ramaphosa in 2018, there was hope that his administration would be able to restore order, ensure consistent rates of economic growth and promote a more inclusive society. However, the government's handling of the July riots coupled with the economic divide as a result of COVID-19 has left a lot to be desired. Part of the problem is that the ability of the president to fulfil his duties effectively is being hindered by factionalism within the ANC, compromising the consolidation of the proposed renewal project (Hogg 2021). This chapter argues that the biggest threat to social stability in South Africa today is the government's inability to reduce unemployment, poverty, corruption, and inequality. This view was reinforced by the Centre for Risk Analysis, which says that South Africa will probably experience more frequent bouts of violent protests unless the government fast-tracks growth-enhancing structural reform (Naidoo 2021). The violence reflects an economy that has been "stagnant for more than a decade and data show that there is a strong correlation between economic growth and social stability, and rioting and looting could become more prevalent in the next few years unless the authorities are serious about implementing reforms. Therefore, this chapter argues that the jailing of the president alone did not give rise to the riots of July 2021; rather, some factors had already consolidated societal discontent. Sadly, looting made life for South Africans even harder and made it difficult to ensure inclusive socioeconomic development as the riots resulted in massive economic losses for both the country and the provinces.

THE GOVERNMENT'S RESPONSE TO LOOTING IN SOUTH AFRICA

On the 15th of July 2021, South African ministers representing the presidency and correctional services officials met with thirty-four CEOs of South Africa's largest companies and multinational corporations to talk about the unrest in both KZN and Gauteng province (Vhumbunu 2021). Amongst the other things discussed were the challenges faced by businesses, workers, and communities, and how to stabilize the provinces, re-establish supply chains and repair critical damaged infrastructure. It was urgent to design a recovery plan to rebuild destroyed factories (Visser, Rangongo and Esterhuizen, 2021). The South African government took serious actions to respond to the economic, social and security aspects of the crisis. The businesses also recommended the government's intervention in the economy as well as a collaborative way forward (Vhumbunu 2021). This unity between the government and business reset South Africa for growth, re-establishing the confidence of the people, industries, and investors. The goal of the South African government was not only to recover the country's economy but to bring a brighter future in which all our people will enjoy a higher standard of living, with highly skilled youth (Oxford Analytica, 2021).

CONCLUSION

This chapter has provided a content analysis of how inequality and poverty have contributed to looting and the extent to which the looting (itself) contributed to inequality and poverty. With reference to the violent unrest and looting in KwaZulu Natal and Gauteng in July 2021 over the jailing of Jacob Zuma, the findings of the book chapter show that poverty and inequality stand as a catalyst and main cause of looting in South Africa. This is because South Africa is the most unequal society in the world, with the wealth owned by the minority, and the majority of people suffering from extreme poverty. As a result, when there is unrest or riots, the poor simply opt for looting with the hope of overcoming poverty. However, some aspects of the findings show that the looting has a negative impact on the country's economy, which in turn exacerbates the level of inequality and poverty in South Africa. This is because the violent unrest has resulted in the torching of malls and business properties, which results in the loss of jobs and disturbances of the food supply chain.. The looting might have brought disruption and stagnation to the country's economy, but it reflected how the needs of the poor are neglected by the government. The looting of shops shows the extent to which poverty and inequality are entrenched in South African society.

Therefore, the government must look to issues of poverty and inequality by addressing and prioritizing the needs of the poor. By doing so, the government will be able to prevent and manage unrest and looting in the future and thereby prevent disruption of economic activities.

REFERENCES

Aryeetey, Ernest, Devarajan, Shantayanan, Kanbur, Ravi, and Kasekende, Louis, eds. 2012. *The Oxford companion to the economics of Africa*. Oxford: Oxford University Press.

Ben Amar, Mohamed, and Zghidi, Nahed. 2016. The relationship between inclusive growth, inequality and poverty in Africa. *Theoretical & Applied Economics* 23(2).

Bowden, Robyn. 2021. Food inequality in South Africa. Southern African Faith Communities' Environment Institute. October 22. https://safcei.org/15293-2/.

Breakfast, N., Bradshaw, G., and Nomarwayi, T. 2019. Violent service delivery protests in post-apartheid South Africa, 1994–2017: A conflict resolution perspective. *African Journal of Public Affairs* 11(1): 106–26.

BusinessTech Staff Writer. 2021. South Africa has a New COVID-19 Vaccine Target for Christmas. *BusinessTech*, July 22. https://businesstech.co.za/news/trending/508010/south-africa-has-a-new-covid-19-vaccine-target-for-christmas.

———. 2021b. South Africa's GDP shrinks by 1.5% as lockdowns and looting bite. *Business Tech*, December 7. https://businesstech.co.za/news/business/544686/south-africas-gdp-shrinks-by-1-5-as-lockdowns-and-looting-bite/.

Chawane, Midas. 2016. The development of Afrocentricity: A historical survey. *Yesterday and Today* 16: 78–99.

Chukwuokolo, J. Chidozie. 2009. Afrocentrism or Eurocentrism: The dilemma of African development. *OGIRISI: A New Journal of African Studies* 6: 24–39.

Cokayne, Roy. 2021. Vital links taken out of the supply chain by unrest and looting. Tech Central, July 16. https://techcentral.co.za/vital-links-taken-out-of-the-supply-chain-by-unrest-and-looting/170621/.

Cotterill Joseph. 2021. South Africa struggles to contain worst unrest in decades. *Financial Times*, July 13. https://www.ft.com/content/9ab45599-ea5c-405e-99b9-f69a497ec0bc

———. 2021b. South Africa Counts the Cost of its Worst Unrest Since Apartheid. *Financial Times*, July 25. https://www.ft.com/content/1b0badcd-2f81-42c8-ae09-796475540ccc.

Creswell, John W., and Creswell, J. David. 2017. *Research design: Qualitative, quantitative, and mixed methods approaches*. Thousand Oaks, CA: Sage.

de Villiers, Katusha. 2021. Bridging the health inequality gap: an examination of South Africa's social innovation in health landscape. *Infectious Diseases of Poverty* 10(1): 1–7.

Elo, Satu, and Kyngäs, Helvi. 2008. The qualitative content analysis process. *Journal of advanced nursing* 62(1): 107–15.

Heiberg, Tanisha. 2021. Unrest hits farmers as food supply threatened. *Business Live*. https://www.businesslive.co.za/bd/national/2021-07-13-unrest-hits-farmers -as-food-supply-threatened/.

Henning-Smith, Carrie. 2020. The unique impact of COVID-19 on older adults in rural areas. *Journal of Aging & Social Policy* 32(4): 396–402.

Hogg, Alec. 2021. Is ANC set to splinter? Ramaphosa vs corrupt, anti-white RET faction—expert insights. *Biz News*, April 16. https://www.biznews.com/thought-leaders/2021/04/16/ramaphosa-anc-faction.

Isike, Christopher. 2019. Factionalism and corruption could kill the ANC—unless it kills both first. The Conversation, May 12. https://theconversation.com/factionalism-and-corruption-could-kill-the-anc-unless-it-kills-both-first-116924.

Khumalo, Juniour. 2021. Durban looting aftermath: 45 000 businesses affected, R16 billion in lost stock and damaged infrastructure. News24, July 14. https://www.news24.com/citypress/news/durban-looting-aftermath-45-000-businesses-affected-r16-billion-in-lost-stock-and-damaged-infrastructure-20210714.

Lateef, Husain. 2015. Afrocentricity theory revisited: An alternative framework for assisting Black youth. *University of Houston Libraries*.

Lamb, Guy. 2021. Why have South Africans been on a looting rampage? Research offers insights. The Conversation, July 15. https://theconversation.com/why-have-south-africans-been-on-a-looting-rampage-research-offers-insights-164571.

Leibbrandt, Murray, Wegner, Eva, and Finn, Arden. 2011. The policies for reducing income inequality and poverty in South Africa. Working paper. Southern Africa Labour and Development Research Unit (SALDRU).

Lephakga, Tshepo. 2017. Colonial institutionalisation of poverty among Blacks in South Africa. *Studia Historiae Ecclesiasticae* 43(2): 1–15.

Majola, Nokulunga. 2021. Health services in KZN struggle to function amidst looting and violent unrest, *Round-Up*. July 12. https://www.groundup.org.za/article/health-services-kzn-struggle-function-amidst-violent-protests/.

Malan, Mia. 2021. Half of KZN Patients have no chronic medication: Here's how looting affected SA's COVID-19 vaccine roll-out, *Mail & Guardian*, July 16. https://mg.co.za/health/2021-07-16-half-of-kzn-patients-have-no-chronic-medication-heres-how-looting-affected-sas-covid-19-vaccine-roll-out

Maphumulo, Winnie T., and Bhengu, Busisiwe R. 2019. Challenges of quality improvement in the healthcare of South Africa post-apartheid: A critical review. *Curationis* 42(1): 1–9.

Martin, Michaela Elsbeth, and Solomon, Hussein. 2016. Understanding the phenomenon of "state capture" in South Africa. *Southern African Peace and Security Studies* 5(1): 21–35.

McKenna, Amy, ed. 2010. *The history of southern Africa*. London: Britannica Educational Publishing.

Naidoo, Prinesha. 2021. There'll be more riots and looting if govt doesn't grow the economy, think tank says. News24, August 5. https://www.news24.com/fin24/economy/therell-be-more-riots-and-looting-if-govt-doesnt-grow-the-economy-think-tank-says-20210805.

Ndou, Clive. 2021. Zuma sentenced to 15 months imprisonment by ConCourt. News24, June 29. https://www.news24.com/witness/news/breaking-zuma-sentenced-to-15-months-imprisonment-by-concourt-20210629.

Niyimbanira, Ferdinand. 2017. Analysis of the impact of economic growth on income inequality and poverty in South Africa: the case of Mpumalanga Province. *International Journal of Economics and Financial Issues* 7(4): 254–61.

Oxfam South Africa. 2020. *Reclaiming power: Women's work and income inequality in South Africa*. Johannesburg: Oxfam South Africa. https://www.oxfam.org.za/wp-content/uploads/2020/11/oxfam-sa-inequality-in-south-africa-report-2020.pdf.

Parnell, Sue. 2005. Constructing a developmental nation-the challenge of including the poor in the post-apartheid city. *Transformation: Critical Perspectives on Southern Africa* 58(1): 20–44.

Payi, Bulelwa. 2020. Retrenchments on the rise, *Independent Online*, November 17. https://www.iol.co.za/weekend-argus/news/retrenchments-on-the-rise-78039c4f-f8fc-4317-af3e-28d83173ab74.

Schneider, Geoffrey. 2003. Neoliberalism and economic justice in South Africa: Revisiting the debate on economic apartheid. *Review of Social Economy* 61(1): 23–50.

Sihlobo, Wandile. 2021. South African riots and food security: Why there's an urgent need to restore stability, July 14. The Conversation. https://theconversation.com/south-african-riots-and-food-security-why-theres-an-urgent-need-to-restore-stability.

Smit, Sophie. 2021. The effects of looting on the South African health care system at a time when it is most needed. Helen Suzman Foundation, July 26. https://hsf.org.za/publications/hsf-briefs/the-effects-of-looting-on-the-south-african-health-care-system-at-a-time-when-it-is-most-needed.

Spaull, Nicholas. 2013. Poverty and privilege: Primary school inequality in South Africa. *International Journal of Educational Development* 33(5): 436–47.

Statistics South Africa. 2021. Towards measuring food security in South Africa: An examination of hunger and food inadequacy. July 14. https://www.statssa.gov.za/publications/03-00-14/03-00-142017.pdf.

Thabang, Motsohi, 2017. Transformation of South Africa needs a high sense of consciousness for social justice to succeed. *Daily Maverick*, February 23. https://www.dailymaverick.co.za/article/2017-02-23-letter-to-editor-transformation-of-south-africa-needs-high-sense-of-consciousness-for-social-justice-to-succeed/.

Tshishonga, Ndwakhulu. 2019. The legacy of apartheid on democracy and citizenship in post-apartheid South Africa: An inclusionary and exclusionary binary? *African Journal of Development Studies* 9(1): 167–91.

Van der Merwe, Christiaan. 2021. South Africa's riots take a bite out of food security. *Research professional news*. https://www.researchprofessionalnews.com/rr-news-africa-south-2021-8-south-africa-s-riots-takes-a-bite-out-of-food-security/.

Visser, Jaco, Rangongo, Timothy and Esterhuizen, Zerelda. 2021. Looting following Zuma's arrest raises SA' s risk premium. *Fin-week*. https://www.scribd.com/article/517185665/Looting-Following-Zuma-s-Arrest-Raises-Sa-S-Risk-Premium.

Vhumbunu, C. Hazvinei. 2021. The July 2021 protests and socio-political unrest in South Africa: Reflecting on the causes, consequences and future lessons. *ACCORD*, December 10. https://www.accord.org.za/conflict-trends/the-july-2021-protests-and-socio-political-unrest-in-south-africa/.

Williams, Melvin H., Rawson, Eric S., and Branch, J. David. 2017. *Nutrition for health, fitness, and sport*. New York: McGraw-Hill Education.

Chapter Nine

The Looting Culture and Its Value in the Transformation of Higher Education

Primrose T. Sabela

INTRODUCTION

This chapter questions the value of the looting culture in higher education transformation, looking specifically at how it has reinforced and directed attention to the need for changes in a bid to ascertain equal access to quality education by all in a spatially just environment. The chapter analyses the looting culture and its influence in changing the higher education landscape. The question emanates from different perspectives on looting and protests, where some conceive looting as destructive while others look at it as an indispensable revolutionary violence to bring about meaningful transformation. Varied views are attributed to a number of issues that are conceived as having sparked violent protests, and these include inequalities, various forms of discrimination, unequal financial support and of late lack of security and safety experienced in certain higher education spaces. The lens used in this chapter acknowledges the protests and looting culture as an inherited ideology used to pressurize higher education institutions to transform. The reasons for looting in higher education are, however, complex and require understanding of what lies behind the growing violent protests and looting. The analysis focuses on how looting has contributed to the transformation of higher education, based on the fact that protest marches and looting have had a profound influence on teaching and research space in higher education.

While we cannot shy away from the fact that looting is destructive, we should also acknowledge that there a number of complex and intersecting factors that spark the violence. The incidents have been a major political and transformation force in the struggle against inequality and exclusion, including persistent unequal distribution of benefits. There is a strong belief that disgruntled students have engaged in protest marches and looting as a way of highlighting desperation and putting pressure on structural imbalances, inequalities and injustices. Looting is also driven by the value of the loot and assumed benefits.

Ayodeji-Falade and Osunkunle (2021) characterize the violence of students as vandalism, looting, harassment, and intimidation, bringing loss of assets and other consequences. On the other hand, it can be argued that the use of violence and looting is a means of making management in higher education institutions and government to listen to the demands and challenges experienced by students. The stance of the chapter is that transformation needs to be prioritised in higher education institutions (HEIs), especially since they are also expected to lead the transformation in their local communities. This chapter acknowledges the fact that there has been work done towards transformation of HEIs, but the pace has been too slow and has been limited to changes in policy, pedagogical instructions and ill-defined access. It is argued that looting, though damaging in the education space, has played a crucial role in bringing transformation.

Ayodeji-Falade and Osunkunle (2021) maintain that the focus should not be on the violence and looting but on how to discourage acts of violent protests. In addition, Mavunga (2019) argues that protests continue to be characterized by violence and looting, which culminate in suspensions of lectures and examinations, damage to property, injury and arrest of students. Mavunga (2019, 82) uses Critical Realism Theory (CR) to describe the character of the protests and describes the student movements such as #FeesMustFall and #RapeMustFall as a culture of engagement whereby different stakeholders belonging to different structures perceive and exercise their agency. Ndebele (2007) argues that access to education by all should not be treated as a moral issue dependent on the conscience of decision makers, but as an inherent struggle for liberation. He describes access as a logical outcome of the history of liberation, but this has proven difficult to achieve.

The student movements are viewed as a conduit through which various forms of inequality, gender-based violence and other injustices experienced in higher education are channelled for attention. The movements are further described as a means through which transformation has been solicited and enforced in most African higher education institutions. Ndebele (2007) raised a question of whether the institutions of higher learning are embracing transformation by themselves or are forced to do so. Mavunga (2019) also confirms that students perceive violence and looting as the only weapons freely available for achievement of desired goals. However, it is not all students who approve of violence and looting, and this is reiterated by Jansen (2015), who describes the radical behaviour as 'new anger' demonstrating the daily sufferings as a result of untransformed universities and the persistently white-dominated economy. However, it seems strange that uprisings persist in the post-1994 era and Jansen (2015) associates these with the complexity of the challenges and the intense and threatening anger surprisingly from people who had no encounter with the colonial apartheid's atrocious cruelties and violation of human rights. Violence and looting can sometimes be fuelled by beliefs held about benefits expected while the resolutions are dependent on the interests of all stakeholders.

The concept of looting in the higher education context and in this chapter is therefore not limited to callous destruction of infrastructure and theft of equipment and learning materials; rather, the focus is on planned restructuring and transformation. In the same vein, the focus of the chapter does not downplay the negative consequences of looting such as destruction of property, development of toxic relations among students, staff and other stakeholders affiliated to tertiary institutions. Ginty (2004) identifies the dimensions of looting as comprising the redistributive looting where people loot to liberate the wealth or assets for all to gain access. Other approaches relate to looting as a by-product of violent protest, looting for appropriation and looting in terms of the greed thesis. The last approach is flash looting which is difficult to predict and is short lived. Higher education looting usually takes one or two of the approaches listed depending on the context. Furthermore, Ginty (2004) raises concern that the concept 'looting' is under-conceptualized, arguing that the emphasis and belief is placed on looting as constituting a cause and a component of armed conflict and theft.

EDUCATION AS A SOLUTION TO INEQUALITY AND DEPRIVATION

One percent of the population in the world controls 50 percent of the wealth, meaning 99 percent share the remaining half (Stober, 2019). Wealth inequality often results to inequality in educational outcomes, yet education is viewed as a solution out of poverty and inequality. Van Der Berg et al. (2011) confirm the scope for education to challenge and transform individual lives and social structure but argue that the education system itself perpetuates inequalities. Success has always been equated with education, but the system generates outcomes that tend to reinforce patterns of poverty and privilege. In addition, Nabassaga et al. (2020) report that education plays a role in reduction of inequality. However, Bandala and Andrade (2017) contend that poverty and illiteracy persists despite the fact that the World Bank founded in 1944 adopted two objectives, namely, to end poverty and to promote shared prosperity.

Notwithstanding, access to education has remained a challenge and the differentiated schooling system at all levels in terms of public institutions for the poor and private institutions for the well-off has perpetuated inequalities. Madikizela-Madiya (2021) confirms that access to higher education is always taken lightly but seems to be more complicated than frequently depicted. A number of questions are raised in Madikizela-Madiya (2021, 2) relating to access to education such as: *what access should be for and whether the space enables the attainment for this purpose.* The author further argues that access to higher education requires taking into consideration inclusion, justice, capabilities and quality of education. The poor tend to be excluded, discriminated against and marginalised by the education system (Madikizela-Madiya, 2021). Access is sometimes conceived as gaining entry into higher education. However, this ignores other issues related to exclusion and injustices that students come across. Madikizela-Madiya (2021) relating exclusion and injustices in higher education, presents the South African differentiation in terms of the predominantly white institutions that were much more advantaged during the apartheid era and the less empowering institutions that were disadvantaged. The argument raised relates to exclusion in the more empowering institutions, which leaves students with no choice. Adonis and Silinda (2021) caution us against the assumption that access for all groups within an institution does not translate to transformation, as it involves more than mere access. That is, students encounter challenges and drop out due to injustices and inequities in higher education and challenges stemming from writing, language, communication and poverty. Student protests accompanied by looting and sometimes the consequent closure of higher learning institutions emanate from these challenges.

Furthermore, access to poor-quality basic education tends to result in exclusion from post-matric quality education, and most students coming from poor socioeconomic background have found themselves in less empowering higher education institutions with inequal opportunities. This could be interpreted as blaming and punishing the poor for their poverty. Santos (2011) confirms that poor-quality education traps the poor in poverty. Meanwhile, Stober (2019) maintains that investment in education is essential but more critical is the structure and conditions of education. On the other hand, Nabassaga et al. (2020) maintain that inequality in education stems from inequality of results and inequality of opportunities. This implies that the results of inequality could be measured by income or wealth accumulated by individuals, or it could be determined by the socioeconomic background of individuals, locality and ethnicity. Nabassaga et al. (2020) maintain that education plays a vital role in addressing inequalities, however, the household's socioeconomic status and other factors do have an influence on the access to education and postgraduation opportunities.

The conditions associated with inequality of results and inequality of opportunities have significantly affected access and success in higher education. African higher education institutions have encountered unprecedented, massive and destructive uprisings that have culminated in suspension of lectures, looting, imprisonment, and even murder. The insurrection and looting indicate the profoundness and pervasiveness of the frustration with the higher education system and differentiated access to education. Waghid (2012) contends that higher education institutions in Africa have failed to competently address inequities and associates the situation with domination by those with superior knowledge who in most cases do not recognise the need to democratise knowledge. The student movements and protests worldwide have proved to be one of the major tools in transforming higher education. This has been a worldwide challenge in higher education, and most of the protests are mainly rooted in a number of issues such as the disproportionate distribution of access to education-related benefits (Dlamini, 2019). Protests and resultant looting over inequality in institutions of higher learning have widened the gap between the rich and the poor. Fomunyam (2017) asserts that student protests, though viewed as unsavoury, have played a major role in fighting discrimination worldwide and continue in Africa due to the poverty and misery that students find themselves faced with.

THE IDEA OF HIGHER EDUCATION

Higher education is a contested concept. However, the emphasis is on the importance of understanding and adhering to the fundamental principles on which higher education is anchored. Centre stage has always been the educational experience of the student as an independent and critical learner. Barnett (2012) describes higher education as a social institution that it is comprised of individuals collaborating to acquire knowledge and truth. Research universities are expected to create new possibilities and "develop the cross-disciplinary concepts that are increasingly vital that will enable students to address many of the complex challenges to national and global societies" (Boulton and Lucas 2008).

In the same vein, Boulton and Lucas (2008) propound that universities are spaces where innovative and critical thinking and circulation of these thoughts takes place. Assie-Lumumba (2006) argues that higher education embodies all organized learning activities at the tertiary level and defines the university as a subset of higher education. Universities are viewed as "agents of social justice and mobility". They are seen as vehicles for societal transformation_both within campus and in local communities. Universities are expected to influence change (Boulton and Lucas 2008). However, although major transformational changes have been noted, particularly in the academic culture universities, in some cases they are still exclusionary. Barnett (2014) argues that in the past, the university was characterized by elitism, exclusion and inequalities, whereas today's university is viewed as more diversified, marketized, technologized, borderless and globalized, with persistent inequality and discrimination. This current view raises questions such as the extent to which the changes highlighted challenge the middle-class capture of higher education. Who is influencing policy futures in higher education? How inclusive is the higher education environment? What drives instabilities faced by higher education institutions? And are the universities, particularly in Africa, well-prepared to meet societal demands and needs? Ndebele (2007) sees higher education, in particular the universities, as the cultural reproduction of Europe in Africa. He raises concerns about the extent to which Africans bring into higher education their African experiences and whether African epistemologies are ever considered in pedagogical practices. Furthermore, Ndebele (2007) argues that European liberals believe that the oppressed would develop much better with prescriptions of European standards, while the apartheid system was anchored on separate development, ignoring the fact that Bantu education was designed such that mass ignorance was produced and reproduced. Ndlovu-Gatsheni (2017) views the struggles as emanating from the colonial education system and Eurocentric thinking arguing that this calls for African intellectuals and academics to come up with interventions that provide solutions on 'how to change the rules of the game' without solely focusing on increasing the number of African Black students entering the higher education system. Nevertheless, Nyerere cited by Ndlovu-Gatsheni (2017, 62) stated that it is good to change but identified possible dangers facing a university in a developing nation, such as:

> the danger of blindly adoring mythical 'international standards' which may cast a shadow on national development objectives, and the danger of forcing our university to look inwards and isolate itself from the world.

Fomunyam (2017) in support of this assertion argues that the waves of protests and looting are based on the demand to eradicate injustices which relate to social, political, economic, cultural and personal issues. The author also sees the African elite that took power after independence as an extension of the colonialists.

On the other hand, Morley (2012) and Fomunyam (2017) note the persistence of toxic correlations between poverty, the misery that students are faced with and the inadequate access to higher education, including the elitism which continues to prevail despite calls for increased access, inclusion and affirmative action programmes. In the same vein, Aina (2010) and Morley (2012) raise issues that could precipitate the violence and looting higher education is perpetually faced with. These issues relate to policy upheavals, rapid and extreme transformation influenced by needs of the economy rather than academic imaginaries, irrelevant pedagogies, the prevalence of inherited colonial governance and academic systems with minimal transparency and inclusiveness, including cultural practices that encourage the growth of violent societies and the interference of political parties and other associations. Assie-Lumumba (2006) concurs, stating that higher education institutions in Africa are in continuous social and political crisis, but maintains that students and other stakeholders are major contributors to the turmoil. Assie-Lumumba (2006) further states that the development agenda of the African continent is in need of higher education systems that are capable of using knowledge for the construction of stable and solid societies and not systems that implant the seeds of self-destruction.

As much as the protests and looting have had a profound influence on the teaching and learning space in higher education, they have to a great extent contributed to the struggle against inequality and exclusion, and therefore have been a major force in higher education transformation. Sabela and Ndlovu (2022) notes that African higher education has experienced a remarkable transformation in post-independence Africa, driven by a desire to change the colonial higher education architecture and to address issues of marginalization and discrimination of certain sectors of the population. However, the African voice is still missing, and they suggest a need to take a breath and reflect on transformative framework guiding transformation of the higher education agenda in Africa (Sabela and Ndlovu 2022). Higgs and Van Wyk (2007) maintain that the overall character of most of the educational theory and practice is informed by European or Eurocentric philosophies. The South African Union of Students (SAUS) states that all sectors have a role to play in the transformation of higher education and looks at the role of higher education as going beyond that of knowledge production. SAUS argues that the universities specifically should pay more attention to the development of students in all areas if economic transformation, equality and inclusion are to be achieved so students can participate in discussions on issues that affect them, otherwise the poor will continue to suffer.

EXPERIENCES AND DRIVERS OF LOOTING IN HIGHER EDUCATION

Reinders (2019) regards protests as having illuminated issues that have long been on public record but ignored, and these include demands for decolonisation of the curricula, discrimination and inequalities. The author further maintains that students resort to violence when frustrations overflow and authorities on the other hand use force, which aggravates the situation, leading to violent protests which mostly culminate in looting, vandalism and various types of losses. The protests have taken place intermittently for decades in higher education. Fomunyam (2017) traces student activism from 1766 at Harvard University where students were fighting for their basic rights or necessities, Fisk University between 1924 and 1925, Columbia University in 1968 and student violence in the same year in France, which saw about 422 students arrested and 345 police injured in the struggle. Student activism in Africa is traced from the early 1940s as part of the struggle for independence. Khanyile (2020) is of the opinion that violence is a dynamic phenomenon that shifts with time, context, effects and meaning and could be mobilized to attract attention to socio-political and economic challenges experienced.

This raises a question of whether violence and looting could be justified particularly in the context of higher education students organizing and mobilizing against inequalities and other injustice such as discrimination and exclusion. Chinguno (2017) argues that universities as environments of learning and knowledge construction and production are contested and mostly characterised by inequalities and prejudices. Students from poor socioeconomic backgrounds find it difficult to gain access to the higher education institutions. Education, based on the human capital theory, has been viewed as an investment, while, within the liberal arts tradition, it has been interpreted as means for equipping people with knowledge to enable them to make free and autonomous choice about their lives (Chinguno 2017). Butler-Adam (2014) hammers on the essentiality of higher education for the design and productive use of new technology and states that it lays a solid foundation for the innovative capacity of a nation and contributes to a country's development. Beliefs created by these views confirm that access to education frees one from the deprivation trap. The words of Nelson Rolihlahla Mandela cited by Seepe (2015, 10) state: "Education is the great engine of personal development. It is through education that the daughter of a peasant can become a doctor, that the son of a mineworker can become the head of the mine, that a child of farmworkers can become president of a great nation."

Santos (2011) maintains that education is acknowledged as an instrumental value with high impact for other development outcomes. Access to quality higher education has become a struggle of the poor and working class. Deprivation could lead to anger, disruptions, including violent uprisings, and related consequences such as looting. In support, Ndebele (2007) stated: "Surely the children of the masses are destined to invade the universities." This implies that radical transformation remains in the hands of the students, particularly those coming from poor socioeconomic backgrounds who cannot afford a university education. The uprooting of entrenched inequities and discrimination in higher education cannot be overemphasised. Reinders (2019) and Adonis and Silinda (2021) assert that when students' voices are not attended to, frustrations overflow, opening the floodgates for unrest and looting.

In addition, Jansen (2015) confirms that some of the historically white institutions still have a problem with provision of access to higher education and points out that the complexity of interracial friendships has no value and that the challenge of social, cultural, intellectual and symbolic recognition remains a powerful lament. The quote from Langston Hughes that Mpofu (2017, 351) uses perfectly fits the growing rage, frustration and explosion, which will never be corrected by large injections of finance in higher education or the pacifiers used to contain the anger of those feeling various forms of exclusion such as an unwelcoming institutional culture, language barriers with no attempts to accommodate other languages, inadequate access to resources and other forms of inequality. Hughes asks: "What happens to a dream deferred? Does it dry up like a raisin in the sun? Or fester like a sore—And then run? Does it stink like rotten meat? Or crust and sugar over—like a syrup sweet? Maybe it just sags like a heavy load. Or does it explode?"

Mpofu further argues that inequality has changed its form and is manifesting itself as violence, looting, poverty, exclusion and subtle discrimination. Gómez González and Gutiérrez (2022) assert that improving educational equity has proven to be a challenge and the surrounding environment affects how students learn and how teaching occurs. Chinguno (2017) concurs that gaining access is a struggle for the disadvantaged and in some instances shifts in power have been observed where the powerless take control from the powerful. Understanding the historic context and drivers could assist with situational analysis and shed some light on the extent to which the looting culture has pressurized higher education transformation. The drivers identified in this chapter are associated with inequality, discrimination and exclusion linked to unequal access to resources, group dynamism and other socio-political and economic issues.

INEQUALITY AS A DRIVER OF VIOLENCE AND LOOTING

Higher education institutions are the key agents for countries to build capacity, growth and progress through creation and implementation of knowledge. Aina (2010) argues that although the higher education sector remains a significant part of the overall social, economic, political and cultural constitution of societies, most institutions are faced with challenges, including mass looting which has caused damage and losses in higher education and massive destruction of infrastructure. Kromydas (2017) and Barnett (2017) ague that higher education must serve the intellectual development of individuals, but currently is criticised for encaging students within the system instead of emancipating them. Within the African context, Mpofu (2017) argues that it has become a norm for students to demonstrate acts of violence, destruction of property and disruption of classes as a way of communicating their grievances. The author alludes to human security threats faced by the poor in higher education, and these include suppression of rights and freedom and deprivation of resources, with the majority living in poverty. Seepe (2015) and Madikizela-Madiya (2021) both share the same view that mere access to higher education is incomplete if issues related to inclusivity, affordability and access to quality education are not addressed. Constrained freedom of choice, hassles associated with lack of finance for tuition and accommodation ignites anger, frustration and student violence and looting to fight for justice and transformation.

Madani (2019) maintains that the main objective of any system of education is to provide quality education for all learners, arguing that the indicators for quality is reflected through the student/teacher ratios, learning environment, curriculum and a host of other indicators. However, Aina (2010) and Woldegiorgis and Doevenspeck (2013) maintain that it is crucial to understand the historical context concerning the changes that have occurred and are currently taking place and to identify what drives the changes and the direction higher education is heading to. This assertion is informed by the current situation, which is characterised by the absence of a dominant framework and that higher education systems continue to use a European framework.

Ndebele (2007) alludes to proclamation of high standards adopted by some institutions as a function of active involvement in combating inequalities, exclusion and injustice, while others use high standards which tend to be exclusionary in that they prevent participation or access to higher education. Furthermore, opening access to higher education is not an end in itself, as it requires adequate attention to be given to democratization of the process of access and the manner knowledge is acquired and communicated (Ndebele 2007; Heleta 2016). In support, Morley (2012) opines that social justice seems to be less of a priority, and quality and equality have been placed in opposition. Further noted is entry of students from poor socioeconomic backgrounds, which is viewed more as reproduction of injustices than transformation in that the majority find themselves gaining entry into dysfunctional institutions, which could suggest middle-class capture of higher education. Also, Adonis and Silinda (2021) maintain that transformation is sometimes interpreted as providing Black students with access to higher education, ignoring that some students find themselves excluded and marginalised by the institutional culture of certain institutions, leading to exasperation culminating in protests and looting.

GROUP DYNAMICS, ORGANISING AND MOBILISING

The argument concerning group influence and dynamics relates to the theory that individuals who have a predisposition to violence become initiators of violence and acts of looting are contagious. This means that the act of looting by some may encourage others to follow suit. The members of the aggrieved group in one way or another become more influential but on their own, individuals cannot succeed, hence the tendency to influence others. So they start by organising and mobilising others before engaging in the protest. Usually, the protests start as peaceful protests (Khanyile, 2022). Violence, in most cases, ensues when the institution's management response not favourable or delayed, when students feel that their demands are ignored and/or when the institution involves private security or police (Khanyile, 2022). The violent acts include looting teaching and learning equipment, burning property and vandalizing, acts which disrupts the academic progress and lives of other students. The groups labelled as instigators justify looting against specific targets as permissible and justifiable. Chinguno (2017) alludes to the importance of collective solidarity in fighting persistent inequality, poverty and lack of access to education for all and by all. The need to remain strong and united is recognised as a pillar when violence is used to forge violent solidarity. Alekseyeva (2019) refers to the speech by Martin Luther Jr. who stated that "a riot is socially destructive and self-defeating, but it remains the language of the unheard." This quotation applies to violence and looting in higher education inasmuch as it is destructive but pressures the university management to listen. Jansen (2015), Seepe (2015) and Mpofu (2017) alluded to the growing rage, anger and frustration experienced by the poor in higher education. Higher education is rapidly becoming unaffordable and this has culminated in intensification of student protests and the resultant looting.

POLITICAL AND GOVERNANCE ASPECT

The International Covenant on Civil and Political Rights (1966) states that human beings have to enjoy their civil and political rights with freedom from fear and want. Furthermore, governments have to ensure that everyone enjoys civil and political rights including economic, social and cultural rights. And Section 17 of the Bill of Rights in the Constitution of the Republic of South Africa states that everyone has a right, peacefully and unarmed, to demonstrate, picket and present petitions. Nevertheless, Fuo (2020) argues that the policy positions of some institutions are not compliant and fail to consider the rights as stipulated in the constitution and associated responsibilities of higher education institutions emerging from the Bill of Rights. Inconsistencies could be attributed to the provision which puts emphasis on peaceful demonstrations and protests. Masilela (2017) argues that certain sectors of the population are largely disadvantaged and find themselves restricted from gaining entry due to gatekeeping procedures and processes put in place. Anger is sometimes fuelled by the manner in which institutions respond to protests and the media. Lancaster (2016) and Moyo (2017) confirm that the nature and drivers are complex; one has to understand the context underlying the protests and the risk factors and dynamics including social factors that are ignited.

In the same vein, Wicomb (2018) argues that people who are without political or economic power have only protests as a strategy to communicate their concerns and grievances. In addition, Mpofu (2017) and Wicomb (2018) also maintain that protests and looting seem to be the only tool that students have at their disposal, and if silenced, the plight of the poor and marginalised continues unabated. Fuo (2020) proposes that higher education institutions have to revisit how they respond to protests in order to ensure that they comply with the constitution. On the other hand, Reinders (2019) and Khanyile (2022) allude to securitisation and militarisation of learning institutions which come with brutality and aggravation of violence. The authors argue that the presence of armed forces, court interdicts and suspension and arrest of students are viewed as sanctions without trial that deprive students of their rights to protest, but also result in looting.

Governments could find it politically difficult to enforce the law against the looting activities particularly when the action addresses pressing issues affecting society. A good example within the South African context relates to violence of the FeesMustFall riots, which seemed to be the only strategy available. In support, Mavunga (2019) cited Mantashe, declaring that the current South African ruling party has always supported the provision of free education, and this has been an important aspect of the ANCs' policies, suggesting that it is politically difficult to enforce the law. The wave of violent protests and looting, though not openly supported, has laid the foundation for the transformation of higher education in terms of access.

THE EFFECTS OF THE LOOTING CULTURE IN HIGHER EDUCATION

Hungwe and Divala (2020) opine that students' protests seem to be a threat to entrenched order or sanctioned authority or norms. The authors further state that in some African states such as Zimbabwe, Sudan, Uganda and others, students have been abducted, murdered, tortured for expressing their grievances and issues of concern. The chapter acknowledges that violent protests and looting are associated with destruction of property, intimidation and has to be condemned. However, Hungwe and Divala (2020), Khanyile (2022) and Osterweil (2020) argue that protests and looting continue to be the revolutionary mechanisms to force the higher education leadership listen to problems experienced by students. The acts contradict efforts towards enhancing the ideals of responsible citizenship. Furthermore, violence and looting are regarded as extreme actions by opportunists and an action which reflects false consciousness and ignorance (Osterweil 2020). The author further argues that the belief in law and order trivialises issues of equality and freedom. In the same vein, there is also a belief held by society that law enforcement reduces violent protests and looting. This could be partially true. On the other hand, violence and looting are viewed as the failure of higher education institutions to embrace those who are marginalised and economically underprivileged or to act transformatively. Moyo (2017) contend that transformation in education and in society should be shaped by those who have interest in its improvement and are not engrossed with self-gain. Looting is considered to have played a major role in pressuring for transformation concerning the need for economic and epistemic decolonisation in higher education. Certainly, the focus on numbers enrolled by institutions of higher education is inadequate, particularly if the numbers cloud issues of access and success in higher education. Stealing equipment and objects at higher education institutions is viewed as disruptive, but the act sends a message and draws attention to issues that serve as hindrances to access and success.

CONCLUSION

Violent protests and looting are inherited acts that were used for liberation from the colonialists. Universities are viewed as place of struggle for change and disruptive rage and subsequent violence and looting. The disruptions and violence can either be useful or detrimental. Proponents of protests and looting in the context of higher education have viewed looting from different perspectives and have provided varied complexities and historical experiences. Some criticise the phenomenon of looting as having paralysed academic activities and characterize it as the highest level of criminality. The dominant view adopted in this chapter relates to its recognition as a weapon of fighting social, economic, cultural, political and personal injustices. It is concluded that the looting culture has positive implications for the transformation of HEIs. To this effect HEIs are seeing significant shifts in areas such as the curriculum. Looting, together with protests, is viewed as the language best understood and responded to, bringing about transformation by government and university management within the African context. The universities have developed new policies and frameworks concerning equality, equity, transformation and change but the implementation requires a complete reframing, rethinking and reconstruction of the education system and curriculum. Although there is a strong belief that violence and looting need to be condemned, the acts have proven to be a means of gaining access to higher education and a strategy that seems to work well in fighting inequality, discrimination and transformation. Education is viewed by most underprivileged and economically marginalised as a tool to break down intergenerational deprivation. However, access to quality education can only be realised with equitable distribution of resources and acknowledging the need to transform the higher education landscape such that issues of economic and epistemic decolonization are given adequate attention. Depriving those without power and resources will ignite violent protests and strikes, which in turn could lead to looting, a wilful destruction of property and infrastructure including suspension of lectures and other activities in a bid to fight for justice, equality and transformation of higher education. Violence and looting in higher education have exposed the plight of the economically marginalised. However, it needs to be seen with more emphasis given to clear lines of open and honest communication among stakeholders in higher education. The top-down approach perpetuates inequalities and tensions including the use of force to silence the powerless. Equal access to higher education and equity in the quality of education for all sectors of the population is viewed as a solution to restrain violence and looting. Lastly, the institutions of higher learning have to instil a strong institutional culture; this includes values and attitudes of respect for each other that define what is acceptable and unacceptable in interactions.

REFERENCES

Adonis, Cyril K., and Silinda, Fortunate. 2021. Institutional culture and transformation in higher education in post-1994 South Africa: A critical race theory analysis. *Critical African Studies* 13(1): 73–94.

Aina, Tade Akin. 2010. Beyond reforms: The politics of higher education transformation in Africa. *African Studies Review* 53(1): 21–40.

Alekseyeva, Julia. 2019. "'A Riot is the Language of the Unheard': The Grassroots Activism of Whose Streets? (2017)." *Middle West Review* 6, no. 1 (2019): 222–24.

Assie-Lumumba, Ndri. T. 2006. *Higher education in Africa: Crisis: Reforms and transformation* Dakar, Senegal: CODESRIA.

Ayodeji-Falade, Monisola B., and Osunkunle, Oluyinka O. 2021. Framing of FeeMustFall students' protest by *Daily Dispatch* Newspaper and the effect on readers' perceptions. *Heliyon* 7(8): e07782.

Bandala, Carlos Alberto Jiménez, and Andrade, Luis Antonio. 2017. Education, poverty and the trap of poor countries in the face of development. *Journal on Efficiency and Responsibility in Education and Science* 10(4): 101–8.

Barnett, Ronald, ed. 2012. *The future university: Ideas and possibilities*. London: Routledge.

———. 2014. *Thinking about higher education*. Cham, Switzerland: Springer.

———. 2017. *The ecological university: A feasible utopia*. London: Routledge.

Boulton, Geoffrey, and Lucas, Colin. 2011. What are universities for? *Chinese Science Bulletin* 56(23): 2506–17.

Butler-Adam, John. 2014. The statesman of education, science and technology. *South African Journal of Science* 110(1–2): 1–2.

Chinguno, Crispen. 2017. A comrade from beyond the frontier. In *Rioting and writing: Diaries of Wits fallists*, edited by Crispen Chinguno. Johannesburg: Friedrich Ebert Stiftung, 2017.

Dlamini, Sipho. 2019. # FeesMustFall: Lessons from the post-colonial Global South. *Journal of Student Affairs in Africa* 7(1): 47–59.

Fomunyam, Kehdinga George. 2017. Student protest and the culture of violence at African universities: An inherited ideological trait. *Yesterday and Today* 17: 38–63.

Fuo, Oliver. 2020. Rethinking the regulation of university students' protests in light of *Mlungwana v The State* 2018 ZACC 45. *De Jure Law Journal* 53(1): 369–92.

Ginty, Roger Mac. 2004. Looting in the context of violent conflict: A conceptualisation and typology. *Third World Quarterly* 25(5): 857–70.

Gómez, Viviana, González, María Paz, and Gutiérrez, Pablo. 2022. Teachers' beliefs about poverty: A barrier we must face. In *Pedagogy-Challenges, Recent Advances, New Perspectives, and Applications*, edited by Hülya Şenol and Katherine K. M. Stavropoulos. London: IntechOpen, 2022.

Heleta, Savo. Decolonisation of higher education: Dismantling epistemic violence and Eurocentrism in South Africa. *Transformation in Higher Education* 1(1): 1–8.

Higgs, Philip, and Van Wyk, Berte. 2007. The transformation of university teaching and learning: An African philosophical perspective. *Indilinga: African Journal of Indigenous Knowledge Systems* 6(2): 177–87.

Hungwe, Joseph Pardon, and Divala, Joseph Jinja. 2020. "Burn to be heard": The (in) dispensability of "revolutionary" violence in student protests and responsible citizenship in African public universities. In *University education, controversy and democratic citizenship*, edited by Nuraan Davids and Yusef Waghid, 147–66. Cham, Switzerland: Palgrave Macmillan.

Jansen, Jonathan D. 2015. A quiet contemplation on the new anger-the state of transformation in South African Universities: Student movement. *New Agenda: South African Journal of Social and Economic Policy*, no. 60: 6–8.

Khanyile, Buhle. 2021. Violences in the South African student movement. In *The Oxford Handbook of Global South Youth Studies*, edited by Sharlene Schwarts et al., 185–200. Oxford: Oxford University Press.

Kromydas, Theocharis. 2017. Rethinking higher education and its relationship with social inequalities: Past knowledge, present state and future potential. *Palgrave Communications* 3(1): 1–12.

Lancaster, Lizette. 2016. "At the heart of discontent-measuring public violence in South Africa." *Institute for Security Studies* Papers, no. 292: 1–20.

Madani, Rehaf A. 2019. "Analysis of Educational Quality, a Goal of Education for All Policy." *Higher Education Studies* 9, no. 1: 100–09.

Madikizela-Madiya, Nomanesi. 2021. The question of access and spatial justice in universities in sub-Saharan Africa: A capabilities approach. *Transformation in Higher Education* 6: 10.

Masilela, Bafana Nicolas. 2017. "Free Education." *Rioting and Writing: Diaries of Wits Fallists.* Chinguno, C., Kgoroba, M., Mashibini, S., Masilela, B. N., Maubane, B., Moyo, N., Mthombeni, A., and Ndlovu, H. University of Witwatersrand, Johannesburg.

Mavunga, George. 2019. # FeesMustFall protests in South Africa: A critical realist analysis of selected newspaper articles. *Journal of Student Affairs in Africa* 7(1): 81–99.

Morley, Louise. 2012. Researching absences and silences in higher education: Data for democratisation. *Higher Education Research & Development* 31(3): 353–68.

Moyo, Nhlanhla. 2017. The gates. In *Rioting and Writing: Diaries of Wits Fallists*, edited by C. Chinguno, Johannesburg: University of Witwatersrand.

Mpofu, Shepherd. 2017. Disruption as a communicative strategy: The case of# FeesMustFall and# RhodesMustFall students' protests in South Africa. *Journal of African Media Studies* 9(2): 351–73.

Nabassaga, Tiguene, Chuku, Chuku Agbai, Mukasa, Adamon N., and Amusa, Hammed Adedeji. 2020. How does educational inequality affect income inequality in Africa? Working Paper no. 343. African Development Bank.

Ndebele, Njabulo Simakhale. 2007. *Fine lines from the box: Further thoughts about our country*. Compiled by Sam Raditlhalo. Cape Town: Random House.

Ndlovu-Gatsheni, Sabelo J. 2017. The emergence and trajectories of struggles for an African university: The case of unfinished business of African epistemic decolonisation. *Kronos* 43(1): 51–77.

Osterweil, Vicky. 2020. *In defense of looting: A riotous history of uncivil action*. New York: Bold Type Books.

Reinders, Michael Bongani. 2019. Militarisation, the state of exception, and fascism in South African universities. *Acta Academica* 51(1): 72–87.

Sabela, Primrose T., and Busile Cynthia Ndhlovu. 2022. African transformation agenda to promote inclusive education. In *Handbook of research on creating spaces for African epistemologies in the inclusive education discourse*, edited by Mbulaheni Obert Maguvhe and Mfundo Mandla Masuko, pp. 220–35. Hershey, PA: IGI Global, 2022.

Santos, Maria Emma. 2011. Human capital and the quality of education in a poverty trap model. *Oxford Development Studies* 39(1): 25–47.

Seepe, Sipho. 2015. Dismantling the false post-1994 narrative: Student movement. *New Agenda: South African Journal of Social and Economic Policy* 2015(60): 9–11.

Stober, Emmanuel Olusegun. 2019. Breaking the poverty trap: Is education the solution? *Journal of Humanities and Social Sciences Studies* 1(5): 1–14.

Van der Berg, Servaas, Burger, Cobus, Burger, Rulof, de Vos, Mia, du Rand, Gideon, Gustafsson, Martin, Moses, Eldridge, et al. 2011. Low quality education as a poverty trap. Stellenbosch Economic Working Papers: 25/11.

Waghid, Y. 2012. The decline of the university in South Africa: Reconstituting the place of reason. In *The Future University: Ideas and possibilities*, edited by R. Barnett, 71–83. New York: Routledge.

Wicomb, Wilmien. 2018. What does the constitutional courts judgement on protests mean? GroundUp. https://www.groundup.org.za/article/what-does-constitutional-courts-judgment-protests-mean/#.

Woldegiorgis, Tadesse, Emnet, and Doevenspeck, Martin. 2013. The changing role of higher education in Africa: A historical reflection. *Higher Education Studies* 3(6): 35–45.

Chapter Ten

Looting, Wealth, Security and Prestige

Detailed Modern Schemes for Education Oppression and Exclusion

Mbulaheni Obert Maguvhe

INTRODUCTION

This chapter endeavours to show how looting perpetuates wealth, security and prestige for the minority while to the majority those are detailed modern schemes for education oppression and exclusion. Research reveals that education is strongly related to both income and wealth. Therefore, the value of wealth and income should not be underestimated when discussing education matters. Some education programmes and projects are also funded by wealthy philanthropists. Children from poor families more often than not, start school already far behind their peers from rich families. A child from a well-to-do family who is ready to attend school will have the ability to succeed both academically and socially in the education context, while one who is not ready might encounter both academic and social challenges. It is a given that for children to succeed, their physical well-being, emotional health and a positive approach to new experiences are key. Poverty engenders problems with health, home life, and neighbourhood safety, reducing to a large extent the child's readiness for school. South Africa in particular, and many African countries in general, thus have deep and historical education issues.

It should be borne in mind that poverty diminishes children's hope, and often diverts their attention, aspirations and focus on life. As a result, instead of children focusing on education to improve themselves by getting good jobs, some children involve themselves prematurely in economic activities. Their involvement in economic activities compromises their childhood, sound education and development. Such children who have dropped out of school usually work in labour markets, household enterprises or as street vendors.

They work to augment the meagre incomes of their parents and guardians for basic survival purposes. These children could be classified as child labourers because of the nature of the activities they engage in. Their human rights, including privacy, respect and dignity, among others, are seriously violated.

Children from impoverished families become victims of child labour, child abuse and neglect, child trafficking, sexual exploitation, and killings, and they lack access to education, health care and safe water and sanitation. Even though education is recognised as one of the basic human rights in many parts of the world, many children still do not access it. Instead of playing, socialisation and learning, many children are forced to work in degrading conditions that not only interfere with their education but are harmful to their health and full development. The wealthy, conversely, are able to ensure that their children receive a quality education.

It would be of great importance at this juncture to define the following terms/concepts: *looting*, *wealth*, *prestige* and *security*. *Looting* can be defined as stealing goods, such as electronic equipment, food, medicines, cleaning material, and so on from shops during a violent event.

Wealth can be defined as the value of all assets owned by a person, community, company, or country. Wealth is further determined by the total market value of all physical and intangible assets owned minus all debts. Essentially, wealth is the accumulation of scarce resources. *Prestige* can be defined as respect and admiration given to someone or something, usually because of a reputation for high quality, success or social influence. *Security* is defined as freedom from danger or threat.

In 2021, Kwazulu-Natal and Gauteng provinces of South Africa experienced a great deal of looting in which according to government reports, 139 schools in Kwazulu-Natal and 4 in Gauteng were targeted. It is estimated that it would cost more than R300 million to repair them and replace their stolen infrastructure and equipment. Yet this level of looting was not without precedent. In the past, for example, looting took the form of forced tribal removals from homelands, either to appropriate the land for farming purposes or to acquire huge mineral deposits. A good example of that looting was the promulgation of the 1913 land act, where white settlers took 87 percent of the land and the Black majority retained only the remaining 13 percent, which was mostly sterile. When land was forcefully taken from blacks, no negotiations or compensations took place. The present government is now not even sure what mechanisms it might put in place to bring about land restoration and redistribution.

Friedman (2009) postulates that even if governments try to reduce or eradicate poverty through social security schemes, those schemes under the best of circumstances still leave people in abject poverty. Incidents of high-ranking government officials, including presidents and ministers, siphoning money and investing it in offshore markets continue to occur. In the last decade, looting of state resources in South Africa took place through what is called 'state capture'. Money earmarked for the provision of services and other needs found itself in the hands of officials and individuals owning companies. Such looting of resources results in poor service provision/delivery and basic human rights such as education being compromised. Manaka (2021) maintains that the South African government has persistently been plagued by exploitation and corruption which includes nepotism and fraudulent awarding of tenders, as well as the fraudulent circumvention of protocols.

Corruption is one of the major reasons why poor children in poor countries may not have access to well-funded education systems and programmes by governments. Some countries opt to spend money on construction of dams or roads or acquisition of defence hardware. Such projects, unlike education enhancements, are likely to provide kickbacks to government officials. Furthermore, where tenders for the provision of teaching and learning materials are concerned, it is possible to advise tender holders to inflate prices so that they also can get those kickbacks. Foreign donations tend to account for the lion's share of poor countries' budgets. Donors in many instances favour or prefer capital spending over recurring school expenses like salaries and teaching materials.

In South Africa, there are two education systems, viz. Curriculum Assessment Policy Statements (CAPS) grades one to twelve and the Independent Examination Board (IEB). The former is for the children whose parents are less privileged while the latter is for children whose parents are wealthy. It is most likely that the less privileged children will receive inferior education. Further, poor communities may be excluded, and their views suppressed when it comes to the formulation and implementation of education policies.

LOOTING OF RESOURCES AND HOW IT AFFECTS EDUCATION PROVISION

No education system, no department of education/ministry, no school, no teacher and no learner can function well without resources. The utilization of resources in education brings about fruitful learning outcomes, since resources motivate students and stimulates their learning (Okongo et al. 2015). Therefore, teaching students who are experiencing barriers to learning must deviate from the normal programme. In emerging countries, the distribution of services and the belief that citizens are a liability to the system is a common hindrance to the provision of education (Chataika et al. 2012). This view overlooks the possibility that certain cases in which people have completed their education and yet have not been able to become economically self-sufficient may be due to the system failing to provide them with the educational opportunities that a person needs, namely, to be encouraged to engage in development efforts and develop his/her own skills (Pidgeon et al. 2021). Education provision depends on good and reliable resources. If resources in the form of money and other essential things such as assistive devices and technologies are looted, education will bear the brunt of insignificance, low quality, inefficiency and ineffectiveness.

Children experiencing barriers to learning in most instances require more teaching and learning time, adapted teaching and learning methods and professional knowledge. This can only be achieved by an increase in resources as well as through a re-arrangement of available resources. Children experiencing barriers to learning are not expected to meet the classroom standards; rather, the classroom must strive to meet the individual needs of all children (Bargsma 2000). On the other hand, Puri and Abraham (2004) maintain that both school management and teachers should make efforts to identify and attend to learners experiencing barriers to learning' dietary needs especially pre-school children. Oyugi and Nyaga (2010) suggest that teaching and learning resources include and are not limited to: peripatetic services, support staff (such as Sign Language interpreters and braille transcribers), community involvement, orientation and mobility instructors, regular and special teachers, and so on.

Looting of resources by any person, rich or poor, sentences poor communities and their children to hardships, illiteracy and poverty because of the weak foundations of education. Schools are expected to break the cycle of poverty experienced by poor communities. In a country where resources are plundered, instead of schools breaking the cycle of poverty, they perpetuate the same situations and conditions their parents went through. Unlike the poor, the middle class and the wealthy have means to fend for the type of education they cherish for their children. It is the type of education one receives that determines what type of life one will lead in the future, the job one will secure and most importantly, one's success and wealth, ultimately leaving a huge gap between the wealthy and the poor.

Since teachers are human resources, they must receive quality training, as inadequate training more often than not acts as a major hindrance to the effective implementation of any education system, including inclusive education (Kochung 2011). To raise the quality of education, better learning materials, physical facilities and human resources are needed (Okongo et al. 2015). Textbooks and other resource materials such as pens, pencils, notebooks, calculators, files, typing sheets, chalk boards and chalk, and so on are basic for effective teaching and learning. Lack of resources resulting from looting is likely to make subjects dry and less interesting. The importance of always having appropriate personnel, plans for adequate instructional materials and physical facilities to fully support educational efforts cannot be over-emphasised. It is highly likely that the scarcity of learning materials, libraries and physical facilities may prevent education systems from positively responding to the needs of learners in particular and the demands of education in general.

THE EFFECTS OF LANDLESSNESS ON EDUCATION

Perhaps it is prudent to try to answer the following questions:

How does landlessness contribute to inequalities in education?
In what way is looting, wealth, security and prestige related to education provision?
On what basis does the author of this chapter discuss land and looting?

Land grabs through legislation and forced removals by the colonisers of Africans rendered them powerless because land means both power and nationhood. Expropriation of land accompanied by inequitable distribution thereof, make poor people more powerless while the wealthy continue wielding power and have enormous influence over programmes, systems and above all, use the economy to fund the type of education they aspire to, including model C schools and independent examination boards. Wolfe (2006, 387) posits that land in its true intense and purpose is life, and people cannot live without land. People fight for land. In other countries, for example, farmers fight over pastoral land and water holes. Such battles are severe, and people lose lives, land and even livestock.

Conversely, the arrival of the Dutch colonialists in South Africa in 1652 was based on land, as the Dutch wanted to establish a refreshment station. Land was crucial for this venture. Therefore, if it were not for this need, the natives would not have experienced forced removals, the creation of "bantustans" with useless and infertile soil, and a lack of minerals.

The question that needs to be answered is: in what way is looting, wealth, security and prestige related to education provision? According to Danielsen et al. (2022) every mortal, system, practice, programme and project needs land for total independence, self-determination, means of production, growth, and financial resources that result in the provision of quality education and other social needs. Because the wealthy have the financial muscle, they can give their children quality education at the expense of the less privileged. It is worth noting that the majority of past revolutions were about land. The American Civil War was about land; the Russian Revolution was about land and the Chinese Revolution was about land to cite a few examples.

IN ALL THOSE REVOLUTIONS, IT WAS THE LANDLESS VERSUS THE LANDOWNERS

Campsie (2021) is of the view that revolutions recorded in history were about economics, dignity, nationhood, and self-determination. In England to give but one example, "land hunger" was rife among all classes. This explains why it is difficult to overestimate the psychological importance to people in whose minds land had always been identified with security, success and the good things life had to offer (Rosher 2022) . The advent of democracy in South Africa did not bring any significant change in terms of status between the poor, wealthy, secure and prestigious. Blacks are still confined to rural areas slums and townships. The schooling of African children takes place under rural, slum and township conditions. It is only a handful of Africans who can afford to buy education for their children from private proprietors. It is only the privileged who can afford this type of education, and Africans send their children there at double the price. Good education in Africa is an expensive commodity. Landlessness/poverty have serious implications on the provision of education. The Dutch robbed Africans of their valuable land, and in 1852, the English toppled the Dutch government in South Africa. Cecil John Rhodes was instrumental in leading that conquest. He once uttered these words: "Every black man cannot have three acres and a cow or four morgen and a commonage right. We have to face the question and it must be brought home to them that in the future nine-tenths of them will have to spend their lives in daily labour" (Hendricks quoted in Mngxitama 2006, 42).

According to Appadurai (2004) poverty is many things, all of them bad. Poverty is material deprivation and desperation. It is lack of security and dignity. It is exposure to risk and high costs for thin comforts. It is inequality materialized. It diminishes its victims. It is also the situation of far too many people in the world, even if the relative number of those who are escaping the worst forms of poverty is also increasing. The number of the world's poor, their destitution, and their desperation now seem overwhelming by most measures.

COMMUNITY SUPPORT FOR EDUCATIONAL VENTURES

Education in historically disadvantaged schools has been subjected to problems that undermine parental involvement. Communities in this instance fail dismally to take ownership of neighbourhood schools (Halata 2011; Naong and Morolong 2011). Community support is needed to first improve the education situation and second, communities are instrumental in bringing back discipline and safety in schools. Communities influence either negatively or positively what is happening at schools and the school projects the image of the community within which it is situated (Ngqela and Lewis 2012).

Literature reveals that the bulk of the world's poor live in East Asia, South Asia, the Pacific and sub-Saharan Africa. School enrolment in these regions reflects their economic performance. Many children in poor countries drop out of school before completing the school programme. In 1999, the completion rate, the percentage of children of graduating age who in fact completed primary school that year, was 73 percent in developing countries. East Asia was 81 percent while south Asia and sub-Saharan countries obtained 50 percent. Even though children complete primary school education, this is no guarantee that children have acquired basic academic skills. Literature further reveals that adults who have received five or six years of education are functionally illiterate and innumerate. That is why some countries embark on literacy campaigns to solve the literacy problem.

What is more troubling are the disparities in educational attainment between different groups within countries and regions. Sadly, but not surprising, in poor countries and regions, children from poor families are much less likely to be in school than children of the wealthy and financially secure. This disparity is even bigger between genders. Girls feature very high among children from poor countries and regions. This bias is obvious in Asia and Africa. Children with disabilities are particularly marginalized and disadvantaged. It is estimated that only 5 percent of children with disabilities go to school. Seventy percent of children with disabilities could go to school only if there are appropriate facilities for them. It is argued that even if schools are accessible and accommodating, parents may opt to send their children out to beg instead of allowing them to receive education.

HOW INFERIOR EDUCATION CONTRIBUTES TO OPPRESSION, MARGINALISATION AND EXCLUSION

The first South African democratically elected president Mr. Rolihlahla Nelson Mandela once uttered the following words: "Never, never, and never again shall it be that this beautiful land will again experience the oppression of one by another and suffer the indignity of being the skunk of the world. Let freedom reign" (Twenty Year Review by the Presidency Office, 2014, 3). Nelson Mandela said these words on his inauguration day 27 April 1994 as the first Black African president after languishing in jail for twenty-seven years fighting the unjust system and apartheid policy.

Heldke and Peg O'Connor (2004) and Freire and Macedo (1995) describe oppression as the social, economic, and cultural conditions that lead to savage inequalities resulting in the loss of dignity, denial of human citizenship, and outright violent and criminal acts committed by the institutions responsible for implementing the law or practices. Oppression could also be understood as the exercise of tyranny by a ruling group. Heldke and Peg O'Connor (2004) argue that in education, the notion of oppression traces back to slavery when laws in the south made it illegal for anyone to educate a slave. The view or mentality not to educate a slave was perpetuated by the belief that African slaves were incapable of higher learning. Europeans feared that should Africans be educated, they will be in a strong position to fight these injustices that they were encountering including segregation as well as oppression laws.

Camangian and Cariaga (2021) argued that inferior education perpetuates oppression and oppressed people become powerless that they do not even talk about their oppression. In instances they reach the oppression stage, they land in situations and conditions wherein it is forbidden to even mention the injustices that are being committed. Inferior education contributes to the oppressed people not challenging or questioning the status quo. Inferior education takes away oppressed people's voice and the will to stand up for their basic human rights. This marginalises and excludes them from participating in activities necessary to improve their lives. Heldke and Peg O'Connor (2004) describe marginalisation as the act of relegating or confining a group of people to a lower social standing or outer limit or edge of society.

Overall, marginalisation it is a process of exclusion. Heldke and Peg O'Connor (2004) further posit that people are generally marginalised based upon race. One outstanding example is the Aboriginal communities of Australia that were excluded from society and pushed farther and farther away from their homelands as cities and towns grew. Marginalisation of various racial groups took place when societies met the needs of Europeans and not the needs of the marginalised themselves. Therefore, marginalisation is closely linked to the idea of whiteness. Research indicates that social exclusion to a large extent deprives people of benefits, privileges, choices and opportunities to escape from poverty and silences them from claiming their human rights (DFID 2005; UNESCO 1998a; UNESCO 1998b). Apparently, one of the major problems facing the world currently, is the exclusion of the majority of people from meaningful participation in the economic, social, political, cultural and education endeavours of their respective communities.

Research further indicates that current programmes, measures and strategies have largely fallen short in terms of addressing the needs of children and youth who are vulnerable to marginalisation and exclusion. In instances where programmes are geared towards targeting people who are marginalised and/or excluded, more often than not they have functioned outside the mainstream and special programmes, specialised institutions and specialist educators. Furthermore, poor, marginalised and excluded people are not just like "poor people" but are further hard done by the fact that their living conditions are very bad and consequently this deprives them of the privilege and/or benefit of development.

According to A DFID Policy Paper (2005) the problem of exclusion and marginalisation of the poor can be addressed by adopting the following measures: Ensure that socially marginalised groups equally benefit from public expenditure. Improve economic opportunities and access and services for discriminated, marginalised and excluded groups. Promote their political participation in society and their capacity to mobilise and organise themselves. Let them advocate for themselves and others like them. Increase accountability to protect citizens' basic rights. And Tackle prejudice and changing behaviour by all costs.

It is also believed that affirmative action in various forms could be a catalyst for addressing discrimination, exclusion and marginalisation, as this could foster and enhance access to education. Affirmative action alluded to here could be in the form of reserved spaces in educational institutions for the poor and minorities, designated scholarships for the poor and minorities as well as serious investment of much needed additional resources into education and poverty-stricken regions or where minorities live. Education for all programmes or systems should by all means endeavour to take into account the needs of the poor and the most disadvantaged, including and not limited to: working children; remote rural dwellers and nomads; ethnic and linguistic minorities; young children, young people and adults affected by conflict, HIV/AIDS, hunger and poor health; and those with special learning needs (UNESCO 1998a; UNESCO 1998b).

HOW QUALITY EDUCATION PERPETUATES WEALTH, DOMINATION, SECURITY AND PRESTIGE

A growing body of literature recognises education as one of the most important drivers of both social and economic development. It is an undisputed fact that higher levels of literacy lead to greater economic output, higher employment levels, better health, better social structures and number of other development indicators. To be more specific, the impact of education has been shown to result in rapid improvements in family planning, nutrition, health and income and is also seen as one of the best tools for promoting social and economic development (Gao et al. 2021; Misra 2012)

In addition, Woessman (2015) posits that if people disregard the economic value of education, the prosperity of future generations will be endangered with widespread repercussions for poverty, social exclusion, and sustainability of social security systems. It is however interesting to note that spending on quality education according to McDaid, Park and Chadha (2021) has become more of a priority worldwide as the majority of countries have increased education spending as a share of national income since 1999. Hence Misra (2012) regards education as a key factor in determining whether a country is a developed, developing, or underdeveloped country.

According to Crosweller and Tschakert (2021) the lack of accountability and responsibility could be attributed to policy makers and policy implementers alike. In 2008 the then Australian prime minister, Kevin Rudd, officially apologised on behalf of the government to indigenous people for their role in the stolen generation. Colonisers not only looted wealth (in the form of minerals and precious stones), land, knowledge, artifacts, and so on but looted generations as well. An example of stolen generations could be people taken by force as slaves from mainland Africa, India, China and elsewhere to the Americas and the Caribbean Islands/West Indies. This confession and acceptance of stealing generations in Australia led to the closing the gap policy (Niesche 2017). Many countries to-date that have colonised Africa still owe the Africans that confession and apology.

If attempts to normalise or make education issues equal are overlooked, overcoming disadvantages, exclusion and marginalisation will just be a pipedream. The wealthy, secure and prestigious will continue receiving quality education while the poor and marginalised will continue receiving inferior education. Quality teaching and learning is the only way or means to address inequality and disadvantage (Charles et al. 2014; Brooks 2012).

The individual classroom teacher is the central player in imparting quality education, but this also requires quality content, adequate human and material resources and various levels of support and intervention. Schools from affluent areas enjoy all the afore-mentioned things and benefit middle- and upper-class students. Authors such as Heslop (2003), Allard and Santoro (2004) and Jorgensen and Niesche (2011) argue that there should be recognition of complexities teaching in remote and rural contexts. Further, these authors believe that the support from principals and teachers could go a long way in making new teachers appreciate working in both remote and rural areas.

Looting has long lasting legacies of white Anglo privilege and cultural dominance (Forrest and Dunn 2006). Looting has therefore disadvantaged many children of school age. Schools have been identified as places where children most commonly experience racism, exclusion, prejudice and marginalisation (Forrest, Lean and Dunn 2016; Mansousi and Jenkins 2010).

Schools whether in affluent or rural areas must strive to address issues of exclusion, discrimination and marginalisation. Schools that embrace diversity/multiculturism have to be supported for taking that stance. To eradicate dominance, it is advised (Charles et al. 2014; Brooks, 2012) that there needs to be a focus on how social, historical, political and cultural factors underpin forms of domination and prestige. Leaders, students, government officials, parents, administrative staff, and others should do some self-introspection about whether in this day and age giving irrelevant or inferior education to the poor is necessary and good for countries.

CONCLUSION

This chapter has endeavoured to show that misuse or looting of resources result into poor service provision/delivery and basic human rights such as education, health, and so on, become just a pipedream. Corruption contributes largely to poor funding of education systems and programmes. The wealthy avoid this dire education system by sending their children to independent/private institutions. On the other hand, the poor are marginalised, oppressed and in some instances excluded from receiving education (a basic human right).

Looting of much needed resources compromises in a big way the provision of education. No education system, no department of education/ministry, no school, no teacher and no learner can function properly and effectively without resources. It is an undisputable fact that education provision depends on good and reliable resources. If resources in whatever form and magnitude are looted, education will bear the brunt of low quality, inefficiency and ineffectiveness. In a country where resources are scarce and plundered, instead of education or schools breaking the cycle of poverty, they perpetuate the same historical situations and conditions. Unlike the poor, the middle class and wealthy have means to acquire the type of education they cherish. In order to eradicate this inequality, there needs to be a focus on how social, historical, political and cultural factors underpin forms of domination and prestige.

REFERENCES

Allard, Andrea, and Santoro, Ninetta. 2004. Making sense of difference? Teaching identities in postmodern contexts. In *Doing the public good: Positioning educational research*. AARE 2004 International Education Research conference proceedings, 1–20.

Appadurai, Arjuna. 2004. The capacity to aspire: Culture and the terms of recognition. In *Culture and public action*, edited by V. Rao and M. Walton, 59–84. Stanford, CA: Stanford University Press.

Bargsma, Sijtze. 2000. *The regular classroom as battle for inclusive special needs education: An assessment of options of special needs education in the commonwealth Caribbean*. Series editor L. Quamina-Aiyejina, Education for All in the Caribbean. Kingston: UNESCO.

Brooks, Jane. 2012. *Black school white school: Racism and educational (mis)leadership*. New York: Teachers College Press.

Camangian, Patrick, and Cariaga, Stephanie. 2021. Social and emotional learning is hegemonic miseducation: Students deserve humanization instead. *Race Ethnicity and Education* 25(7): 901–21. https://doi.org/10.1080/13613324.2020.1798374.

Cambridge Dictionary. 2019. Exclusion. Cambridge: Cambridge University Press, Available online: https://dictionary.cambridge.org/dictionary/english/exclusion.

Campsie, Alexandre. 2021. Socialism, nationalism and Tom Nairn's dream of escape, *Twentieth Century British History* 32(4):509–32. https://doi.org/10.1093/tcbh/hwab013.

Charles, Claire, Mahony, Caroline, Fox, Brandi, and Halse, Christine. 2014. School principals and racism: Responding to Aveling. *Discourse: Studies in the Cultural Politics of Education*, 37(2): 230–44. https://doi.org/10.1080/01596306.2014.985634.

Chataika, Tsisi, Mckenzie, Judith, Swart, Estelle, and Lyner-Cleophas, Marcia. 2012. Access to education in Africa: Responding to the United Nations Convention on the Rights of Persons with Disabilities. *Disability and Society* 27(3): 385–98. http://dx.doi.org/10.1080/09687599.2012.654989.

Crosweller, Mark, and Tschakert, Petra. 2021. Disaster management leadership and policy making: A critical examination of communitarian and individualistic understandings of resilience and vulnerability. *Climate Policy* 21(2): 203–21. DOI: 10.1080/14693062.2020.1833825.

Danielsen, F., Eicken, H., Funder, M., Johnson, N. L., Theilade, I., Argyriou, D., and Burgess, N. 2022. Community Monitoring of Natural Systems and the Environment. *Annual Review of Environment and Resources*. 47 (1): 1–38.

DFID. 2005. Reducing poverty by tackling social exclusion. Department for International Development, September 2005.

Grant, Cathrine. 2017. The contribution of education to economic growth. Institute of Development Studies.

Gao, Chao, Xu, Jiao, Liu, Yang and Yang, Yuexin. 2021. Nutrition policy and healthy China 2030 building. *European Journal of Clinical Nutrition* 75(2): 238–46. https://doi.org/10.1038/s41430-020-00765-6.

Halata, Chantal. 2011. Gangsters enter school to attack learner. *Diamonds Fields Advertiser*, 5.

Heldke, Lisa M., and O'Connor, Peg. 2004. *Oppression, Privilege, And Resistance: Theoretical Perspectives on Racism, Sexism, and Heterosexism*. Boston: McGraw-Hill.

Heslop, Jim. 2003. Living and teaching in Aboriginal communities. In *Reform and Resistance in Aboriginal Education*, edited by Q. Beresford and G. Partington Perth: UWA Press. https://www.nintione.com.au/resources/rao/living.

Kochung, Edwards J. 2011. Role of higher education in promoting inclusive education: Kenyan perspective. *Journal of Emerging Trends in Educational Research and Policy Studies* 2(3): 144–49.

Forrest, Jim, Lean, Garth, and Dunn, Kevin. 2016. Challenging racism through schools: Teacher attitudes to cultural diversity and multicultural education in Sydney, Australia, *Race Ethnicity and Education* 19: 618–638. https://doi.org/10.1080/13613324.2015.1095170.

Forrest, James, and Dunn, Kevin. 2006. Racism and intolerance in eastern Australia: A geographic perspective. *Australian Geographer* 37: 167–86.

Friedman, George. 2009. *The next 100 years: Forecast for the 21st Century*: New York: Doubleday.

Freire, Paulo, and Macedo, Donald P. 1995. A dialogue: Culture, language and race. *Harvard Educational Review* 65(3): 377.

Jorgensen, R., and Niesche, R. 2011. Curriculum leadership in remote indigenous communities. *Leading and Managing* 1(17): 45–58.

Manaka, Phuthi. 2021. Fraudulent award of tenders and South African government (Doctoral dissertation). https://hdl.handle.net/10500/28404.

Mansousi, Fethi, and Jenkins, Louise. 2010. Schools as sites of race relations and intercultural tension. *Australian Journal of Teacher Education* 35: 93–108.

McDaid, David, Park, A-La, and Chadha, Shelly. 2021 Estimating the global costs of hearing loss. *International Journal of Audiology* 60(3): 162–70. DOI: 10.1080/14992027.2021.1883197.

Misra, Srikant. 2012. *Contribution of education in the socio-economic development: An empirical study*. Lucknow, India: Faculty of Management and Research Integral University.

Mngxitama, Andile. 2006. The taming of land resistance: Lessons from the National Land Committee. *Journal of Asian and African Studies* 41(1–2): 39–69. doi:10.1177/0021909606061747.

Naong, Matsidiso, and Morolong, Itumeleng. 2011. Challenges to parental involvement in school governance. Acta Academica, 43(2): 236–63.

Ngqela, Nozuko, and Lewis, Andrew. 2012. Exploring adolescent learners' experiencesof school violence in a township high school. *Child Abuse Research: A South African Journal* 13(1): 87–97.

Niesche, Richard. 2017. Perpetuating Inequality in Education: Valuing Purposes over Process. *Educational Leadership,* Volume 36, 235–52.

Okongo, Rachel B., Ngao, Gladys, Rop, Naftal K., Nyongesa, Wesonga J. 2015. Effect of availability of teaching and learning resources on the implementation of inclusive education in pre-school centers in Nyamira, North Sub-County, Nyamira County, Kenya. *Journal of Education and Practice* 6: 35.

Oyugi, Ndanu L., and Nyaga, Margaret M. 2010. *Introduction to contemporary issues affecting education.* Kenya Institute of Special Needs.

Pidgeon, Nick, Groves, Christopher, Cherry, Catherine, Thomas, Gareth, Shirani, Fiona, and Henwood, Karen 2021. A little self-sufficient town close to the beach: Local energy system transformation through the lens of place and public things. In *Research Handbook on Energy and Society*, edited by Janette Web, Faye Wade and Margaret Tingey, 299–316). Cheltenham, UK: Edward Elgar Publishing. https://doi.org/10.4337/9781839100710.00033.

Presidential Foreword. 2014. *Twenty years review South Africa.* South African Presidency Office: Pretoria: Oxford University Press.

Puri, Madhumita, and Abraham, George. 2004. *Inclusive education.* London: Sage.

Rosher, Ben. 2022. "And now we're facing that reality too": Brexit, ontological security, and intergenerational anxiety in the Irish border region. *European Security* 31(1): 21–38. DOI: 10.1080/09662839.2021.1949297.

UNESCO. 1998a. From special needs education to education for all. Tenth Steering Committee Meeting UNESCO, Paris, 30 September–1 October 1998. Unpublished manuscript.

UNESCO. 1998b. *Wasted opportunities: When schools fail. education for all, status and trends*. Paris: UNESCO.

Woessmann, Ludger. 2015.The economic case for education, *Education Economics* 24. http://www.tandfonline.com2015.1059801?journalCode=cede20.

Wolfe, Patrick. 2006. Settler colonialism and the elimination of the native, *Journal of Genocide Research* 8(4): 387–409, DOI: 10.1080/14623520601056240.

Chapter Eleven

The Impact of Looting in the South African Tourism Sector

Lombuso Precious Shabalala

INTRODUCTION

This chapter explores the impact of looting in South African Tourism. The term *looting* is defined as an act of stealing from a person or place, it could be money or property. In South Africa, looting took place in two forms the first in in April 1652 and the second in July 2021, which attests that looting is not something new.

The first looting is still evident and its impact continues to be felt today. This looting began when land was sighted on 5 April 1652 at the Cape of Good Hope by Jan van Riebeeck and his team. The aim of the expedition was to establish a refreshment station to supply the crews of the company's trading ships as they sailed to the East. They would here be able to stock their ships with fresh water, vegetables and fruit, meat, medical supplies and other needs (South African History Online 2012). The presence of Van Riebeeck along with the Council of Policy, which would be the governing body for the station, predicted the beginning of a permanent European settlement inasmuch as they already had drawn up around the year 1649 the 'Remonstrantie', a document of recommendations for Van Riebeeck that emphasised the suitability of the Cape for the VOC (Dutch East India Company) project (South African History Online, 2012). The indigenous people, lacking a legal system of land ownership did not have deeds for their land or the bureaucratic framework within which to negotiate the sale or renting of land with strangers. Van Riebeeck and his team were thus in a position to appropriate the most suitable tracts and begin looting the ancestral lands of the native inhabitants. This looting impacted people such as the seminomadic Khoikhoi and the San because the land the Dutch took for farming had been traditional hunting and gathering areas. It is regarded as an example of how indigenous groups are still suffering the impacts of this form of looting. Later, males were forced to leave their families to seek work, as they could no longer grow their own food due to lack of land and livestock. It can be debated whether the establishment of protected sites and other properties such as World Heritage sites, National parks, private game reserves and so forth are the results of institutionalised looting, enabled by the 1913 Native Land Act. The "1913 Natives Land Act was one of the first pieces of legislation that limited property rights of Africans in South Africa; as before the pass of this Act Africans were able to purchase land outside of their reserves" (South African History Online 2014). This act did away with the freedom of ownership and replaced it with poverty and sorrow. Today the majority of indigenous peoples lack access in protected areas.

The other form of looting was witnessed in July 2021, when tourism activities were suspended in KwaZulu-Natal and Gauteng because of the violence and looting that took place. In addition, job losses in the area will translate to households being without income. During the looting, safety for tourists became a major concern and some major roads were blocked by the looters, followed by the closure of key tourist attractions as well as shortages of basic essentials such as petrol and food. For instance, officials were forced to close several beaches in Durban, usually popular with visitors both local and foreign, for fear of chemical contamination following nearby industrial arson. The real struggles of the poor thus become a serious crisis. The impact of this looting was felt mainly by tourism business owners, the majority of whom are white people and their employees. According to the *Mail & Guardian* (2004) report about ownership in the tourism sector a study done by Empowerdex in 2003 estimated only 6 percent of JSE-listed tourism entities had BEE ownership. Management and control of these companies was vested in, on average, 81 percent white male, 15 percent Black male, and only 2 percent Black women. The goal of apartheid was to uphold the status quo of white supremacy as well as control the African labour needed for rapid industrial development (Baldwin 1975, 218).Separate development was supposed to allow Africans to develop themselves under their own self-government, but this was impossible due to then South African economic structure. For instance, the 1913 Natives Land Act "limited the landmass where they were allowed to own land" (South African History Online, 2014). The act resulted in the land being owned mostly by the minority (whites) and leaving the majority (Blacks) with less land and little tourism or revenue-generating activities.

Tourism is described as the largest and fastest-growing sector in the world, a sector that employs the most people (Saayman 2016, 2). Tourism can be defined as the temporary, short-term movement of people to destinations outside the places where they normally live and work and their activities during their stay (Gautam 2007). Tourism is divided into eight types namely: leisure tourism (adventure and recreational), cultural tourism, religious tourism, family tourism, health (medical) tourism, sports tourism, business tourism, and educations tourism. In addition, there are also forms of tourism such as ecotourism, food tourism and agro-rural tourism. The tourism sector has eight industries, namely: accommodation, adventure tourism and recreation, attractions, events and conferences, food and beverage, tourism services, transportation and travel trade. Tourism is a sector that is unquestionably growing rapidly in developing countries, which is regarded as an enormous economic activity (McIntosh et al. 1995, 22). A study conducted by Al-Ansi, Lee, King and Han (2021) explored the previously neglected concerns of local communities towards the smuggling of cultural heritage property with particular reference to Yemen. The flourishing global art market is in fact behind the phenomenon of blockbuster exhibitions in leading tourism cities throughout the world. The United Nations World Tourism Organisation (UNWTO) maintains that looting involves international organised crime syndicates that threaten global tourism development and sustainability and is aimed at vulnerable communities. Byrne (2016) notes that such acts cause extreme harm to aesthetic, historical and spiritual legacies, thereby harming present and future generations (Byrne 2016). Appreciating the overwhelming data presented by the Empowerdex (2003, as cited in *Mail & Guardian* 2004) in sync with the study conducted by Al-Ansi et al. (2021) proposing the six constructs that contribute significantly to sustainable tourism: direct protection management, trust in government, community participation and support for sustainable tourism could be answer to mitigate with the shortage of people of colour in the tourism industry and also assist with inclusion or businesses ownership of indigenous/people of colour since the globally showed cased assets were looted from their forefathers.

CONCEPTUALISATION OF LOOTING IN THE TOURISM CONTEXT

As indicated by UNESCO (2003), Cultural Heritage Tourism (CHT) is a growing sector that allows sustainable development through sustainable cultural tourism projects and other related practices within the space of the local people. The July 2021 looting directly interfered with the provision of the above-stated White Paper as the whole tourism value chain was placed on standstill in KwaZulu-Natal and Gauteng provinces and safety of the destination was in question. Therefore, due to this unanticipated act, it is understood that South Africa tourism is suffering long effects. Looting is defined as the crime of stealing money or property from a person or place (Oxford Learner Dictionary 2022). Gauteng Province known as the country's economic hub, and KwaZulu-Natal on the east coast bore the brunt of the July 2021 Looting. People stole items from shops and businesses and committed vandalism. Looting is not something new. "Despite growing global efforts and rules that track illegal cultural markets, the looting of cultural heritage is accelerating, with art houses, museums and auction centres in several European countries and the USA continuing to exhibit stolen cultural properties" (Al-Ansi et al. 2021, 1). In addition, findings by Keitumetse and Nthoi (2009, 144) have pointed out that giving a site a World Heritage status in the developing world encourages tourism. South Africa is home to ten declared World Heritage Sites (WHSs), which are expected to lead to the economic development associated with tourism products and services, contributing to improving the standards of living of the local people. The South African Heritage Resources Agency (SAHRA) "has been given a mandate by the National Heritage Resources Act, Act No. 25 of 1999, to protect, monitor and, manage the country's heritage resources, while also providing, guidance to the communities who reside in those area where there are National Heritage Sites" (South African Heritage Resources Agency 2022). South African National Parks (SANParks) is also trusted with the World Heritage Sites, and World Heritage Sites managers are employed and report to SANParks. A healthy relationship between SAHRA and SANParks is vital. It must be noted that the ten sites are inscribed as World Heritage sites and also declared as National Heritage sites through the South African Heritage Resources Agency. The World Heritage Convention: UNESCO (1992–2022) presents the ten South Africa World Heritage Sites as follows:

Five *Cultural Sites*

1. Fossil Hominid Sites of South Africa (1999, 2005)
2. Mapungubwe Cultural Landscape (2003)
3. Richtersveld Cultural and Botanical Landscape (2007)
4. Robben Island (1999)
5. *Khomani* Cultural Landscape (2017)

Four Natural Sites

1. Barberton Makhonjwa Mountains (2018)
2. Cape Floral Region Protected Areas (2004, 2015)
3. iSimangaliso Wetland Park (1999)
4. Vredefort Dome (2005)

One Mixed Sites (Natural and Cultural)

1. Maloti-Drakensberg Park (2000, 2013).

The 1996 White Paper on the Development and Promotion of Tourism confirmed "South Africa's approach to tourism as one which is government-led, private sector driven and community-based, and grounded in cooperation and close partnerships between all stakeholders". At the same hand, tourism is perceived to be one of the most powerful economic, social, cultural, ecological and political forces in the world today. However, benefits to local communities and heritage custodians from cultural heritage tourism in heritage sites remains a concern, including the realisation of social and economic development in its true sense. Therefore, community support and involvement on how the past is presented, as well as understanding the economic impact of the tourism industry, becomes paramount for any heritage tourism project or activity. The 2003 UNESCO Convention took a stance by calling up nations to commit to develop inventories of their intangible cultural heritage and to work with local communities, practitioners and other concerned/affected stakeholders towards safeguarding those traditions. The convention further called upon nations and communities to work together on developing action plans for safeguarding their cultures. The developed action plans will play a vital role in the protection and preservation of the culture because it entails research and documentation, education and transmission, as well as legal protection and forms of public recognition and support (Kurin 2004, 71). Concurrently, taking into account land grabbing in Africa, a study conducted by Obeng-Odoom and Gyampo (2017, 131) note that, Rights-based approaches to development tend to exclude land while land rights research tends to be focused on land law and law courts without analysing 'the right to land'. The scholars further posed an intriguing question in relation to transformation: "Is it possible for the courts to play a key role to shape the current transformation of property relations?" In addition to this question, it must not be taken lightly that the connection between indigenous peoples and their traditional lands largely defines these peoples' identity, both historically and in relation to present-day threats to their physical and cultural integrity (Pentassuglia 2011, 165). Therefore, the evolving research interest in the role of the courts to guarantee land rights, tries to link the dispossession of land to human rights abuse and hence invoke the power of the judiciary to bring about social justice (Obeng-Odoom and Gyampo 2017, 131).

The 1996 White Paper on the Development and Promotion of Tourism in South Africa provides for the promotion of domestic and international tourism. Patel and Everatt (2021) are of the opinion that looting or violence are due to:

- The frustration of being hungry and cold, people whose prospects were already constrained by the pandemic
- Inequality between rich and poor
- Tensions within the governing party
- Racial tensions in the country

Therefore, it is understood that South Africa tourism is suffering long effects from looting, particularly KwaZulu-Natal and Gauteng provinces. During the looting the safety of tourists was a major concern. The looters blocked some main roads and evidence indicates that closure of key tourist attractions led to shortages of essentials such as petrol and food from shops, which have a direct impact on tourism. For instance, the government was forced to close several beaches in Durban, usually popular with visitors, both local and foreign, for fear of chemical contamination following nearby industrial arson. It is understood that, when tourists are not visiting a destination, it translates to no generation of revenue. Secondly, the poor suffer from the lack of sustainable job opportunities, one of the possible motives for the looting. Another factor is lack of community involvement in and benefit from projects.

Research by Hall and Ntsebeza (2007) present the 1913 Native land Act, whereby the white settlers forcefully took more than 90 percent of the land forced some of the indigenous people, in particular males, to leave the rural in search of work. The appropriation of land was administered in a forceful manner which scattered families due to borders that were put in place by white settlers. Their land was demarcated into farms and protected areas that we see today; such as Kruger National Park and the Mapungubwe World Heritage Site. Moreover, the discovery of minerals in the 1860s contributed to the forced removal of the indigenous people from their forefathers' land. Evidently, there are mining activities taking place not far from these protected sites and some have been stopped due to new policies around mining near protected areas. Such policies have contributed to people of colour not seeing protected areas as their own and perceiving tourism as foreign concept, which may explain the lack of BEE ownership in the sector. Historically, Mapungubwe lands now known as the Mapungubwe World Cultural Heritage Site (MWCHS) belonged to its indigenous inhabitants, who were forcibly removed. The area today has gained universal value. Mapungubwe was the site of the earliest kingdom in Southern Africa, with extensive regional and continental links spreading to East Africa, the Arabian Peninsula, the Persian Gulf, India and East Asia (Schoeman and Pikirayi 2011, 1). According to Carruthers (2006) the Mapungubwe World Heritage cultural landscape is situated on the farm Greefswald at the junction of the Limpopo River (Limpopo Province, South Africa) and south of Shashe River (Zimbabwe). The

Site borders three countries, namely, South Africa, Zimbabwe and Botswana, and falls under the management of South African National Parks. Carruthers further outlined MWCHS as an important contemporary economic and cultural driver and described the effect that the Mapungubwe site may have on elevating South Africa's international profile and on African national pride (Carruthers 2006, 1). The site offers two key attractions:

- Confluence: The meeting point of the three countries and the two rivers.
- Heritage tour: Mapungubwe hill is the mountain were the famous golden rhino and other artefacts were excavated from one of the graves by archaeologists. This is the same mountain where some of the descendants' ancestor's remains are presently reburied (22 remains) in one ceremonial grave.

MAPUNGUBWE LAND CLAIM BY THE DESCENDANTS, "THE OWNERS OF THE LAND"

As Al-Ansi et al. (2021) and Hall and Ntsebeza (2007) show, the claims of ownership of the land are rather complex, as people living there today are believed to have migrated there to seek farming jobs after the land was seized from its original owners by colonialists. Six groups claim the Mapungubwe World Heritage site as their ancestral land. The Mapungubwe descendants' groups are n: the Vhangona Cultural Movement, the Tshivhula Royal Family, the Lesheba Royal Family, the Machete Royal Council, the Lemba Cultural Association and the Sematla people. The six groups of Mapungubwe descendants are presently scattered all over the Limpopo province and country (South Africa) today, and some are even found in Zimbabwe. The late Chief Petrus Lahlang Machete (Figure 12.1) was very instrumental in pushing the land claim agenda on behalf of the Mapungubwe descendants. He had the first meeting with the Land Claim Commission Officials at Masisi with an aim to reclaim their land. The land claim was lodged just after the democracy but only three out of fifty-six farms were officially given back to the descendants by time of the interview. Danstaart farm is one that has been claimed. It is regarded as a rich area along the banks of a river. The connection between indigenous peoples and their traditional lands largely defines these peoples' identity and cultural integrity (Pentassuglia 2011, 165). Therefore, the power of the judiciary to bring about social justice in matters involving land rights, restitution and ownership should be regarded as a matter of urgency. The saying goes, "*Justice delayed is justice denied*". With only three farms awarded, two questions arise: Is Chief Machete resting in peace? Are his

Figure 12.1. The Late Chief L. P. Machete and the researcher (Mapungubwe WCHS)
Source: Researcher's own photo (2017).

people, the Mapungubwe descendants, at peace? At the present moment, a firm yes to both questions from the people concerned is unlikely.

The results of the forceful removal include challenges of access and meaningful benefits from proceeds derived from the site. In addition, due to borders imposed by the colonial government following their removal from lands that have now gained universal value, some descendants presently reside outside the borders of South Africa. For instance, some of the Machete people are found in Botswana, and they have recently appointed a traditional leader in a ceremony in which representatives of the Machete royal family from across the border in South Africa were required to officiate. Chirikure et al. (2010, 36) recommended community tourism development projects aimed at benefitting the descendants and local communities and sustaining the site through the Greater Transfontier Conservation Area (GTFCA). The Transfontier was aimed at benefiting and involving all three countries that border the site, namely, South Africa, Botswana and Zimbabwe. Moving forward, as a new disandourse, community involvement has steadily gained importance as archaeologists endeavour to enhance the social relevance by engaging with local and indigenous communities, in particular the communities that own and have an interest in archaeological sites (Chirikure and Pwiti 2008, 467). Scholars such as Mulale et al. (2013, 9) define community as "a group of people from one or more villages living within a defined location and for whom the meaning they attach to the natural resource provides a foundation for social cohesion". An important lesson is presented on how a traditional top-down Community Based Tourism (CBT) network was created in Nicaragua and fully funded by external organisations, which reflected the general criticisms of the approach, while bottom-up CBT born of a local initiative demonstrated longer life expectancy, faster growth and more positive impacts on the local economy (Zapata, Hallb, Lindo and Vanderschaeghe 2011, 725).

METHODOLOGY

Explanatory sequential mixed methods were adopted for this study. Data were collected using a structured questionnaire. Self-administered interviews were conducted with focused groups, namely the Mapungubwe Traditional leaders and the South African National Parks.[1] A focus group research discussion method was adopted for this study whereby qualitative data were collected through planned discussions with the aim of obtaining the perspectives of the focus group regarding the subject matter. It was important to first collect the qualitative data, analyse the data and develop questionnaires from the analysed data. This method worked because the analysed quantitative data validated qualitative data. Content analysis was used to analyse the data. Quantitative data were collected using a structured questionnaire. Mapungubwe descendants' community and local communities were the respondents. Qualitative questions were imbedded in the quantitative data collection instrument. Methodological triangulation was utilised in order to increase the credibility and validity of research findings. Government documents, scholarly articles, published these and other online sources around the subject matter were consulted. The results and findings are presented in a form of excerpts and graphs.

FINDINGS AND DISCUSSIONS

The chapter presents the three types of looting, namely:

1. The looting of 90 percent of the land from indigenous people by the white settlers;
2. Looted /stolen artifacts and other cultural properties, some of which are being exhibited in European US museums; and
3. The recent looting that took place in KwaZulu-Natal and Gauteng Province.

Impact of Looting and Scholarly Recommendation

Looting has taken place in different forms, degrees and eras. Regardless, the real struggles in relation to poverty in society are perceived to be some of the outcomes of delayed justice for looting that took place during colonial era and further perpetuated by the apartheid regime. Correcting the injustices of the past include land reappropriation, addressing inequality and lack of job opportunities, and allowing transformation of and renewal of benefits to custodians/indigenous people. The high rate of unemployment, inequality and lack of transformation were identified as some of the possible motives for the looting that we witnessed in July 2021. The finding concurs with a recommendation by Chirikure et al. (2010, 36) of projects aimed at benefitting the descendants and local communities and sustaining the MWCHS through the Greater Transfontier Conservation Area (GTFCA). This recommendation is still viewed as relevant to mitigate the 2021 occurrence, which is a decade later. In this case, project developments will not only benefit the descendants whose land was looted from by the whites, but will be expected to also benefit the local communities residing around/closer to the site who are not related to the site by blood.

Community Participation on Site Activities and Descendants' Perspective

Another factor that was a result of the looting and now calls for an urgent intervention is lack of community involvement on identification of projects and implementation and benefiting from those projects. This factor is linked with lack of access to these protected areas since they were demarcated and privatised during the looting era. The descendants of MWCHS indicated that they are not being consulted or involved in any activities or projects taking place in the site. The findings suggest that community involvement and participation is important in any site such as MWCHS, as it may translate to fair benefits sharing from the proceeds derived from the park. The findings also demonstrate that community members, in particular the descendants' community, are under the impression that they are not taken seriously by site management due to the lack of communication, minimal (or no) community involvement or engagement and benefiting from the park and the other cultural/traditional and socioeconomic matters. These include the protocols to be observed when one is visiting the hill, the meaning of Mapungubwe (which the descendants argue is not 'the place of jackals'), the descendants' history, tour guide scripts, rebranding of the park and the construction of a cultural village on the sites. Most importantly, how you are being referred to or addressed is crucial. Therefore, it must be noted that the descendants prefer to be referred to as the owners of the land, not stakeholders, because they regard themselves as the heirs to the land where their forefathers were forcibly removed. One traditional leader, noted that "if we are stakeholders we become like anybody, an interested party, we don't just have an interest there, we are the owners of the place."

The positive thing is that the descendants still believe that a partnership with the site management could bear fruit, though it may not be an easy journey at the beginning, and they also are convinced that their input could take the site to new heights. According to descendants' Group 6: "They believe that they should go back to the drawing board with the park management to involve us"; also, there are calls for unity with the site management, whether management accepts that in the past they did not take them seriously or not. The descendants indicated that after receiving the park guidelines, management should have asked them, as the owners of the culture, about their traditional practices, customs and its application. The matter regarding lack of consultation by the site management is viewed by the descendants as something that can be dealt when they go back to the drawing board with management. In addition, a feeling was voiced noting that management should consult them and find out how they feel when management plans to do things in a certain manner or allow them to guide management about how they wish things to be done so that they can feel comfortable as descendants and feel confident that the site is representing their heritage and adhering to their traditional way of doing things. Thought it should be noted that the descendants do not want to be viewed as dictators but wish to be engaged and be involved. "Let's go back to the drawing board like we did during the reburial" (Pers.com 2019f), said one traditional leader. This assertion is supported by scientific evidence presented in Figure 12.2.

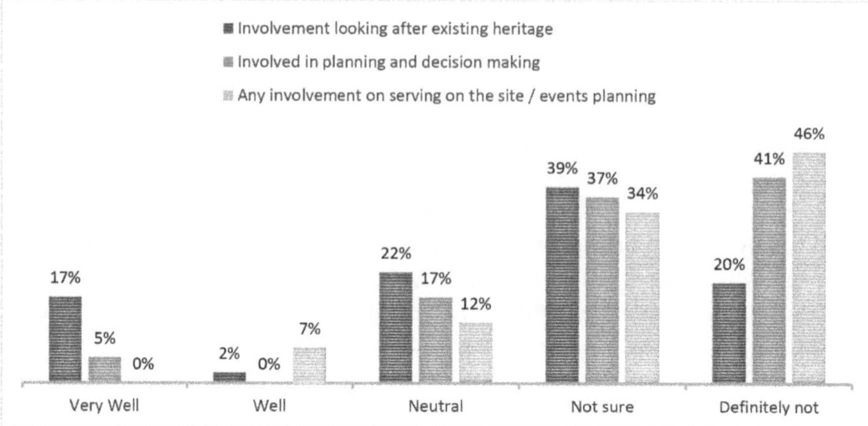

Figure 12.2. Community Involvement
Source: Shabalala (2020)

Descendants Group 2 shared the same sentiments as Group 6 and indicated that some of their challenges is that "They are just being told when things are at the advanced stage or about to be finalised, not on the initial stage" (Pers. com 2019b). This assertion is supported by scientific evidence presented in Figure 12.2.

Drawing from the descendants' perspectives, Figure 12.2 presents three variables, namely: Involvement regarding the existing heritage; involvement in planning and in decision making; and involvement on serving on the site/ events and planning. The answers were categorized as very well, well, neutral, not sure, and definitely not.

The graph shows the relations between variable quantities and also that the descendants and local communities are not holding any roles in the Mapungubwe World Cultural Heritage Site. The results indicate 46 percent of respondents reporting that they are definitely not involved in serving the site or any events planning and only 7 percent reporting that they are well involved. Furthermore, 41 percent of the respondents reported that that they are definitely not involved in planning and decision making and only 5 percent reported that they are very well involved. In addition, 20 percent reported that they are definitely not involved in looking after the existing heritage, while 2 percent reported well involved and 17 percent reported very well involved. On the other hand, as presented above in Figure 12.2, "neutral" and "not sure" had larger percentages in all three questions than "very well involved" and "well involved." The results are evidence that involvement of the descendants and community members is something that seriously requires the management's attention, and it calls to be treated as a matter of urgency. According

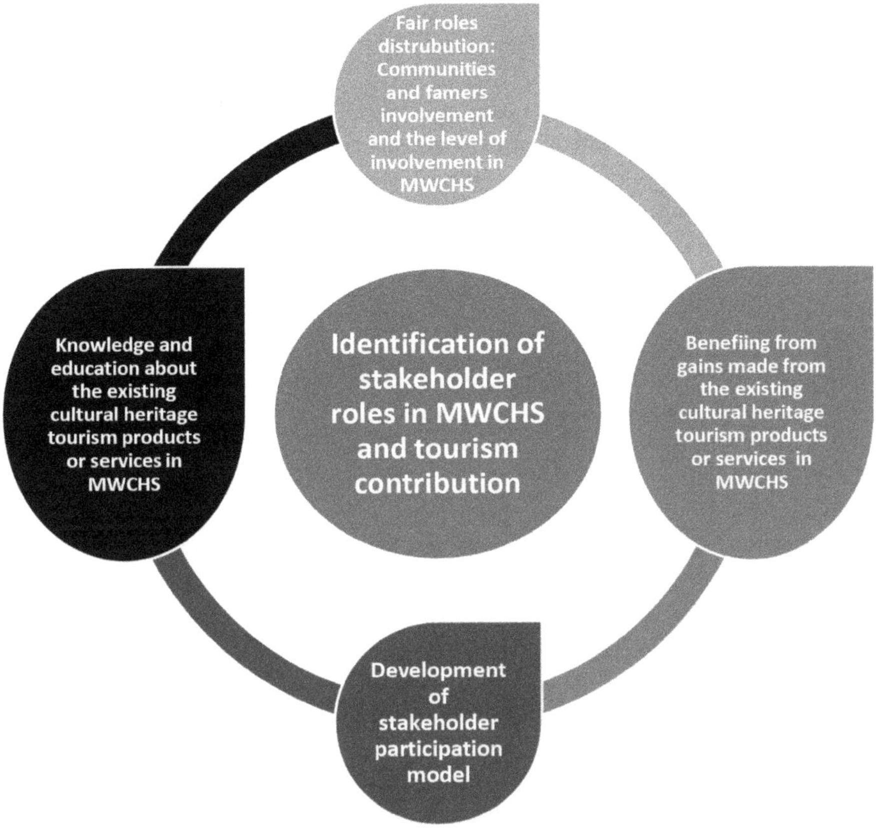

Figure 12.3. The subthemes of stakeholder roles in MWCHS and tourism contribution
Source: Shabalala (2019).

to the sub-themes in Figure 12.3, the descendants' perspectives demonstrate that some of the unfortunate outcomes of looting are real and are affecting the lives of the owners of the land in daily bases. Some of the scares cannot be seen through the naked eye, since they are spiritual/traditional.

Community Benefits

As stated by the descendants' traditional leaders, going back to the drawing board could be the answer to start healing the gaping wounds and correcting the injustice that was brought by the colonial government / apartheid regime. Benefiting from the gains derived from MWCHS is one of the challenges faced by these communities. This finding is consistent with the findings from the prior findings from traditional leaders. The respondents who reported that they are not benefiting also reported that they are not being consulted or engaged by the park and that they do not have any knowledge about representation in committees. The same respondents also indicated that they are not involved in activities that are taking place in MWCHS. Those who reported that they benefitted from the park also reported that the park management engaged or consulted them and that they were involved in activities in the site. This means that all items are measuring the same underlying characteristic, and they do have an impact on fair benefit sharing. The findings revealed that the descendants believe that "not being involved and also not being engaged by the park management plays a role on them not receiving any benefits derived from the park."

Descendants Group 2 voiced out their view thus: (Pers.com 2019b) "*From management site, when they send buses to the community to collect them to go to Mapungubwe during Tourism Month in September they regard it as a benefit.*" This assertion is supported by scientific evidence presented in Figure 12.3.

Descendants Group 1 recalled what used to happen before the current management came on board (Pers.com 2019a) saying: "*Before the current management, there was some efforts from the park management in line with benefiting the community but it stopped.*" Further, "*Last year for the first time, Mapungubwe had a day were all the Mapungubwe descendants were catered for food and other things by the park. Though few challenges were experienced, at least the park is starting to recognise them. Nevertheless, apart from that, the new draft plan will sort of cater for that as well.*" (Pers.com 2019a). This assertion is supported by scientific evidence presented in Figure 12.3.

The MWCHS staff said: "*In terms of Mapungubwe, so far there is nothing much happening when it comes to community participation. The only participation of local communities that has been witnessed by the participant is during the annual event during Tourism Month in September where all the descendants' groups are invited to the park. Even so, the participant noted that there is a missing link that resulted in disconnection between the community and the park. The participant is under the impression that the fact that the park is away from the communities could be one of the reasons why there is a disconnection. MWCHS is located about 70 kilometres away from both sides, east (Musina), west (All Days) and the descendants are about 250–350 kilometres or more.*" (Pers. com 2019h). This assertion is supported by scientific evidence presented in Figure 12.2.

Findings presented by a study conducted by Chirikure and Pwiti (2008) alluded to a new discourse where community involvement has suddenly gained importance as archaeologists attempt to enhance the social relevance by engaging with local and indigenous communities, in particular the communities that own and have an interest in archaeological sites, in this case are the Mapungubwe descendants. Community involvement and engagement in its true sense and application of bottom-up strategy becomes vital for mitigating the undesirable results presented by this study.

Stakeholders' Roles and Tourism Contribution to the Site

The challenges inherited due to looting are assumed to contribute to the lack of stakeholder's participation or lack or stakeholder roles in activities taking place in the site, eventually contributing to the significant spread of poverty. Such occurrences defeat the purpose of the 2003 UNESCO Convention advocating for community involvement in protecting their culture and could prompt the desire for one to take part in the mass looting of businesses and property, hoping for some sort of a gain. But some of the real results of such unfortunate activities are the negative effects on the country's tourism economy and the poor being the ones feeling the cost of looting most. Criminal activities and lawlessness could result in more job losses and delay of tourism recovery.

In addition, our country's promotion of domestic and international tourism campaigns will suffer, as no tourist wishes to visit an unstable destination, where safety is not guaranteed. In order to address the situation, Keitumetse and Nthoi (2009) suggest a usage of research to restore good heritage management strategies that will include community engagement and development at all stages. In addition, research could provide tailor-made options for MWCHS management in regard to safeguarding the intangible elements of heritage in Mapungubwe that incorporate community participation and benefit. As noted by Chellan and Bob (2008), the involvement of all stakeholders including the concerned communities has the potential to stimulate efficient decision-making processes by improving and legitimising them.

On that note, Figure 12.3, present the possible areas whereby site management could be utilised to involve stakeholders in a meaningful manner. The involvement should be aimed at taking the sites to the next level while contributing to tourism through culture/heritage while benefiting the descendants in its true sense. It must be noted that those who reported being involved also reported benefiting. With that notion, meaningful roles for stakeholders in the sites is crucial, as most respondents indicated that they are not presently involved. In addition, as these communities gets involved, the challenge of educating the communities about the existing cultural heritage products/services offered in the site will be taken care off. When they get involved, they will start to learn and thereafter transfer the knowledge in different forms, working together with the site management. Lastly, stakeholder participation will assist with reporting structure and communication channels for both site management and concerned communities. It will also outline who is responsible for what and encourage transparency.

South African Heritage Laws

The approved South African Heritage Laws must be taken into consideration by site managers as guidelines and points of reference when developing conservation strategies for heritage sites. The manner in which the strategies are implemented influence the recognition of the importance of stakeholder and community involvement. The stated South African Heritage Laws includes the following:

- Indigenous Knowledge Systems Policy
- National Heritage Resources Act no. 25 of 1999
- Intellectual Properties Laws Amendment Bill, 2007
- Heritage Resources Agency Policy, Living Heritage
- World Heritage Convention Act
- Protected Areas Act
- Forestry Act, 1998

If communities or key stakeholders are not included, managers will run a risk of the people not owning and valuing the site or even appreciating efforts to safeguard the assets. Protecting historic landmarks and places, unique qualities, and special traditions that attract visitors is a way of safeguarding these resources for the future. In this way, increased tourism, can be promoted while the very qualities that attracted tourists in the first place, remain preserved.

South African Heritage Laws are key as they are the guideline to practitioners and site managers to adhere to and also a way to address the injustice that was inherited from the old regime. These laws also symbolise the new democracy which is now affiliating to UNESCO and other important bodies that work hard to protect artefacts and other cultural properties/assets, including advocating for community benefit and sustainable development.

CONCLUSION

This chapter concludes by noting the two different types of looting that South Africa has experienced as a country over the years. With no doubt, the July 2021 unrest, looting and violence interfered with the provision of the 1996 White Paper on the Development and Promotion of Tourism in South Africa. Therefore, due to this unanticipated act, South Africa tourism is suffering long effects. Perpetrators are being brought to book. On the other hand, the historical looting of land and forceful removal of descendants from their ancestral land interfered with human rights. Failure to correct the injustices that were caused by the then colonial government could mean a challenge to the Constitution of South Africa, which is the supreme law of the Republic of South Africa. The importance of community engagement and consultation as well as transparency and accountability by leaders is vital. It is evident that any type of looting has severe negative impact on South African Tourism, either economic, cultural or any other form. In addition, the findings of this chapter clearly indicated that the custodians of the culture are not in control in sites such as Mapungubwe. Lastly, with no reasonable doubt, we may close by saying tourism (in this case cultural heritage tourism) is not in the hands of the owners or previously disadvantaged communities, instead it is still in the hands of the minority, who are also majority landowners.

The author dedicates this book chapter to the late Chief Petrus Lahlang Machete, Chief Tshivhula and the six groups of Mapungubwe descendants. "Not Yet Uhuru"!

NOTE

1. All interview participants are anonymised to protect their identities.

REFERENCES

Al-Ansi, Amr., Lee, Jin-Soo., King, Brian, and Han, Heesup. 2021. Stolen history: Community concern towards looting of cultural heritage and its tourism implications. *Tourism Management* 87 (December). https://doi.org/10.1016/j.tourman.2021.104349.

Baldwin, Alan. 1975. Mass removals and separate development. *Journal of Southern African Studies* 1(2). DOI: 10.1080/03057077508707934.

Byrne, Denis. 2016. The problem with looting: An alternative perspective on antiquities trafficking in Southeast Asia. *Journal of Field Archaeology* 41(3). DOI:10.1080/00934690.2016.1179539.

Carruthers, Jane. Mapungubwe: An historical and contemporary analysis of a World Heritage cultural landscape. *Koedoe* 49(1). DOI: https://doi.org/10.4102/koedoe.v49i1.89.

Chellan, Noel and Bob, Urmilla. 2008. Sustainable Ecotourism in the uKhahlamba Drankensburg Park: A stakeholder Analysis. *Alternation*, 15 no 1. 290–315.

Chirikure, Shadreck, and Pwiti, Gilbert. 2008. Community Involvement in Archaeology and Cultural Heritage Management. An assessment from case studies in *Southern Africa and Elsewhere, Current Anthropology* 49 no 3. 467–85. DOI: 10.1086/588496.

Chirikure, Shadreck, Manyanga, Munyaradzi, Ndoro, Webber, and Pwiti, Gilbert. 2010. "Unfulfilled promises? Heritage management and community participation at some of Africa's cultural heritages sites." *International Journal of Heritage Studies* 16(1–2)(February). DOI: 10.1080/13527250903441739.

Department of Environmental Affairs and Tourism. 1996. White paper on Tourism. Pretoria: Government Printers.

Hall, Ruth and Ntsebeza, Lungisile. 2007. *The land question in South Africa: The challenge of transformation and redistribution*. Cape Town: HSRC Press.

Keitumetse, S., and Nthoi, O. 2009. Investigating the impact of world heritage site tourism on the intangible heritage of community: Tsodilo Hills World Heritage site, Botswana. *International Journal of Intangible Heritage* 4 (April). SSRN. https://ssrn.com/abstract=2249856.

Kurin, Richard. 2004. Safeguarding intangible cultural heritage in the 2003 UNESCO convention: A critical appraisal. *Museum International* 56(1–2). https://doi.org/10.1111/j.1350-0775.2004.00459.x.

Mail & Guardian. 2004. Who owns tourism? November 30. https://mg.co.za/article/2004-11-30-who-owns-tourism/.

Mulale, K., Matema, C., Funda, X., Slater-Jones, S., Njovu, D., Kangueehi, G., Hay, D., and Crookes, V. 2013. *Community-Based natural resource management in Southern Africa*. Bloomington, IN: AuthorHouse.

Obeng-Odoom, Franklin, and Gyampo, Ransford. 2017. Land grabbing, land rights, and the role of the courts, *Geography Research Forum*, no. 37 (December).

Oxford Learners Dictionaries. 2022. looting. https://www.oxfordlearnersdictionaries.com/definition/english/looting?q=looting+.

Patel, Ozayr, and Everatt, David. 2021. *What Drove South Africa's recent violence and looting and what to do about it*. University of Witwatersrand. https://www.wits.ac.za/news/latest-news/opinion/2021/2021-07/what-drove-south-africas-recent-violence-and-looting-and-what-to-do-about-it.html. Access date: 22 March 2022.

Pentassuglia, Gaetano. 2011. Towards a Jurisprudential articulation of indigenous land rights. *The European Journal of International Law* 22, no. 1 (February). Doi: 10.1093/ejil/chr005.

Pers.com 2019f. Interview with a Traditional leader at Dzanani Township, Ndzhelele area in Limpopo (Mar 2019).

Saayman, Melville. 2013. *En Route with Tourism - An Introductory*. South Africa: Juta Books.

Schoeman, Maria H., and Pikirayi, Innocent. 2011. Repatriating more than Mapungubwe human remains: Archaeological material culture, a shared future and an artificially divided past. *Journal of Contemporary African Studies* 29(4). DOI:10.1080/02589001.2011.600847.

South African Heritage Resources Agency. 2022. *Heritage protection*. https://www.sahra.org.za/heritage-protection/. Access date: 12 September 2022.

South African History Online. 2012. The arrival of Jan Van Riebeeck in the Cape—6 April 1652. https://www.sahistory.org.za/article/arrival-jan-van-riebeeck-cape-6-april-1652.

———. 2014. The Group Areas Act of 1950. Available from: https://www.sahistory.org.za/article/group-areas-act-1950.

UNESCO. 2003. Convention for the Safeguarding of the Intangible Cultural Heritage. https://ich.unesco.org/doc/src/15164-EN.pdf. Access date: 7 February 2018.

World Heritage Convention: UNESCO. 1992–2022. South Africa: Ten world heritage sites. https://whc.unesco.org/en/statesparties/za. Access date: 17 May 2022.

Zapata, Maria Jose, Hall, C. Michael, Lindo, Patricia, and Vanderschaeghe, Mieke. 2011. Can community-based tourism contribute to development and poverty alleviation? Lessons from Nicaragua. *Current Issues in Tourism* 14(8). DOI: 10.1080/13683500.2011.559200.

Index

About the Editors and Contributors

ABOUT THE EDITORS

Mfundo Mandla Masuku is associate professor in the School of Built Environment and Development Studies at the University of KwaZulu-Natal. He is supervising at master's and PhD level from different universities and has been actively involved in curriculum development. He is very passionate about research, and he has published more than thirty-five scholarly articles in accredited journals on his area of expertise, which includes food security, inclusive education, local economic development, governance and scholarship of teaching and learning, as well as five book chapters. He has also presented papers at both local and international conferences. He has worked with different government institutions including the Department of Planning, Monitoring and Evaluation and has been appointed by different local and international journals as the reviewer and external examiner for different universities. He recently published an edited book on African epistemologies and inclusive education.

Dalifa Ngobese is senior lecturer in culture and heritage studies and program leader at the University of Mpumalanga. He was a lecturer and acting HOD at the University of Zululand and has been teaching history, culture, and heritage since 2014. He also has a vast experience in archives and museum institutions, and has worked as a museum curator, manager and deputy director in the heritage sector. He has read papers at numerous national and international conferences and has published more than ten articles in peer-reviewed, accredited journals and contributed two book chapters. His main research focus areas are African studies, culture and heritage, archives, museums, South African history, sacred sites, indigenous knowledge systems

(IKS), and decoloniality discourse and writings. He explores these research areas within the framework of Afrocentric approaches, Ubuntu and African traditional religion. He has been an external examiner to various institutions for higher learning and reviewed numerous book chapters and book manuscripts. He has been appointed by the minister of sport, arts and culture to serve as a council member for Ditsong Museums of South Africa.

Mbulaheni Obert Maguvhe is a full professor. Prof Maguvhe's research has concentrated on education for learners with disabilities and has largely been interdisciplinary, combining his two disciplines, special and inclusive education, with a focus on human rights, social justice and Ubuntu, and applied mainly within education for all and no-child-left-behind paradigms. His output has consistently been with a critical inclusivist stance (initiated in his PhD dissertation on the inclusion of blind and visually impaired learners in the teaching and learning of biology) merging theory on disability and theory of mind and drawing on the theories of cognitivism and the relationship between accessing information and knowledge tactually. His research collectively demonstrates his relating voluntarism, advocacy and agency to his research praxis, intertwining both the theoretical and ontological rationale across inclusion, reasonable accommodation and differentiated instruction and assessment. To date he has coedited four books on disability and inclusive education matters. He has recently been appointed UNESCO's chair of inclusive education in higher education.

Sifiso Ndlovu is political science lecturer at the University of Mpumalanga. She previously held a post-doctoral research fellowship at the Johannesburg Institute for Advanced Studies (JIAS),University of Johannesburg and Public Affairs Research Institute. Her PhD project—obtained from the University of the Witwatersrand—broadly examined intersections and divergences in the articulations of belonging to ethnic identity and nation-building in post-apartheid South Africa in the culturally heterogeneous KwaMhlanga region. She also holds an MA in political studies, an honours degree in political studies and a BA in political studies and sociology, all from the University of the Witwatersrand. Her research interests include the state in Africa; African politics; public policy; democratization; social justice; and the politics of nation building, ethnic identities, and belonging and citizenship, and she has published journal articles and book chapters on the politics of belonging, nation building and Ndebele ethnicity. She is a budding academic who has received academic awards and scholarships, including the Next Generation Social Sciences in Africa doctoral fellowship, University of the Witwatersrand's Council Postgraduate Merit Scholarship, National Research

Foundation bursary, and University of the Witwatersrand's Postgraduate Merit Award Doctoral Scholarship.

ABOUT THE CONTRIBUTORS

Annah Dudu is a doctor of inclusive and special needs education at Great Zimbabwe University. She obtained a doctorate in education in learner support from the University of North West. She holds a master's in special needs education from the Great Zimbabwe University. Dudu's research interests are teacher education for inclusive and special needs education and inclusivity of learners with diverse disabilities. Her research articles appear in internationally accredited journals. She has authored and co-authored several book chapters with established researchers. She has presented at several national conferences and has successfully supervised master's students to completion.

Nirmala D. Gopal (PhD) is a member of the SABTT and professor in criminology at the University of KwaZulu-Natal, Durban. Her teaching and learning passion facilitate her current position as a criminology professor. An NRF-rated researcher, she enjoys scientific writing and publishing. Her most recent research niche areas are peace and security, including cyber-security. These niche areas are not just current and provocative but ideally situated to inform policy and suggest practical interventions. Having served as external examiner for a variety of PhD and master's students across various South African universities contributed to her perspective on the nature and quality of research in South Africa. In addition, her frequent invitations to review national and international journal articles, NRF rating applications and PhD proposals have helped shape her research trajectory. She is passionate about various facets of transformation and is a keen researcher in the 4IR space.

Tawanda Majoko is professor of inclusive and special needs education at Great Zimbabwe University. He obtained a doctorate in inclusive education from the University of South Africa. He holds a master's in philosophy of education in curriculum policy, development and management from the Nelson Mandela Metropolitan University. Prof Majoko's research interests are teacher education for inclusion and inclusivity of learners with diverse and unique needs. His research articles appear in internationally and nationally accredited journals. He has authored and co-authored several chapters with early-career scholars and has presented at numerous international and national conferences. He has successfully supervised master's and doctoral students' theses and is an external examiner for several universities in Africa.

Dina Mokgadi Mashiyane is assistant director (campus librarian) at the University of the Free State, with a demonstrated history of working in higher education library and information services. She is skilled in electronic resources, knowledge management, digitization, information literacy, research methodology, library marketing and liaison. She is also a researcher who has published in reputable academic journals, including a book chapter, and is an accredited facilitator. She was one of the candidates for the Carnegie CPD Programme "Enhancing librarians' ICT skills for research enablement in African universities". Her research interests include information literacy, information ethics, inclusive education and social media in libraries/teaching and learning. She has presented papers at both local and international conferences.

Mfaniseni Wiseman Mbatha is researcher in the Chief Albert Luthuli Research Chair at the University of South Africa. He is also doing his PhD in the Department of Development Studies at the University of Zululand. His research interests revolve around rural development, rural agriculture, food security, local economic development, rural migration, and the sustainable livelihood approach.

Methembe Mdlalose is lecturer at the School of Built Environment and Development Studies, University of KwaZulu-Natal. Dr Mdlalose previously worked as a researcher at the Regional and Local Economic Development Unit based at the University of KwaZulu-Natal's Graduate School of Business and Leadership. He is passionate about issues that have an immediate social and economic impact on the lives of citizens. Specifically, Dr Mdlalose specializes in regional and local development, political economy and state institutions, focusing on the role of the state in economic development. His recent work focuses on regional coastal development, social safety nets and COVID-19, political economy of COVID-19, blue economy and community development, local government and spatial issues in coastal areas.

Victor H. Mlambo is lecturer at the University of Johannesburg, School of Public Management, Governance and Public Policy. Victor's research interests include conflict and migration studies, political geography, regionalism and security studies.

Mandla A. Mubecua is currently a PhD scholar in development studies at the University of Zululand and also works as a research assistant at the Moses Kotane Institute. He has worked as a research assistant for the Human Science Research Council (HSRC) and the University of Zululand, where he focussed on writing papers and research proposals for the Community Engagement Department. In 2018, he was selected to participate in the Young African Leaders initiative (YALI) and in 2019 was invited to participate in the review of the National Development Plan (NDP) of 2030. In the same year, the eThekwini Metro Municipality selected Mubecua to contribute to the research symposium which was based on the nexus of water, hunger and energy.

Bhekani Ngwenya is a history educator from Qiko High School, UGu District in South Coast, South Africa and is currently registered with the University of South Africa for a master's degree in history. He is an experienced marker in history with the Examination Section of the Department of Basic Education. He will be pursuing his PhD studies in the 2023 academic year with an intention to publish. His interest is global terrorism, which has plagued the world and already has its tentacles in Africa. He believes in a United Africa free from Western neo-colonialism and economic prosperity.

Primrose Thandekile Sabela is senior lecturer at the University of Mpumalanga in the School of Development Studies, Faculty of Economics, Development and Business Sciences. She holds a PhD in the field of development studies. Her diverse research areas of interest are influenced by the diversity inherent in the discipline of development studies. She has vast experience in the higher education space, has presented papers at international and national academic conferences and has published peer reviewed articles. Her research areas of interest include African development, gender and development and inclusive education.

Dr Lombuso Precious Shabalala is a lecturer in the College of Economic and Management Sciences at the University of South Africa. Her focus area is Cultural Heritage Tourism. She holds a PhD from the University of the Witwatersrand. She made history for being the first nGAP Lecturer hosted by the University of Mpumalanga to complete and graduate with a PhD. She is a member of the Golden Key International Honour Society. She is an emerging researcher, who is actively involved in community engagement and enjoys working with students. She successfully established and maintained relations and partnerships with stakeholders, which include traditional leaders, business owners, government organisations/parastatals, including tourism educators. She has presented papers in both local and international conferences; and reputable publishers such UNESCO UNITWIN Network (Culture, Tourism, & Development) has published some of her work. She recently contributed a chapter in an ebook published by Springer. She has reviewed conference papers and a book chapter. Her collaboration institutions include University of the Witwatersrand and University of Zululand. In addition, she holds a vast amount of experience in the tourism sector.

Kemist Shumba (PhD) is an avid researcher. He has an interdisciplinary background and holds a BA in English from the University of Zimbabwe, PGCE from Great Zimbabwe University, bachelor's of social science honours in cultural and media studies from the Centre for Communication and Media Studies (University of KwaZulu-Natal), a master's in social science in health promotion (cum laude), and a PhD in health promotion (University of KwaZulu-Natal). Shumba's areas of interest include gender-based violence, HIV and AIDS, African indigenous knowledge systems, adolescent health and social justice. Health and well-being constitute an integral component of his research, illuminating a gamut of contemporary social issues.

Philangani Sibiya is lecturer at the University of South Africa in information science. Mr Sibiya is currently doing his PhD with the University of South Africa in the Department of Information Science. His research interests are digital scholarship, libraries as community information hubs, information organisation and retrieval, computer literacy skills training and indigenous knowledge documentation and dissemination.

Mbongeni Shadrack Sithole is currently serving as a lecturer in the School of Applied Human Sciences at the University of KwaZulu-Natal. He is a qualified social work educator with eleven years of academic experience. He has field-practice expertise in public service, having practiced in the areas of social development, corrections and skills development. The author's research interest is mainly in the area of inclusive education, corrections, supervision, trauma debriefing and Afrocentricity as an alternative knowledge system. As a self-driven and results-oriented lifelong learner, the author prides himself on demonstrable skills in facilitation, coordination, organisation, report writing, monitoring and evaluation, amongst others. He has a working knowledge of legislative prescripts and policy frameworks pertaining to higher education, criminal justice systems and inclusive education. He embraces practice-related skills, namely reflective practice, problem solving, critical thinking and managing change and diversity.

Kutenda Trinos is a doctoral candidate at the University of KwaZulu-Natal. His primary research interests are decolonial praxis, curriculum dialogue, curriculum transformation, social justice and coloniality. Mr Trinos received his science teaching certification prior to entering decoloniality, which is where the idea for the ontological orientation originated. His epistemological perspective as a teacher and aspiring philosopher is described as encouraging context-based learning, where curriculum links to and is a result of daily lived experience.

Lightning Source UK Ltd.
Milton Keynes UK
UKHW040605060323
418056UK00018B/12

9 781666 919905